Science Adventures
with Children's Literature

Science Adventures
with Children's Literature

A Thematic Approach

Anthony D. Fredericks

Illustrated by
Anthony Allan Stoner

1998
Teacher Ideas Press
A Division of
Libraries Unlimited, Inc.
Englewood, Colorado

To Bonnie Blake-Kline, my partner in crime, for warm friendship and support, collegial joie de vivre, and constant good times.

❧❧❧❧❧❧❧❧❧❧❧❧❧❧

Teacher Ideas Press
A Division of
Libraries Unlimited, Inc.
P.O. Box 6633
Englewood, CO 80155-6633
1-800-237-6124
www.lu.com/tip

Production Editor: Stephen Haenel
Copy Editor: Brooke Graves
Proofreader: Matthew Stewart
Typesetter: Michael Florman

Library of Congress Cataloging-in-Publication Data

Fredericks, Anthony D.
    Science adventures with children's literature : a thematic
approach / Anthony D. Fredericks.
        xi, 233 p. 22x28 cm.
    Includes bibliographical references and index.
    ISBN 1-56308-417-1 (pbk.)
    1. Science--Study and teaching (Elementary)--United States.
2. Children's literature--Study and teaching (Elementary)--United
States. 3. Education, Elementary--Activity programs--United States.
I. Title.
LB1585.3.F72 1998
372.3'5044--dc21   98-34268
                                                        CIP

CONTENTS

viii   **Contents**

PREFACE

One of my favorite "Far Side" cartoons by Gary Larson shows a group of dinosaurs standing outside a cave. The dinosaurs are lighting up some cigarettes and furtively glancing in several directions. The caption reads, "The real reason dinosaurs became extinct." I like that cartoon for several reasons, but most of all because it illustrates the fun that can be had with science. Although Larson frequently gave science and scientists a gentle "jab" now and again, he also demonstrated how much science is a part of everyday life, too.

I, too, think science can be fun. I also believe that science can be one of the most exciting subjects of the elementary curriculum. A major impetus for the creation of this book was the fact that children are naturally curious about the world around them ("Why is the sky blue?," "Why do geese fly south?," "Where do babies come from?") and that the investigation of their world can be made a stimulating and meaningful part of their lives, particularly when presented by teachers who can teach the fun and excitement of science every day.

I think it important at this point that you understand how this book came to be and what propelled me as I prepared the manuscript. Basically, I was driven by three mutually exclusive, yet highly related concepts. First, through my conversations with educators around the country, work with fellow teachers, observations of elementary classrooms, and some detailed interviews, I became convinced that science was the area of the elementary curriculum teachers feared most. Several theories have been proposed for these fears, including teachers' own dismal experiences with science when they were students, a feeling that science is too complex and too difficult to teach, and the belief that there is not enough time or resources to teach science during the normal school day. Suffice to say that many teachers place "Science" last on a list of their favorite subjects to teach.

Second, my research and interviews also revealed that teachers of science *do not* need to be repositories of vast sums of statistical data, factual information, and chemical equations to be effective teachers. More important is the concept of teacher as learner; the most successful teachers of science are those who are willing to learn along with their students, providing the models, processes, and a supportive arena in which students can begin making their own discoveries and pursuing their own self-initiated investigations. To that end, effective and successful science instruction should be "hands-on/minds-on"—designed by teachers who are as much learners as are their students.

Third, I earnestly believe that successful teachers of science have the same sense of wonder, awe, curiosity, and creative spirit that children are noted for. Science, for both students *and* teachers, should be touchable, smellable, tasteable, hearable, and seeable—in other words, it should not be book-bound or confined to the limits of a curriculum guide. Rather, science can and should be a participatory subject that offers opportunities to "get down and dirty" with the world and the way it operates. In essence, effective science teaching is a constant process of involvement—involvement on the part of students as well as teachers.

Given the fact that many teachers are uneasy with science, and with the teaching of science, I wanted to create a resource book that was both comfortable and useful. In so doing, I tried to create a book that emphasized *practicality* as well as *utility*. I also included several other features throughout the book, including:

- A process/discovery approach: I believe that science is best learned and best taught when it involves students completely in all its dynamics. This book is designed to help teachers promote a participatory approach to science—one in which students are actively engaged throughout the science curriculum.

- An integrative approach: One of the major trends in science education is the integration of science throughout the entire elementary curriculum. I believe that science should not be taught as an isolated subject area, but rather as a continual process of investigation that can be infused throughout all subjects and certainly throughout any child's life.

- Children's literature: Another exciting and dynamic trend in elementary education is the systematic inclusion of trade books throughout the science curriculum. Given the significant number of quality science books published each year, a major element in the design of a meaningful science curriculum is the thematic arrangement of that literature.

This book is designed for anyone wishing to actively engage children in all the dynamics and possibilities of science. Here you will discover a wealth of learning opportunities and teaching possibilities for all your students. I encourage you to consider this book a resource that helps elementary students of all ages, grades, and ability levels participate actively in the wide-ranging dimensions of science. I sincerely hope this book stimulates and encourages your students' active participation—learning, growing, and discovering throughout the entire science curriculum.

—Tony Fredericks

ACKNOWLEDGMENTS

For guidance, support, and encouragement throughout the creation of this book I am particularly grateful to the following:

A standing ovation and a crescendo of cheers goes to my friend and illustrator—Tony Stoner. Once again, Tony has lent his considerable talents and magnificent drawings to another TIP book. His extraordinary artistic abilities and incredible creative vision have added immeasurably to the ideas within these pages.

To Steve Haenel, my production editor, goes thunderous applause for, once again, shepherding another volume through the labyrinth of decisions, details, and deadlines.

To Nancy Coulter, my webmaster, whose remarkable creativity and superior technical talents have produced a magical Web site (http://www.afredericks.com) through which classroom teachers can obtain a rich array of practical and dynamic ideas.

I am particularly indebted to all the teachers around the country who have participated in my Bureau of Education and Research (B.E.R.) science seminars over the years. They have shared countless successes and challenges, and their ideas have been both the inspiration and foundation for the creation of this book. May their contributions be celebrated throughout every page.

Part I

Expanding the Science Curriculum

1 INTRODUCTION

 ## Into the Rainforest

Long, arcing liana vines hang down from every light fixture and corner of the room. An array of greens and golds and reds and blues splash across the walls and down the window panes. Illustrations of tapirs, harpy eagles, and long-tongued bats, and photos of passionflower butterflies, marmosets, and orchid bees are posted throughout the room. The distant cries of macaws, parrots, and toucans fill the air with a medley of sounds. Occasionally, the flapping of wings and the muted callings of distant monkeys can be heard in the distance. Insects of every dimension, size, and shape are heard buzzing and whirring through the air, while unseen reptiles slither across the weather-hewn bark of ancient trees. The lyrical gurgling of a hidden stream mixes with animal sounds to create an orchestral blend of basses and trebles that ebbs and flows across the landscape. To any visitor, it is evident that this place is filled with a rich diversity of life—and an incredible assortment of learning opportunities.

Janice Corbella has been a third-grade teacher in eastern North Carolina for the last seven years. Visitors entering her classroom often feel as though they have been transported to some lush Amazonian forest. Janice, along with her students, has transformed the room into an ecological wonderland awash in magnificent sights and sounds. This tropical rainforest simulation is so authentic that one almost expects an emerald boa to slither out of the shadows or a flock of ruby topaz hummingbirds to hover overhead.

Janice knows that most of her students may never have the opportunity to travel to Brazil or another tropical rainforest country to experience the sounds and sights of this endangered environment. She also realizes that the rainforests of the world are seriously endangered and that the next generation of kids must work together to help preserve the flora and fauna that live in this fragile ecosystem.

To actively involve her students in a host of positive science experiences, increase their awareness of this valued environment, and offer hands-on/minds-on activities and projects, Janice presented them with a thematic unit on rainforests (see page 62). Let's take a few moments and look in on Janice's class as her students explored some of the mysteries and marvels of this magical world.

A small group of three girls was comparing notes on information they had obtained from back issues of *International Wildlife* and *Wildlife Conservation* about the status of selected endangered species in the rainforests of South America. Hector and Christian had elected to contact various environmental organizations throughout the country (e.g., Rainforest Alliance [270 Lafayette St., Suite 512, New York, NY 10012], Rainforest Action Network [450 Sansome St., Suite 700, San Francisco, CA 94111], Children's Rainforest [P.O. Box 936, Lewiston, ME 04240], and The Nature Conservancy [1815 North Lynn St., Arlington, VA 22209]) to obtain information on each organization's efforts to preserve indigenous peoples. Inez, Diane, Boyd, and Tyrone were working with the school librarian to assemble a bibliography of rainforest literature that could be shared with their pen pals in another third-grade class in Winston-Salem.

Darrell, Bruce, and Tran were constructing a terrarium from a plastic soda bottle, soil, pebbles, charcoal, and an assortment of small plants. The terrarium (one of several) was to be set up on the window sill and the growth of its life forms tracked and recorded over a period of several weeks.

Josh, Connie, and Peter were in the process of drafting a letter to various political leaders sharing their concerns about rainforest destruction. Maurice and Sharon were replaying the rainforest audiotape ("Costa Rica Soundscapes," available from The Nature Conservancy, Merchandise Department, P.O. Box 294, Wye Mills, MD 21679 [1-800-382-2386]) and identifying each of the animal sounds recorded. Amanda and Carole were creating a series of posters focusing on representative animals that live in each of the four major layers of the rainforest.

One group of students was beginning to prepare a short video on the ecology of the rainforest. Sandra, Da'nelle, Janet, and Tim were interviewing other third-grade students to compile a list of questions to pose to the environmental sciences professor who would be visiting from the University of North Carolina the following week. Abraham and Michael began looking through several books to collect information about the poison dart frog and other dangerous animals that live in the rainforest. Roger and Bobbie were setting up an experiment to test the speed of depletion of nutrients from rainforest soil during flooding.

Enthusiasm echoed throughout the classroom. Students were excited by the opportunities to share information, discuss ideas for presenting data with other classes, and make decisions on how their knowledge could be used in productive ways. Some students chose to pursue independent activities while others worked quietly in small groups. Cooperative learning was evident throughout the room as students assembled ideas and shared possibilities in an atmosphere of mutual respect and support. Competition was scarcely evident, as students helped each other with ideas, resources, and extensions of activities. It was clearly apparent that this was a true community of learners, in which students all worked toward common goals, made and followed through on decisions, and took responsibility for how they learned as much as for what they learned.

Janice's students were engaged in a series of well-planned and thoroughly engaging learning opportunities wrapped around a *thematic unit*. The thematic unit was designed to assist students in learning about specific aspects of rainforest life, help them appreciate the various rainforests around the world, and become aware of the factors leading to destruction of the forests. Janice had introduced the unit with a collection of books about the rainforests, including those dealing with the climate, explorations, rates of destruction, medicines obtained from rainforest plants, and some of the most unusual animals found anywhere in the world. Her primary resource was *Exploring the Rainforest: Science Activities for Kids* by Anthony D. Fredericks (Golden, CO: Fulcrum, 1996). Other books included *A Walk in the Rain Forest* by Kristin Pratt

(Nevada City, CA: Dawn Publications, 1992); *Life in the Rain Forest* by Lucy Baker (New York: Scholastic, 1990); *Rain Forest* by Barbara Taylor (New York: Dorling Kindersley, 1992); *The Great Kapok Tree* by Lynne Cherry (San Diego, CA: Harcourt Brace, 1990); *Tropical Rain Forests Around the World* by Elaine Landau (New York: Franklin Watts, 1991); *Welcome to the Green House* by Jane Yolen (New York: S. P. Putnam's Sons, 1993); *Rain Forest Secrets* by Arthur Dorros (New York: Scholastic, 1990); and *Nature's Green Umbrella* by Gail Gibbons (New York: Morrow, 1994). Although these books were the basis of the unit, Janice was also able to offer her students a wide-ranging assortment of hands-on experiences, activities, experiments, and projects that provided engaging and exciting learning opportunities for several weeks.

Janice and thousands of other teachers have discovered that a thematic learning environment has enormous possibilities for "energizing" the science curriculum. A classroom that provides a variety of stimulating activities; a classroom overflowing with books and opportunities to read those books in a productive way; a classroom overflowing with meaningful science activities: This classroom facilitates learning and values the depth and breadth to which students can become immersed in their own scientific endeavors.

In Janice's classroom science comes alive, becoming an exciting and dynamic part of everyday classroom activities. Science is not separated from other subjects but is naturally blended into a coherent curriculum that offers learning opportunities for each student. The obvious advantage is that students begin to see the natural relationships and interrelationships that exist between science and other subjects. Those subjects are an extension of the science program and are equally supported by that program.

 # Science Literacy

The term *science literacy* has become synonymous with the way science is taught in this country. It implies that there is a basic set of concepts, facts, or principles that must be known by all students and that ignorance of those ideas results in a corps of pupils who have little or no knowledge of basic scientific precepts or practices.

Actually, science literacy is more generic and more general. It is more than the memorization of science facts (e.g., the nearest planet to the sun is Mercury) or science principles (e.g., a body in motion tends to remain in motion unless acted upon by an outside force). Rather, science literacy should be defined as a *process* of posing questions and discovering answers. In essence, science is simply a way of looking at the world.

You should infer from this definition that science is much, much more than a series of dry, lifeless facts waiting to be committed to memory. Rather, it is an attempt to take advantage of the natural queries—questions beginning with the words *how* and *why*—that children ask unceasingly about the world around them. Science literacy is the practice of providing youngsters not only opportunities to ask those questions, but also opportunities to pursue the answers. Thus, the inclination to seek out answers, more than the answers themselves, is at the very heart of science literacy.

A scientifically literate environment is one in which thinking is emphasized more than memorization. This means that you do not need to rely on the traditional methods of teaching science—lecture, textbooks, and rote memorization—to create an atmosphere of science literacy in your classroom. Your approach to science literacy should emphasize the *processes* of science, not the *products*. In short, science literacy is students doing and thinking science, not memorizing and regurgitating science.

Principles of Science Instruction

Children need many opportunities to make some sense out of their world and to lay a foundation from which future discoveries can emanate. The following principles should be considered "markers" from which elementary science programs can grow:

1. Students need to be provided with a basic body of knowledge that will form the foundation for future discoveries. Being able to identify certain types of leaves may be important in helping students gain an appreciation for conservation measures. Knowing the different types of simple machines provides a basis for students to comprehend the workings of more complex machinery. Nevertheless, meaningful science programs must move beyond these facts. Contrary to the arguments of some, an accumulation of facts is no more science than a collection of bricks is a house.

2. Students need to develop positive attitudes toward the entire world of science. Those attitudes become the catalyst for comprehension and critical thinking. They also serve as a foundation for a lifelong appreciation of science.

3. Students need to understand the interdependencies and interrelationships that exist among all elements of the world around them. So too do they need to see the role of science in promoting those understandings.

4. Students need to use science information in practical and personal ways. Possessing the skills of science is one thing; being able to use those skills in a meaningful context is quite another. Elementary science instruction should be geared toward offering youngsters a myriad of opportunities to put their knowledge into practice.

The implications for readers of this book are that these principles are naturally and normally embedded in the dynamics of a thematic unit. Thematic instruction offers a panorama of learning opportunities that embrace and enhance a child's sense of curiosity about the world. Teaching science thematically underscores the intellectual and developmental needs of children and presents an arena in which meaningful, hands-on/minds-on discoveries can be made.

 # Five Key Ingredients

Several professional organizations (e.g., The National Science Teachers Association, the American Association for the Advancement of Science) have developed criteria essential to effective science instruction. These criteria are based on the latest research available about how children learn and specifically about how they learn science.

What is most distinctive about these ingredients is that they are all embedded in well-designed thematic units in science. In short, a thematic unit provides a vehicle through which these key ingredients can be promoted and emphasized.

☐ **Hands-on Approach.** Children need active opportunities to manipulate science, to handle science, and to get down and dirty with science. A hands-on approach to science has long been promulgated as one of the most effective instructional strategies for any elementary teacher.

☐ **Process Orientation.** Focusing on the processes of science (e.g., observing, classifying, measuring, inferring, predicting, communicating, and experimenting) helps students appreciate science as a "doing" subject, one that never ends, but rather offers multiple opportunities for continuing examination and discovery.

☐ **Integrated Curriculum.** When science is integrated into all aspects of the elementary curriculum, students begin to understand its relevance and relationship to their daily lives outside the classroom. Children begin to comprehend the effect science has on daily activities, both in the present and in the future.

☐ **Cooperative Learning.** When children are given opportunities to share ideas, discuss possibilities, and investigate problems together, they can benefit enormously from the background knowledge of their peers, as well as from the strength that comes from a group approach to learning.

☐ **Critical Thinking.** One of the issues classroom teachers have wrestled with for many years concerns the need to help students become independent thinkers. In other words, effective science instruction is not dependent on helping students memorize lots of scientific information, but rather on assisting them in being able to use that data in productive and mutually satisfying ways.

Science education, to be fruitful, requires a partnership between the science curriculum, the joy of teaching, and children's inherent curiosity about their environment. Thematic instruction is a vehicle for stimulating science teaching and promoting authentic science learning. The benefits are many and the possibilities unlimited.

CREATIVE SCIENCE INSTRUCTION

 ## Teaching Thematically

Before we look at the design of thematic units, let's meet Glenn Garrison, who has been a third-grade teacher for nearly 14 years. Teaching in an inner-city school in Detroit has given him a unique perspective on the experiences and needs of his students. He had grown frustrated at his inability to transform the facts and concepts of his third-grade science textbook into meaningful and relevant learning experiences for his students. He would "cover" the textbook, but many of his students finished the year with poor attitudes, poor self-concepts, and poor mastery of the science concepts Glenn felt they should know.

One spring Glenn was given the opportunity to travel to the Annual Convention of the National Science Teachers Association. There he attended several sessions and workshops on thematic teaching and began to sense the enormous possibilities a thematic approach could offer his students. In talking with teachers from throughout the United States and Canada, Glenn became equally aware of the energy and enthusiasm evident when thematic teaching was used throughout the day. Throughout the convention, Glenn collected an array of ideas, techniques, and strategies for using thematic units and could hardly wait to return home to plan for the following school year.

Glenn realized that the best kinds of thematic units would be those he built with his students. That is, Glenn wanted to offer his students opportunities to take an active role in pursuing their own questions within a thematic unit, empowering them with a sense of ownership that would be both motivational and intellectually stimulating. He wanted to emphasize the experiences and background knowledge his students brought to class and help his students become actively engaged in selected themes.

Holistic Webbing

As the school year began, Glenn introduced his students to the concept of *holistic webbing*, a strategy that encourages students to tap into their prior experiences and background knowledge as they suggest holistic and cross-curricular extensions related to a science theme. This procedure is a collaborative one—an invitational process in which students are encouraged to contribute ideas and possibilities for exploration. Several of their ideas can then be incorporated into a prepared thematic unit (see Part II of this book).

One thing Glenn knew was that all students, and particularly his third-graders, are fascinated by dinosaurs. He wanted to take advantage of their natural curiosity and work with them in investigating a dinosaur theme, involving them through a host of hands-on/minds-on activities, an abundance of children's literature, and an array of intellectually stimulating projects.

Before initiating the "Dinosaurs" unit (page 53), Glenn drew an outline for a generic web on the chalkboard. In the center of the web he wrote "Dinosaurs" and asked students to 1) discuss what they knew about dinosaurs, 2) raise any questions they might have about dinosaurs, and 3) brainstorm for potential activities and projects that could be used to investigate this topic. The web his students created is illustrated in figure 2.1.

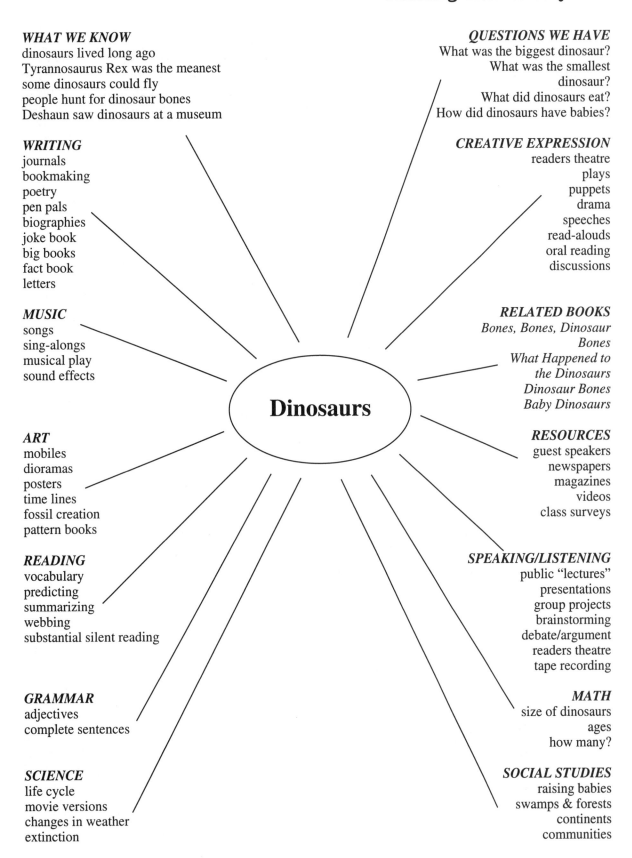

WHAT WE KNOW
dinosaurs lived long ago
Tyrannosaurus Rex was the meanest
some dinosaurs could fly
people hunt for dinosaur bones
Deshaun saw dinosaurs at a museum

WRITING
journals
bookmaking
poetry
pen pals
biographies
joke book
big books
fact book
letters

MUSIC
songs
sing-alongs
musical play
sound effects

ART
mobiles
dioramas
posters
time lines
fossil creation
pattern books

READING
vocabulary
predicting
summarizing
webbing
substantial silent reading

GRAMMAR
adjectives
complete sentences

SCIENCE
life cycle
movie versions
changes in weather
extinction

QUESTIONS WE HAVE
What was the biggest dinosaur?
What was the smallest
dinosaur?
What did dinosaurs eat?
How did dinosaurs have babies?

CREATIVE EXPRESSION
readers theatre
plays
puppets
drama
speeches
read-alouds
oral reading
discussions

RELATED BOOKS
*Bones, Bones, Dinosaur
Bones
What Happened to
the Dinosaurs
Dinosaur Bones
Baby Dinosaurs*

RESOURCES
guest speakers
newspapers
magazines
videos
class surveys

SPEAKING/LISTENING
public "lectures"
presentations
group projects
brainstorming
debate/argument
readers theatre
tape recording

MATH
size of dinosaurs
ages
how many?

SOCIAL STUDIES
raising babies
swamps & forests
continents
communities

Dinosaurs

Fig. 2.1. Student-generated "Dinosaurs" web.

After Glenn's students shared their thoughts, questions, and background knowledge, Glenn was able to integrate several of those ideas into a prepared thematic unit (see the "Dinosaurs" unit on page 53). Of course, not all of those ideas were appropriate, necessary, or complementary to the unit; however, the result was a unit "owned" by students and through which Glenn was able to promote purposeful learning in a variety of contexts. The following example shows the activities his class participated in for one day of the unit.

Theme: Dinosaurs

(Day #3)

8:30–9:00 OPENING

Students work alone or with partners completing activities unfinished from the day before. They may also begin new self-directed activities. Activities may include journal writing, book-related activities, newspaper or magazine research, choral readings, or silent reading time.

9:00–9:45 REQUIRED/OPTIONAL ACTIVITIES

Group 1—Students begin to build a dinosaur diorama. Using plastic figures, clay, pipe cleaners, and a shoe box, a prehistoric scene is created using ideas from several selected pieces of literature.

Group 2—Students are composing a letter to a class in another state, telling about some of the dinosaurs and dinosaur facts they are learning (the pen pals were established by the two respective teachers, who are former college classmates). The pen pals communicate regularly about some of their dinosaur activities.

Group 3—Students visit several classrooms throughout the school collecting data about favorite dinosaurs. Teachers, students, and administrative staff are interviewed about the dinosaurs with which they are most familiar. After students complete their data collection, a large bar graph will be constructed to illustrate their results.

Group 4—After viewing several different fossils (borrowed from the high school biology department), students begin to create their own fossils. Using plaster of paris and animal bones (chicken, turkey, fish, etc., boiled clean), students create several fossils for presentation in a school display case.

Group 5—Students finish construction of a dinosaur joke book. After looking through several examples of humor books, students modify old jokes and create new ones for selected dinosaur facts. The completed books will become a permanent part of the classroom library.

9:45–10:05   SUSTAINED SILENT READING

Students obtain books from the classroom library and scatter throughout the room. Books selected include: *Bones, Bones, Dinosaur Bones* by Byron Barton (New York: HarperCollins, 1990); *What Happened to the Dinosaurs* by Franklyn Branley (New York: Crowell, 1989); *Dinosaur Bones* by Aliki (New York: Crowell, 1988); *Dinosaurs* by Lee Bennett Hopkins (San Diego, CA: Harcourt, 1987); and Dougal Dixon's *Dinosaurs* (Honesdale, PA: Boyd's Mills Press, 1993). Most students engage in independent reading while two pairs of students read their books to each other. Several students share their findings about dinosaurs with the whole class.

10:05–10:25   WRITING PROCESS

Journals—Several students each take on the role of a meat-eating dinosaur. In their journals they write about a day in the life of their dinosaurs as seen through the eyes of the dinosaurs. Students are involved in different stages of the writing process, including drafting, revising, and editing.

Readers Theatre—A small group of four students continues work on a readers theatre adaptation of *Dinosaur Days* by Joyce Milton (New York: Random House, 1985). Students create scenarios about some of the dinosaurs from the book. The readers theatre work will be presented at a later date.

Big Book—Another group of students creates an oversized book that has been cut from cardboard into the shape of a stegosaurus. Sheets of paper have been stapled inside the covers. Students prepare essays about some of the largest dinosaurs. The completed book will be shared with several first-grade classrooms.

Fact Book—A small group of students heads to the library to collect data for inclusion in a "fact book" (a collection of interesting facts about dinosaur life). The final project will be donated to the school library for permanent display.

10:25–10:40   READ-ALOUD/STORYTELLING

Dinosaurs and Their Young by Russell Freedman (New York: Holiday, 1983) is read to the entire class (this book discusses the family life of hadrosaurs). Afterward, discussion centers on comparisons between the family lives of dinosaurs and selected animals of today.

10:40–11:10   MINI-LESSON

Opening—To begin the lesson, students are asked to create a list of all the words used to describe dinosaurs. These words are recorded on the chalkboard in a vertical list. Students are told that these words are examples of adjectives.

Book Study—The book *Discovering Dinosaur Babies* by Miriam Schlein (New York: Four Winds, 1991) is introduced to students. During the oral reading, students are asked to listen for adjectives used in the story. As words are noted, they are added to the list on the board.

Group Work—Students are divided into several heterogeneous groups. Each group is assigned four to five dinosaurs and is asked to generate adjectives (from the list on the board) that could be used to describe each dinosaur. Each group prepares a narrative about their dinosaurs using the identified adjectives. Each narrative is read to the whole class and differences and similarities in adjective use are discussed. Stories are posted on the bulletin board.

11:10–11:40   RESPONDING TO LITERATURE

Students have just completed *If the Dinosaurs Came Back* by Bernard Most (New York: Harcourt Brace, 1978).

Group 1—Students select one of the dinosaurs illustrated and named on the last page of the book and draw its shape on a sheet of construction paper. They cut out the dinosaur and, using it as a pattern, make pages and construction-paper covers for student dinosaur books. Students use these materials to write their own stories about "if dinosaurs came back." Students have time to share their stories.

Group 2—Students select one of the dinosaurs in the story and write a letter to it saying why they would like it to come back.

Group 3—Students are involved in a discussion: If it were possible to bring back the dinosaurs, how would they convince their community that it is a good idea? Students are divided into pairs, with each pair creating a full-page newspaper advertisement that will persuade the community.

11:40–11:50   ASSESSMENT

Students are provided opportunities to share what they have learned during the morning with each other. Students may elect to add new entries to their dinosaur journals or select work to be included in their portfolios.

11:50–12:10   RECESS/SHARING

12:10–12:40   LUNCH

12:40–1:25   SPECIAL CLASS

Students go to music, art, computer room, library, or physical education.

1:25–2:10   MATH

2:10–2:40   TEACHER-DIRECTED LESSON

Opening—Students are asked to brainstorm for various reasons why the dinosaurs disappeared (the earth became too cold, there wasn't enough food, etc.).

Group Work—Students each select a reason and get into groups by identified reason (e.g., all who believe the dinosaurs were eliminated by a meteor shower are formed into one group). Each group prepares a pictorial representation for its selected reason (ice age, no plants, etc.) and presents its picture(s) to the class. Groups research their selected reasons (via interviews, library work, etc.) and share their findings with the whole class.

Closure—A local scientist or college professor is invited to speak on the latest findings or theories about the disappearance of the dinosaurs.

2:40–3:00   DAILY CLOSURE AND ASSESSMENT

Students review daily activities. Summary statements about the day's activities are generated by the class and recorded on a large wall calendar in the front of the classroom. Each student transcribes a summary statement onto a personal calendar, which is taken home and shared with parents at the end of the week. Portfolios are updated and students meet with each other to review each other's portfolio entries.

3:00–3:15   DISMISSAL

As you review Glenn's plan, note how he has successfully integrated the topic of "Dinosaurs" across the curriculum and throughout the day. In a very real sense, Glenn and his students have been able to participate in a series of related activities that expands science into every corner of the schedule and every facet of their academic community. In short, science is now actively pursued for an entire day, rather than for one brief period of that day.

 # The Thematic Approach to Learning

A thematic approach to science is a combination of experiments, activities, children's literature, hands-on/minds-on projects, and materials used to expand a scientific concept or idea. Thematic teaching (and thematic learning) is multidisciplinary and multidimensional—it has no boundaries and no limits. It is responsive to the interests, abilities, needs, and input of children and respects their developing aptitudes and attitudes. In essence, a thematic approach to science offers students a realistic arena within which they can learn and investigate scientific principles for extended periods of time.

Thematic teaching in science is built on the idea that learning can be integrative and multi-faceted. A thematic approach to science education provides children with a host of opportunities to become actively involved in the dynamics of their own learning. In so doing, they will be able to draw positive relationships between what happens in the classroom and what is happening outside the classroom. Thematic teaching promotes science education as a sustaining and relevant venture.

Thematic Teaching and Multiple Intelligences

Thematic instruction in science offers many opportunities for students to actively engage in a constructivist approach to learning. It offers a variety of meaningful learning situations tailored to students' needs and interests. Children are given the chance to make important choices about *what* they learn as well as about *how* they learn it. Thematic instruction provides the means to integrate the science program with the rest of the elementary curriculum while involving students in a multiplicity of learning opportunities and ventures.

Incorporated into thematic explorations are opportunities for students to take advantage of, hone, and build upon one or more of their multiple intelligences. According to Howard Gardner (*Frames of Mind: The Theory of Multiple Intelligences*, New York: Basic Books, 1985), each individual possesses eight different intelligences (see "The Eight Human Intelligences") in varying degrees. These intelligences (as opposed to a single intelligence quotient, as traditionally reported via many standardized intelligence tests) help determine how individuals learn and how they fare in their daily lives. Gardner defines an "intelligence" as consisting of three components:

The Eight Human Intelligences

According to Howard Gardner, individuals possess these eight intelligences in varying degrees:

1. *Verbal-Linguistic Intelligence* involves ease in producing language and sensitivity to the nuances, order, and rhythm of words. Individuals who are strong in verbal-linguistic intelligence love to read, write, and tell stories.

2. *Math-Logic Intelligence* relates to the ability to reason deductively or inductively and to recognize and manipulate abstract patterns and relationships. Individuals who excel in this intelligence have strong problem-solving and reasoning skills and ask questions in a logical manner.

3. *Musical Intelligence* encompasses sensitivity to the pitch, timbre, and rhythm of sounds as well as responsiveness to the emotional implications of these elements of music. Individuals who remember melodies or recognize pitch and rhythm exhibit musical intelligence.

4. *Spatial Intelligence* includes the ability to create visual-spatial representations of the world and to transfer them mentally or concretely. Individuals who exhibit spatial intelligence need a mental or physical picture to best understand new information. They are strong in drawing, designing, and creating things.

5. *Bodily-Kinesthetic Intelligence* involves using the body to solve problems, make things, and convey ideas and emotions. Individuals who are strong in this intelligence are good at physical activities, possess good eye-hand coordination, and have a tendency to move around, touch things, and gesture.

6. *Intrapersonal Intelligence* entails the ability to understand one's own emotions, goals, and intentions. Individuals strong in intrapersonal intelligence have a strong sense of self, are confident, and can enjoy working alone.

7. *Interpersonal Intelligence* refers to the ability to work effectively with other people and to understand them and recognize their goals and intentions. Individuals who exhibit this intelligence thrive on cooperative work, have strong leadership skills, and are skilled at organizing, communicating, and negotiating.

8. *Naturalist Intelligence* includes the capacity to recognize flora and fauna; to make distinctions in the natural world; and to use this ability productively in activities such as farming and biological science.

- The ability to create an effective product or offer a service that is valuable in one's culture.

- A set of skills that enables an individual to solve problems encountered in life.

- The potential for finding or creating solutions for problems, which enables a person to acquire new knowledge.

Individuals differ in the strength (or weakness) of each of these intelligences in isolation as well as in combination. For example, whereas some individuals learn best through linguistic means, others are more kinesthetic learners, and still others are spatial learners. Suffice to say that no two people learn in the same way, nor should they be taught in the same way.

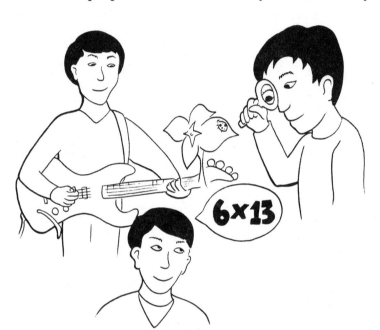

The research on multiple intelligences has revealed that teaching aimed at sharpening one kind of intelligence will carry over to others. There is also mounting evidence that learning opportunities that involve a variety of intelligences allow students to take advantage of their preferred intelligence(s) as well as strengthen weaker intelligences. In short, thematic instruction provides those opportunities.

Thematic instruction allows you to extend, expand, and take advantage of students' intelligences. Thematic instruction also provides you with many opportunities to combine the intelligences of your students with the resources, information, and scientific principles of your entire science curriculum. In short, thematic teaching celebrates multiple intelligences, offering learning opportunities that provide students with a meaningful and balanced approach to science learning. Above all, thematic instruction supports and emphasizes the varied relationships that exist among scientific inquiry, a process approach to learning, and the exercise of multiple intelligences in a positive and supportive environment.

Advantages of Thematic Instruction

Thematic instruction in science offers a plethora of advantages for both teachers and students. Table 2.1 synthesizes some of those benefits.

Traditional approaches to science instruction rely primarily on packaged materials, usually in the form of commercial science series and the ubiquitous teacher's manual and student textbooks. A major disadvantage is that students often have the perception that science is textbook-based or that it takes place only during a specified time period of the school day. Thematic instruction in science, however, provides students (and teachers) with an expanded curriculum—one without limits or boundaries. Table 2.2 compares some of the differences between thematic instruction in science and more traditional forms of classroom organization such as textbooks and school/district curriculum guides.

Table 2.1
Advantages of Thematic Teaching

- Emphasizes and celebrates an individual's multiple intelligences in a supportive and creative learning environment.

- Focuses on the *processes* of science rather than the *products* of science.

- Reduces and/or eliminates the artificial barriers that often exist between curricular areas and provides an integrative approach to learning.

- Promotes a child-centered science curriculum—one in which students are encouraged to make their own decisions and assume a measure of responsibility for learning.

- Stimulates self-directed discovery and investigation both in and out of the classroom.

- Assists youngsters in developing relationships between scientific ideas and concepts, thus enhancing appreciation and comprehension.

- Stimulates the creation of important scientific concepts through first-hand experiences and self-initiated discoveries.

- More time is available for instructional purposes. Science instruction does not have to be crammed into limited, artificial time periods but can be extended across the curriculum and throughout the day.

- The connections that can and do exist between science and other subjects, topics, and themes can be logically and naturally developed. Teachers can demonstrate relationships and assist students in comprehending those relationships.

- Science can be promoted as a continuous activity—one not restricted by textbook designs, time barriers, or even the four walls of the classroom. Teachers can help students extend science learning into many aspects of their personal lives.

- Teachers are free to help students look at a scientific problem, situation, or topic from a variety of viewpoints, rather than the "right way" frequently demonstrated in a teacher's manual or curriculum guide.

- There is more emphasis on *teaching* students and less emphasis on *telling* students.

- Teachers are provided with an abundance of opportunities for integrating children's literature into all aspects of the science curriculum and all aspects of scientific inquiry.

- Teachers can promote problem solving, creative thinking, and critical thinking within all dimensions of a topic.

Table 2.2
Comparison of Thematic and Text-Based Curricula

Thematic Instruction	*Textbook-Based Learning*
Gives students a sense of ownership of their learning.	Teacher makes all decisions as to what will be learned and when.
Facilitates responsible learning.	Students are told what to do, but not always why.
Is holistic in nature.	Is fragmented and disconnected.
Encourages risk-taking.	Emphasizes the accumulation of "right" answers.
Promotes inquiry and reflection.	Teacher asks most of the questions and has most of the answers.
Breaks down artificial curricular boundaries; integrates the entire curriculum.	Segmented and divided curriculum is imposed.
Encourages collaborative and cooperative learning.	Students attempt to get high marks or good grades (vis-à-vis tests and exams).
Has teacher model appropriate learning behaviors.	Teacher dictates learning behaviors.
Uses assessment that is authentic, meaningful, and infused throughout the learning process.	Assessment occurs at the end of learning a predetermined body of knowledge and is teacher-controlled.
Encourages self-direction and individual inquiries.	Everyone must learn the same body of knowledge.
Helps students understand the *why* of what they're learning.	Students are told what to learn.
Allows students to make approximations of learning.	Students must learn absolutes.
Promotes, supports, and stimulates multiple intelligences.	Everyone learns through a formal, standardized lecture/recitation process.

Thematic instruction (and the thematic units that provide the structure for thematic instruction) facilitate the teaching of science as much as the learning of science. The entire science curriculum is broadened, strengthened, and made more attentive to the development of individual science competencies.

Building Thematic Units

This book is designed to offer you an intriguing array of exciting and dynamic thematic units for every area of your science curriculum. These units will energize your entire science program and offer students innumerable opportunities for investigating the dynamics of scientific discovery and enlarging their knowledge and appreciation of the world around them.

The thematic units in this book are built on the idea that science learning can be integrative and multifaceted. Your students will have numerous opportunities to become actively involved in the excitement of learning about, and participating in, science. In so doing, they will become more responsible students and you will become a more effective teacher.

The units and mini-units in Part II of this book are ready to use. That is, you can incorporate them as is into your daily lesson plans. Of course, you are also encouraged to modify, adapt, or revise any section of a particular thematic unit or mini-unit according to the dictates of your specific science program, time allowances, or available materials (see chapter 3).

Although the units in this book are adaptable to any classroom science program, some teachers may wish to design their own units from scratch. It's important to keep in mind, however, that a thematic unit is not simply a random collection of assorted activities, experiments, or science projects. The effectiveness of a unit depends on its being built upon a specific topic, an assembly of major generalizations and/or principles, selected key concepts, certain materials, authentic activities and projects, and a distinctive arrangement of those activities.

Kucer (1993) has outlined a series of procedures that can assist teachers in developing their own thematic units in science. His steps, outlined in table 2.3 offer guidelines that can help you create and structure instructionally effective units. In addition, this sequence of six stages provides the organizational framework for all of the thematic units included in Part II of this book.

Table 2.3
Procedures for Thematic Unit Development

1. Identification of a theme topic.

    a. The topic is relevant and of interest to the students.

    b. The topic is significant; it is important to know about.

2. Identification of major generalizations and/or principles (three to five usually work best) upon which the thematic unit will be based.

    a. The generalizations and/or principles focus on big ideas rather than minor concepts, facts, or details.

    b. The generalizations and/or principles are interrelated.

3. Identification of key concepts that support the generalizations and/or principles.

    a. Each concept is related to several generalizations and/or principles.

    b. The concepts are critical to understanding the generalizations and/or principles.

4. Gathering of thematic materials.

    a. The materials focus on the same set of generalizations and/or principles.

    b. Materials include different types of resources: books, magazines, newspapers, filmstrips, records/audiotapes, movies/videotapes and Web sites.

5. Brainstorming and generation of various activities related to the theme topic, generalizations and/or principles, concepts, and materials.

    a. Activities are authentic in nature: linguistically, cognitively, developmentally, socioculturally.

    b. Activities engage students in the use of various communication systems (reading, writing, listening, speaking, art, music, mathematics, dance/movement) to learn about the generalizations and/or principles and concepts in the theme.

    c. Activities engage students in the use of various thinking processes from different disciplines (science, social science, literature) to learn about the generalizations and/or principles and concepts in the theme.

    d. Activities engage students in both collaborative and independent work.

    e. Activities provide students with opportunities for problem solving, divergent thinking, risk taking, and choice (among activities as well as materials).

    f. Activities take advantage of differing intelligences: linguistic, logical, musical, spatial, kinesthetic, intrapersonal, interpersonal, naturalistic.

    g. Activities help strengthen various intelligences: linguistic, logical, musical, spatial, kinesthetic, intrapersonal, interpersonal, naturalistic.

6.   Arrangement of thematic materials and activities.

a.   There are opening activities that introduce students to the theme and closing activities that draw together and celebrate what has been learned and accomplished.

b.   Materials and activities are arranged around particular generalizations and/or principles and related concepts.

c.   Materials and activities include the most simple/concrete to the most complex/abstract.

d.   Materials and activities include the collaborative and the independent.

e.   Throughout the thematic unit, activities require students to revisit prior meanings and to integrate them with current meanings.

Source: S. B. Kucer, *Procedures for Thematic Unit Development.* Unpublished document, presented at the International Reading Association Annual Convention, San Antonio, TX, April 1993. Used by permission.

Development of a Thematic Unit

To illustrate the development of a thematic unit, let's travel to California and observe Jean Shuker's classroom. Jean teaches fourth grade in San Francisco, where she has worked for the last nine years. Over the past several years she has become increasingly aware of the impact and power of thematic teaching and has read everything she can find on the subject. She has also attended regional and statewide science conferences, visiting many sessions on thematic teaching. At each conference she has taken advantage of the opportunities to talk with other teachers and solicit their ideas about thematic units. As a result of her networking and reading, Jean gained some valuable insights and perspectives on the effective use of thematic units in the science program.

It quickly became apparent to Jean that thematic teaching offered learning opportunities for her students that went far beyond the dictates of a science text or the dry outline of a curriculum guide. Jean became aware of the power of thematic teaching to involve students in their own self-initiated discoveries and participate in collaborative learning ventures. The more Jean read about thematic units, the more excited she became about their utility for her science program.

One year, in preparation for a thematic unit on "The Changing Earth," Jean sat down to craft a basic outline for the unit. Using the six stages outlined in table 2.3, Jean selected specific elements as follows:

1. Identification of a theme topic:

   The Changing Earth

2. Identification of major generalizations and/or principles:

   - The earth is changing all the time.
   - Some changes can be predicted; others cannot.
   - Some changes are dangerous to humans.

3. Identification of key concepts:

   - natural changes versus man-made
   - the earth's surface is changing
   - destruction can be widespread
   - the environment is affected

4. Gathering of thematic materials:

Literature selections:

   - Pringle, Lawrence. *Fire in the Forest: A Cycle of Growth and Renewal*. New York: Atheneum, 1995.
   - Newton, David. *Earthquakes*. New York: Watts, 1993.
   - Simon, Seymour. *Volcanoes*. New York: Morrow, 1988.
   - Hooper, Meredith. *The Pebble in My Pocket*. New York: Viking, 1996.

Web sites:

- http://www.afredericks.com
- http://volcano.und.nodak.edu
- http://athena.wednet.edu/curric/land/todayqk.html

Videos:

- *Living on Our Changing Earth* (No. A51127). National Geographic Society, 1983.
- *Our Dynamic Earth* (No. A51162). National Geographic Society, 1979.

5. Generation of various activities: Several activities were brainstormed with students. Other activities were selected from a variety of professional resources, Internet sites, and collegial input.

6. Arrangement of thematic materials and activities: After gathering an array of potential activities, experiments, and science projects, Jean arranged the ideas into a format that included simple/concrete activities, familiar/unfamiliar, and collaborative/independent activities (see page 28).

This thematic unit design gives you a framework or outline for the development of your own units. With it, you will be able to create units that address specific components of your school or district science curriculum, the unique interests or concerns of your students, and current events (a shuttle launch, the discovery of a new dinosaur, a medical breakthrough). Also, you will be able to keep your science program fresh, current, and invigorating—for you as well as your students!

 # National Science Education Standards

In response to a growing concern about the state of science education in the United States, hundreds of people—including teachers, school administrators, parents, curriculum coordinators, college faculty members, scientists, engineers, and government officials—cooperated in developing an outline of what students need to know, understand, and be able to do to be scientifically literate.

The standards that resulted from this intensive examination of science education focus on a blending of "science as process" and "science as inquiry." This hands-on/minds-on approach to science education helps students actively develop their understanding of science by combining scientific knowledge with reasoning and thinking skills.

The standards are based on the premise that science is an active process and that learning science is something that students do, not something that is done to them.

Not only do the standards provide an outline (as opposed to a curriculum) for the development of science instruction, but they also bring coordination, consistency, and coherence to the improvement of science education. The standards are organized into six broad categories: standards for science teaching, standards for professional development for teachers of science, standards for assessment in science, standards for science content, standards for science education programs, and standards for science education systems. Because effective teaching is at the heart of science education, this chapter focuses on the science teaching standards. These standards are outlined in table 2.4.

Table 2.4
National Science Teaching Standards

Teaching Standard A

Teachers of science plan an inquiry-based science program for their students. In doing this, teachers

- Develop a framework of yearlong and short-term goals for students.

- Select science content and adapt and design curricula to meet the interests, knowledge, understanding, abilities, and experiences of students.

- Select teaching and assessment strategies that support the development of student understanding and nurture a community of science learners.

- Work together as colleagues within and across disciplines and grade levels.

Teaching Standard B

Teachers of science guide and facilitate learning. In doing this, teachers

- Focus and support inquiries while interacting with students.

- Orchestrate discourse among students about scientific ideas.

- Challenge students to accept and share responsibility for their own learning.

- Recognize and respond to student diversity and encourage all students to participate fully in science learning.

- Encourage and model the skills of scientific inquiry, as well as the curiosity, openness to new ideas and data, and skepticism that characterize science.

Teaching Standard C

Teachers of science engage in ongoing assessment of their teaching and of student learning. In doing this, teachers

- Use multiple methods and systematically gather data about student understanding and ability.

- Analyze assessment data to guide teaching.

- Guide students in self-assessment.

- Use student data, observations of teaching, and interactions with colleagues to reflect on and improve teaching practice.

- Use student data, observations of teaching, and interactions with colleagues to report student achievement and opportunities to learn to students, teachers, policy makers, and the general public.

Teaching Standard D

Teachers of science design and manage learning environments that provide students with the time, space, and resources needed for learning science. In doing this, teachers

- Structure the time available so that students are able to engage in extended investigations.

- Create a setting for student work that is flexible and supportive of science inquiry.

- Ensure a safe working environment.

- Make the available science tools, materials, media, and technological resources accessible to students.

- Identify and use resources outside the school.

- Engage students in designing the learning environment.

Teaching Standard E

Teachers of science develop communities of science learners that reflect the intellectual rigor of scientific inquiry and the attitudes and social values conducive to science learning. In doing this, teachers

- Display and demand respect for the diverse ideas, skills, and experiences of all students.

- Enable students to have a significant voice in decisions about the content and context of their work and require students to take responsibility for the learning of all members of the community.

- Nurture collaboration among students.

- Structure and facilitate ongoing formal and informal discussion based on a shared understanding of rules of scientific discourse.

- Model and emphasize the skills, attitudes, and values of scientific inquiry.

Teaching Standard F

Teachers of science actively participate in the ongoing planning and development of the school science program. In doing this, teachers

- Plan and develop the school science program.

- Participate in decisions concerning the allocation of time and other resources to the science program.

- Participate fully in planning and implementing professional growth and development strategies for themselves and their colleagues.

Source: National Academy of Sciences, *National Science Education Standards* (Washington, DC: 1996), pp. 30–52.

In reviewing these standards, it should become evident that many of their elements are embodied in the philosophy and design of a thematic approach to science education. Equally important is the fact that the standards assist teachers in defining the structural components of an effective thematic unit and the environment in which that instruction can take place. The following description illustrates how one teacher integrated these teaching standards into a thematic teaching plan.

A Sample Teaching Plan

Jean Shuker (to whom you were introduced earlier) is a long-time advocate of thematic instruction. In addition, she believes that the National Science Education Standards have helped her create a learning environment in which she and her students can work together as active learners. Her science program is based on four assumptions: 1) a successful science curriculum is never static; 2) science instruction can be extended throughout the curriculum; 3) teachers should be facilitators rather than lecturers; and 4) student understanding of science is actively constructed through a wide variety of individual and social processes. These assumptions are commensurate with a thematic approach to science instruction.

The following example is a single-day lesson plan that Jean used as part of a three-week thematic unit on "The Changing Earth." Each of the activities/designs/experiments has been coded to one or more of the National Science Teaching Standards.

Theme: The Changing Earth

(Day #4 - Volcanoes)

8:30–8:50 OPENING

After putting away their book bags, students assemble around a table on which are several different daily newspapers (e.g., *San Francisco Chronicle*, *Los Angeles Times*, *New York Times*). Students are invited to look through the newspapers for articles regarding changes in the earth (volcanic eruptions, earthquakes, landslides, etc.). Selected articles are cut out and assembled into an ongoing journal. One small group of students is creating a dictionary booklet entitled "My Earth Book." These pupils are creating a page for each letter of the alphabet (i.e., A = Abyss; B = Biosphere; C = Chasm; D = Dangerous). This group is using the book *Earth Words* by Seymour Simon (HarperCollins, 1995) as a reference for their dictionary. [**Teaching Standards A, B, D, E**]

8:50–9:15 WHOLE CLASS INSTRUCTION

Jean shows the video "This Changing Planet" (National Geographic Society, Washington, DC; Catalog No. 30352). (This film explains how the earth is constantly changing its surface through weather, erosion, earthquakes, and volcanoes.) Afterward, she takes the students outside to the playground and constructs a chemical volcano as follows: She sets a soda bottle on the ground and builds up a mound of dirt around it so that only the top of the neck shows. She puts 1 tablespoon of liquid detergent in the bottle. She adds a few drops of food coloring, 1 cup of vinegar, and enough warm water to fill the bottle almost to the top. Very quickly, she adds 2 tablespoons of baking soda (that have been mixed with a little water) to the bottle. She invites students to discuss the similarities between their artificial volcano and the ones depicted in the video. Students record their discussions in their science journals. [**Teaching Standards A, B, D**]

9:15–9:45 WRITING PROCESS

Facts on File—One group of students goes to the school library to search various books for facts about volcanoes. They collect information about the location of major volcanoes around the globe as well as the damage done by each volcano.

Journals—Several students have taken charge of monitoring the events at Mount Kilauea in Hawaii, as reported in the local newspaper. These students record those events in their individual journals and also compare notes on their individual interpretations of those events.

Newspaper—A small group of students has designed a weekly newspaper that reports catastrophic geologic events as they happen around the world. Each event is assigned to a reporter who develops it into an article.

Interviews—A variety of students have initiated a series of interviews with graduate students and professors at San Francisco State University. The interviews center around recent volcanic eruptions in the South Pacific, an earthquake in Eastern Europe, an interpretation of the Richter scale, and the effects of wind erosion in the Midwest. [**Teaching Standards B, D, E**]

9:45–10:30   DRAMA TIME

Students have been divided into four groups. Each group uses various playhouses and other models to create make-believe towns located near major volcanoes (Mount St. Helens, Kilauea, Mount Pinatubo). Each of these towns is assembled on a sheet of plywood along with a clay model of a volcano. Students create skits based on each of the three different types of volcanic eruptions (Hawaiian-type, Strombolian-type, and Vulcanian-type) and the effects on their towns. Students are invited to make videotapes of their skits. **[Teaching Standards A, E]**

10:30–11:30   REQUIRED/OPTIONAL ACTIVITIES

Group 1—Under the direction of the teacher's aide, students watch her manipulate a paraffin block on a hot plate to simulate the formation of a hot-spot volcano (the type that formed the Hawaiian Islands over thousands of years).

Group 2—Students use the Internet (http://volcano.und.nodak.edu) to contact working volcanologists and request information on the effects of volcanoes, eruption rates, and temperatures of different types of lava. The data collected will be organized in the form of charts and graphs.

Group 3—Students have erected a "graffiti wall" outside the classroom and have invited students from other classes to record their information or research about volcanoes. Later, these ideas will be reconstructed in the form of a giant semantic web.

Group 4—After viewing the video "The Violent Earth" (National Geographic Society, Washington, DC; Catalog No. 51234), students compose a book of adjectives and descriptive phrases that have been used to describe various volcanoes around the world.

Group 5—Students who have obtained the address of Hawaii Volcanoes National Park (P.O. Box 52, Hawaii National Park, HI 96718) write to request the park's newspaper, descriptive brochures, and information on recent eruptions of Kilauea. The data will be compared with information collected from a variety of library resources and newspaper clippings. **[Teaching Standards B, D, E]**

11:30–12:00 LUNCH

12:00–12:30   SUSTAINED SILENT READING

Students obtain books from the collection offered by Jean and disperse throughout the room. Books selected include *Earthquakes and Volcanoes* by Fiona Watt (Usborne, 1993); *Mountains and Volcanoes* by Barbara Taylor (Kingfisher, 1993); *Volcano and Earthquake* by Susanna Rose (Knopf, 1992); *Surtsey: The Newest Place on Earth* by Kathryn Lasky (Hyperion, 1992); and *Volcanoes* by Gregory Vogt (Watts, 1993). Several groups of two and three students share their selected books in cooperative reading groups. **[Teaching Standards A, D]**

12:30–1:15   TEACHER-DIRECTED ACTIVITIES

Opening—Jean decides to open the day's lesson with an Anticipation Guide. Using the book *Volcanoes* by Seymour Simon (Morrow, 1988), she has created the following set of statements, which are presented to students before she begins reading the book:

BEFORE   *AFTER*

_____   _____   1. Volcanoes happen all over the world.

_____   _____   2. More volcanoes happen in Hawaii than in any other state.

_____   _____   3. A volcano is the most destructive natural disaster in the world.

_____   _____   4. Volcanoes always occur along tectonic plates.

_____   _____   5. Volcanoes are rare occurrences.

Each student is provided with a duplicated copy of the Guide and is invited to mark "True" or "False" in the "BEFORE" column depending on their personal beliefs.

Class Discussion—The class discusses the responses made on individual Anticipation Guides. Agreements and disagreements are voiced and ideas are recorded on a special area of the chalkboard. Jean invites students to make predictions about the book.

Selected Reading—Jean reads the book *Volcanoes* to the class. Prior to reading she asks students to listen for statements or information that may confirm or modify their responses to the Anticipation Guide statements recorded earlier. She also stops periodically throughout the reading and invites students to change or alter their original predictions based on data in the book.

Closure—Jean has students assemble in small groups and complete the "AFTER" column of the Anticipation Guide (based on the information learned from the book, students mark "True" or "False" in the space in front of each statement). Later, she encourages students to share reasons for their responses and any changes they may have made in their original recordings. Jean urges students to confirm their ideas through additional reading in other pieces of literature. [**Teaching Standards A, C**]

1:15–1:35   STORYTELLING/READ-ALOUD

The students all gather on the large Reading Rug in the back of the classroom to listen to Jean read the book *What If...The Earth* by Steve Parker (Watts, 1995). Afterwards, students discuss volcanoes and lithospheric plates (this discussion will form the basis for extending activities related to other natural changes on the surface of the earth, such as earthquakes, glaciers, and erosion). [**Teaching Standards A, B, C, E**]

1:35–2:10   ART/MUSIC

The art teacher, Mr. Muñoz, has posted a large sheet of newsprint in the school cafeteria. Students, in small groups, have been invited to create a large mural of the events that would happen during and immediately after a volcanic eruption. Mr. Muñoz has shared slides of Diego Rivera's murals, which were painted on public buildings throughout Mexico (this will be extended in later days into a series of geography and history lessons on the land and culture of Mexico). [**Teaching Standards A, B, D**]

2:10–2:40   SELF-SELECTED ACTIVITIES

Group 1—A small group of students creates models of each of the four different types of volcanoes (shield volcano [Mauna Loa], cinder cone volcano [El Misti], strato-volcano [Mount Fuji], and dome volcano [Mt. St. Helens]). The models will be displayed in the school library.

Group 2—Students construct models of the two basic types of lava (*pahoehoe* and *aa*), using modeling clay and photographs from various books. These will be displayed in the classroom with appropriate labels.

Group 3—Students create an extended time line of the major events in the continuing eruption of Mt. Kilauea in Hawaii. Events are selected from those reported on television, those obtained from the Internet, and those appearing in the newspaper (as well as other sources).

Group 4—Students write letters to university students at the University of California-Berkeley, requesting a personal visit. The college students are being invited to share information they learned during a course called "The Geology of North America."

Group 5—Two small groups of students are each compiling bibliographies of current trade books related to "The Changing Earth." These bibliographies will be shared with teachers in other classes. [**Teaching Standards A, B, C, D. E**]

2:40–3:00   RESPONDING TO LITERATURE

Students complete the reading of the book *Volcano: The Eruption and Healing of Mount St. Helens* by Patricia Lauber (Aladdin, 1986). The class has been divided into three separate groups. The first group is discussing the similarities between Mount St. Helens and a volcano erupting in the South Pacific. A second group is developing a story map that outlines the major elements of the book in a graphic representation. The third group is summarizing the major points of the book in the form of a newspaper article to be included in the class newspaper, *Earth Watch*. [**Teaching Standards B, D**]

3:00–3:15   DAILY CLOSURE

The class is divided into teams of three students each. The teams discuss some of the items they learned during the course of the day, items remaining for them to work on in following days, and items on which they would still like to obtain additional information. Each team's recorder shares some of the discussion with the entire class. Students are invited to share their ideas with parents upon their return home. [**Teaching Standards B, C, D, E**]

3:15 DISMISSAL

 # Changing Science Instruction

Jean and thousands of other teachers around the country have discovered that the National Science Education Standards and thematic instruction in science are mutually supportive. Most importantly, they offer classroom teachers multiple opportunities to share the joy and excitement of science education with greater numbers of students. This joining facilitates science instruction (particularly for those who are less than comfortable with their scientific backgrounds) and helps students view science as a process of discovery and exploration rather than of memorization and regurgitation.

The standards in concert with thematic instruction are generating some remarkable changes in the ways science is taught and the ways in which it is learned. These changes are summarized in table 2.5.

Table 2.5
Changing Emphases in Science Education

Less Emphasis on	More Emphasis on
Treating all students alike and responding to the group as a whole	Understanding and responding to individual student's interests, strengths, experiences, and needs
Rigidly following curriculum	Selecting and adapting curriculum
Focusing on student acquisition of information	Focusing on student understanding and use of scientific knowledge, ideas, and inquiry processes
Presenting scientific knowledge through lecture, text, and demonstration	Guiding students in active and extended scientific inquiry
Asking for recitation of acquired knowledge	Providing opportunities for scientific discussion and debate among students
Testing students for factual information at the end of the unit or chapter	Continuously assessing student understanding
Maintaining responsibility and authority	Sharing responsibility for learning with students
Supporting competition	Supporting a classroom community with cooperation, shared responsibility, and respect
Working alone	Working with other teachers to enhance the science program

Source: National Academy of Sciences, *National Science Education Standards* (Washington, DC: National Academy Press, 1996), p. 52.

Thematic instruction not only offers students unique opportunities to process and practice hands-on science, but also provides teachers with integrative strategies and activities that enhance science education in all curricular areas. In addition, students helped to draw realistic parallels between classroom enterprises and events and circumstances outside the classroom. In short, thematic instruction can aid students in understanding the relevance of science to their everyday lives.

HOW TO USE THE THEMATIC UNITS

The thematic units and mini-units in Part II of this book emphasize key concepts throughout the science curriculum. In addition, the activities, experiments, and projects within each unit integrate skills from a variety of areas to ensure a unique, multidisciplinary, interdisciplinary study of science with a strong literature component.

 ## Using a Unit

The thematic units are designed as complete and thorough units of study. However, you are not required to use any single unit in its entirety. You may elect to use selected portions of a unit, to combine one section of a unit with other classroom curricular materials, or to eliminate some sections of a unit (perhaps due to lack of materials or time). The true value of these units lies in the fact that they can be easily adapted, modified, or adjusted according to the dictates of your science program, your level of comfort, and students' interests.

The mini-units (which can be used alone, in conjunction with a corresponding thematic unit, or in concert with another mini-unit), offer engaging literature, activities, and projects for specific scientific concepts. Each mini-unit includes activities, questions, and related works of literature to provide you with a variety of choices through which to develop targeted content objectives and skills.

Each thematic unit contains a wide scope of activities designed to promote growth in critical thinking, creative thinking, problem solving, and scientific investigation, and to give students unlimited opportunities to process and interpret information while learning relevant knowledge and concepts. As you will note, I have suggested a plethora of activities from which you can select the ones most appropriate for your students and your science program objectives.

You are not expected to use all those activities nor all parts of any single activity. Instead, you and your students should decide which activities best serve the needs of the science program and of the students themselves. You will discover activities that can be used individually, in small groups, in large groups, or as a whole class. Providing students with opportunities to make some of their own activity selections can be a powerful and energizing element for the entire science program. When youngsters are given those opportunities, their appreciation of science and their interest in learning important scientific concepts grows tremendously.

As students become involved in the various units, I suggest that you guide them in researching and/or developing other activities based on classroom dynamics and teaching/learning styles. For learning to be meaningful, it must have relevance. I encourage you and your students to adapt the activities included in the units and mini-units to create a challenging learning environment that will arouse each student's natural curiosity and encourage students to pursue new ideas and formulate their own connections.

The literature included within a unit or mini-unit reflects a range of reading levels. Feel free to select and use literature that best meets the needs and abilities of your students in addition to promoting specific scientific concepts. An "energized" science curriculum includes literature selections throughout its length and breadth. You will discover innumerable opportunities for developing, expanding, and teaching scientific principles based on the literature in these units. In that regard, remember that the readability or difficulty level of a single book should not determine if or how it will be used; rather, the emphasis should be on whether students are interested and motivated to pursue literature-related activities that promote learning in a supportive and holistic science curriculum.

To that end, you are encouraged to substitute or include books that you have found to be particularly noteworthy, whether they are old-time favorites, new releases, or recommendations from colleagues or professional resources. The utility of a thematic unit lies in the fact that the literature used can come from a variety of sources; they are not restricted to the suggestions made here. Keeping these units fresh and updated with new literature resources can be a powerful stimulant for both teacher and student interest.

I hope you will make these units your own. Add to them, adapt them, and allow students to help you design additional activities, experiments, and projects (see the section on "Holistic Webbing" in chapter 2) that will challenge them, arouse their natural curiosity, and create a dynamic learning environment.

 # Implementing a Unit

Teaching science thematically is not necessarily an all-or-nothing proposition. That is, it is not necessary to use a thematic unit for a full day, a full week, or a full month. You have several options as to how you present a thematic unit to your class, how much you want it to dominate your daily curriculum, and how involved you and your students want to be. Obviously, your level of comfort with thematic teaching and the scope and sequence of your classroom or district science curriculum may determine the degree to which you utilize a thematic unit or mini-unit. Here are some options for your classroom:

1. Teach a unit throughout a school day and for an extended period of several school days.

2. Teach a unit for half a day for several days in succession.

3. Use a unit or mini-unit for two or more subject areas (e.g., science plus language arts) in combination and the regular curriculum for the other subjects.

4. Use a unit as the curriculum for science and the regular curriculum for the other subjects.

5. Teach a unit for an entire day and follow up with the regular curriculum on succeeding days.

6. Use a unit or mini-unit as a follow-up to information and data presented in a textbook or curriculum guide.

7. Provide students with a thematic unit or mini-unit as independent work upon completion of lessons in the basal textbook.

8. Teach cooperatively with a colleague and present a thematic unit to both classes at the same time (this can be done with two classes at the same grade or with two different classes, each at a different grade level).

9. Use a unit intermittently over a span of several weeks.

How you use a thematic unit or mini-unit may be determined by any number of factors. It is safe to say that there is no ideal way to implement a unit as part of your classroom plans. The preceding listing is only a partial collection of ideas. The dictates of your own particular teaching situation, personal experience, and student needs may suggest other possibilities and alternatives to this register of ideas.

Part II

Thematic Units and Mini-Units

4 LIFE SCIENCE

Thematic Units

ANIMALS—WILD AND WONDERFUL

GENERALIZATIONS/PRINCIPLES:

1. There is a wide variety of animal species throughout the world.

2. Animals have different habits and habitats.

3. Animals grow and develop in different ways.

CONCEPTS:

growth and development
habits and behaviors
physical features and characteristics

MATERIALS:

Primary Literature Selections

Fredericks, Anthony D. *Weird Walkers*.
Minnetonka, MN: NorthWord Press, 1996.

Kitchen, Bert. *Somewhere Today*. Cambridge,
MA: Candlewick Press, 1992.

Tomb, Howard. *Living Monsters: The World's
Most Dangerous Animals*. New York:
Simon & Schuster, 1990.

Wilson, April. *Look!* New York: Dial, 1990.

Secondary Literature Selections

Arnosky, Jim. *Secrets of a Wildlife Watcher*. New York: Beech Tree Books, 1991.
    Takes the reader through important phases of wildlife observation, including the importance of journaling.

Brimmer, Larry. *Animals That Hibernate*. New York: Watts, 1991.
    A well-written introduction to a wide variety of hibernating animals throughout the world.

Brooks, Bruce. *Making Sense*. New York: Farrar, 1993.
    This book addresses animal perception and communication in an amusing, down-to-earth style.

Burns, Diane. *Snakes, Salamanders and Lizards*. Minocqua, WI: NorthWord Press, 1995.
    A take-along guide that identifies and describes some of the most common reptiles and amphibians in the United States.

Chinery, Michael. *Questions and Answers About Polar Animals*. New York: Kingfisher, 1994.
    Lots of information in an easy-to-read format answers many of kids' questions about the polar regions of the world.

Dorros, Arthur. *Animal Tracks*. New York: Scholastic, 1991.
    Using a guessing-game format, the author introduces readers to animals and the tracks they leave behind.

Fredericks, Anthony D. *Clever Camouflagers*. Minnetonka, MN: NorthWord Press, 1997.
    An insect that looks like a flower, a fish that looks like seaweed, a frog that looks like a leaf, and nine more amazing creatures inhabit this book.

Fredericks, Anthony D. *Surprising Swimmers*. Minnetonka, MN: NorthWord Press, 1996.
    Squids that swim at 30 mph, "dragons" that eat underwater plants, animals that jump out of their shells, and nine more unusual creatures populate this book.

Greenway, Shirley. *Animals Homes: Burrows*. Brookfield, CT: Newington Press, 1991.
    Focuses on a dozen animals that live in burrows, reasons why the burrows are built, and how they protect their inhabitants.

Kitchen, Bert. *When Hunger Calls*. Cambridge, MA: Candlewick Press, 1992.
    An examination of 12 creatures, their habitats, and their lifestyles in a variety of environments.

Lacey, Elizabeth. *What's the Difference? A Guide to Some Familiar Animal Look-Alikes*. New York: Clarion, 1993.
    The author examines the differences between 22 pairs of animals often mistaken for each other (e.g., frogs and toads).

Myers, Jack. *Can Birds Get Lost? and Other Questions About Animals*. Honesdale, PA: Bell Books, 1991.
    Dozens of children's questions are accurately answered in a pleasant, conversational tone.

Pringle, Lawrence. *The Golden Book of Insects and Spiders*. Racine, WI: Western, 1990.
    A beautifully illustrated book that include diagrams and information about various insects and spiders.

Thompson, Ruth. *Creepy Crawlies*. New York: Aladdin, 1990.
    An interesting book loaded with inviting and detailed information about some strange critters.

INITIATING ACTIVITY:

Invite students to divide animals into several different categories (e.g., mammals, reptiles, birds, etc.; scales versus feathers; herbivores versus carnivores; polar versus tropical; etc.). Invite them to think of some possible rules for categorizing animals. Next have the children compare several animals and write a list on the board stating the animals' similarities and differences. Compile a list on the board on the general characteristics of each animal classification. Next, divide the students into several groups and assign an animal classification to each group. Encourage groups to record the qualifications of their animal group on a piece of poster board using felt-tip markers. The groups can also provide five sample animals for their animal group (use the secondary literature selections as resources). Invite the groups to present their findings to the class. Allow the students time to debate whether the information provided by each group is complete and accurate. Ask student groups to develop charts explaining general information about the development of their animal classification, and discuss how that information might be shared with students in other classes.

GENERAL ACTIVITIES:

1. Invite students to brainstorm for different types of animals. Show the National Geographic filmstrip, "Fins, Feathers, Fur: Animal Groups" (Educational Services Catalog, Filmstrip No. 30619). This will show how to classify animals into groups. Using the information from the filmstrip, encourage students to create a semantic web, categorizing the animals researched in the initiating activity.

2. Have each student choose an animal to study. Students can pretend that they are writing a newspaper birth announcement for the birth of their animal. They will need to do some research to collect necessary information. Provide the birth announcement sections of daily newspapers for students to use as a reference for writing their articles. Decorate a bulletin board to look like a section of a newspaper and hang the animal birth announcements there. Students can include an illustration of the new "baby."

3. Encourage students to keep an "Animal Journal." This can be a record of all the animals they see during the week. This should include pets, wild animals, insects, and animals seen on television. Hang posters for sightings of mammals, fish, birds, reptiles and amphibians, etc. Students can add to the charts daily.

4. Invite students to create an ongoing trivia game, with each student contributing 5 to 10 questions and answers for the game. The game can be played on a regular basis (as students are accumulating more information about selected animals) or as a "final exam" at the conclusion of the unit.

5. Focus on a different group of animals each day (e.g., Monday—insects, Tuesday—fish, Wednesday—carnivores, etc.). Each day include stories, songs, student-created plays, trivia, games, and environmental concerns related to the subject animal group. Invite a speaker from the community or local college to discuss current issues relating to the animals.

6. Help students to create a variety of bird feeders. These can be hung in various locations around the school. Bird populations, as well as the various varieties of birds in your area, can be recorded over an extended period of time. Following are several possible bird feeders:

- Tie a string to a pine cone. Fill the crevices in the cone with peanut butter and roll the cone in some birdseed. Hang the cone from a tree branch.

- Cut a large section from the side of a waxed or plastic milk carton. Fill the carton with birdseed and hang it from a branch.

- Tie several pieces of orange peel onto lengths of string. Hang these in various locations in a nearby tree.

7. Invite students to create their own classroom terrariums. Provide each of several groups with a clean, two-liter, plastic soda bottle (cut off the top beforehand). Ask students to cover the bottom with a layer of small pebbles mixed with bits of charcoal (aquarium charcoal from a pet supply center works well). A second layer of soil (about twice as deep as the first layer) is then placed in the bottle. Sprinkle the soil with just enough water to keep it moist. Place several plants, such as mosses, ferns, lichens, and liverworts in the soil. Grass seed may be sprinkled, too. Place several rocks or pieces of wood in the bottle. Small land animals (e.g., snails, earthworms) can be added. Cover the top (to allow humidity to build up), ventilate, and keep out of direct sunlight. Invite students to record animal observations over a period of time.

PRIMARY LITERATURE SELECTIONS:

Title: Somewhere Today
Author: Bert Kitchen
Bibliographic Information: Cambridge, MA: Candlewick Press, 1992
   Summary: Somewhere today a sea otter is floating on its back, a chameleon is reaching out for food, a sidewinding rattlesnake is making tracks, and a dormouse is sleeping. This delightful book provides readers with glimpses into the daily habits of selected animals.

1. Invite youngsters to create their own mini-books about animals, people, or events in and around where they live. These compositions can be gathered together into small booklets or newsletters and shared with others. Following are some examples:

    a. Animals in and around the house:
        "Somewhere today two termites were ...."
        "Somewhere today our pet cat was ...."

    b. Family members, neighbors, or friends:
        "Somewhere today my mother is ...."
        "Somewhere today the Smiths are ...."

    c. Trees, flowers, or other plants:
        "Somewhere today a giant pine tree ...."
        "Somewhere today a small underground seed ...."

2. Ask youngsters to keep a journal of the activities, habits, travels, and motions of a single animal. Kids may want to select a house pet or some other animal that can be observed quite regularly throughout the day. Provide youngsters with a "Field Journal"—a simple notebook wildlife biologists frequently use to track the activities of one or more wild animals over the course of an extended period of time.

3. Several of the animals mentioned in this book are endangered, others live in very specific environments, and a few are fascinating simply because they do things no other animals do. Children can learn more about these animals, as well as others throughout the world, by obtaining copies of or subscribing to one or more of the children's magazines listed in the appendix.

4. Provide students with an inexpensive tape recorder that has a corded microphone. Invite them to record and catalog various animal sounds. Help students to tape the microphone handle to the end of a broom handle or a long pole (be sure no tape covers the microphone itself). Encourage students to go outside on a clear and calm day (no wind blowing, for example) and place the microphone near one or more wildlife homes (i.e., a bird's nest, a beehive, a wasp's nest, etc.). The students should check first to be sure the animal(s) are at home.

5. Invite each student to take on the role of a single animal. Encourage students to do the necessary library research on the habits and behaviors of their selected animals. Then have each student write a diary entry, as his or her selected animal might record it, on a day in the life of that species.

Title: Living Monsters: The World's Most Dangerous Animals

Author: Howard Tomb

Bibliographic Information: New York: Simon & Schuster, 1990

Summary: Youngsters will thoroughly enjoy this exciting and intriguing book filled with eye-popping information and delightful illustrations about 18 of the world's most amazing—and dangerous—creatures. A wonderful addition to any animal study.

1. Invite students to survey classmates, friends, and relatives about their choices for the world's most dangerous animals. Encourage students to assemble their data in the form of charts and graphs that can be shared with others. How do the results of their survey compare with the author's selection of the world's most dangerous animals? Some students may wish to do additional research on animals not described in the book.

2. Suggest that youngsters create "Wanted" posters for some of the animals in the book. What information should be included on each poster? What are some of the vital statistics that students would want to share with others via their posters? If possible, obtain one or more "Wanted" posters from your local post office and use them as models for your students' posters.

3. If possible, obtain one or more of the following videos from the National Geographic Society (1145 17th Street NW, Washington, DC 20036-4688 [1-800-343-6610]) or your local video store and share them with your students. Invite students to compare the information on the videos with that in the book. What did they learn in the video(s) that wasn't in the book, and vice versa?

- *Crocodiles: Here Be Dragons* (Catalog No. 51482)
- *Hunt for the Great White Shark* (Catalog No. 51996)
- *Shark Encounters* (Catalog No. 51553)
- *Strange Creatures of the Night* (Catalog No. 51376)
- *Realm of the Alligator* (Catalog No. 50872)
- *The Sharks* (Catalog No. 51593)

4. Students may wish to "capture" their own spider webs. Here's how they can do that:

Materials:

   transparent self-adhesive plastic (clear Contac® paper is available in most hardware or large variety stores)

   dark-colored construction paper

   masking tape

   aerosol hair spray

Invite students to go outside with the hair spray, masking tape, and black construction paper and locate several spider webs. Selected students each make five rings of masking tape (sticky side out) and slip them over the fingers of one hand. Instruct each student to press the construction paper to their hand so that it sticks to the rings of masking tape (this allows them to hold the construction paper vertically so that it doesn't fall). Tell them to carefully hold the construction paper just behind a spider web. With the other hand (or using a friend as assistant), gently spray the web from the other side (this will cause the web to stick to the construction paper). Carefully remove the web; it will stick to the face of the construction paper. When students return to the classroom, they place a sheet of the transparent self-adhesive plastic over the web (or laminate it) to seal it (this will preserve the spider web). *Note:* This process takes some practice, so tell students not to get discouraged if they can't do it the first time. Students may wish to collect several different examples of spider webs from around the school or neighborhood. A scrapbook of different webs can be put together.

Title: Weird Walkers

Author: Anthony D. Fredericks

Bibliographic Information: Minnetonka, MN: NorthWord Press, 1996

Summary: This book offers readers an amazing journey of discovery as they learn about some of the most unusual animals on earth. They meet a fish that walks out of the water, a lizard that walks on the water, and a tree that "walks" through the water.

1. Invite students to locate some land snails around the perimeter of their houses (look in the moist soil of gardens in the early morning hours). Put a 2″ layer of damp soil in a large clear jar and place the snails in it. Place some cheesecloth over the jar opening and fasten it with string or a large rubber band (this will keep the occupants inside— snails can crawl up glass). Instruct children to sprinkle the soil every so often to keep it wet and to keep the jar in a cool, shady place. Small pieces of lettuce can be placed in the jar for food. Encourage children to keep a journal or notebook of the snail's activities. How fast does it move? How much does it eat in one day, one week, two weeks? How active is it? How much does it travel?

2. Invite youngsters to locate animal tracks in soft dirt or mud (these can be cat or dog tracks, or a deer or some other wild animal in your area). Place a circle of cardboard around the track and push it partway down into the soil (be careful not to disturb the track). Mix up some plaster of paris according to the package directions. Pour it into the mold up to the top of the cardboard strip. Wait until the plaster cast hardens and then remove the cast from the ground print. Take off the cardboard strip and clean off the bottom. Students may wish to make several of these (each a separate animal) and display them in the classroom along with pertinent research notes.

3. Invite children to write to one or more of the following environmental agencies to obtain relevant literature on endangered species around the world. When the material arrives, make a list of the animals that are most seriously imperiled, those that are endangered, and those that are threatened.

National Wildlife Federation
8925 Leesburg Pike
Vienna, VA 22184

National Audubon Society
666 Pennsylvania Ave., SE
Washington, DC 20003

Friends of Wildlife Conservation
New York Zoological Society
185 Str., Southern Blvd.
Bronx Zoo
Bronx, NY 10460

4.   Invite children to make a large chart (on an oversized piece of poster board, for example) listing the speeds at which selected animals travel. The chart can rank-order animals from the fastest to the slowest or vice versa. Be sure to encourage kids to place animals with which they are very familiar on the chart (i.e., dogs, cats, guinea pigs, etc.). How much faster is their pet than the slowest animal on the chart? How much slower is the family dog than the fastest animal on the chart?

5.   Encourage students to adopt an endangered animal. Write to the American Association of Zoological Parks and Aquariums (4550 Montgomery Ave., Suite 940N, Bethesda, MD 20814) and ask about their animal adoption program. For a few dollars, kids will be assigned an endangered animal and receive a photograph and fact sheet about their adoptee. The money sent is used to care for and feed selected endangered animals.

Title: Look!

Author: April Wilson, illustrator

Bibliographic Information: New York: Dial, 1990

Summary: Each two-page spread in the book consists of two seemingly identical illustrations. Closer inspection of each pair will reveal 12 vital differences. The differences are all listed in the back of the book, along with a fascinating guide to the wonders of nature portrayed in each pair of pictures.

1. Provide each student with an inexpensive (disposable) camera. Invite each child to set up the camera in a semi-permanent place (e.g., on top of a tree stump, on a sidewalk curb, on a porch railing) outside so that it will not be disturbed or moved for several hours or several days (if possible). *Note:* Many disposable cameras, because they are packaged in cardboard, can be glued to the bottom of a shoe box (for example; see fig. 4.1). The shoe box can then be secured to a permanent place by cutting the sides, folding them out, and nailing or stapling them to a permanent spot (such as a wooden rail). Check the predicted weather conditions for the next several days to make sure the camera won't be harmed.

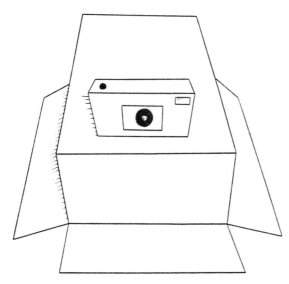

Fig. 4.1.

   Invite youngsters to select a specific object (within 5 to 10 feet) and take a photograph of that item. Ask them to return at regular intervals (every three hours, every other day) and take additional photos of the same spot (with the camera in the same fixed position). Encourage youngsters to keep a running written record of the photos taken and the time and day each one was taken.

   When the photos are developed, have youngsters place two consecutive photos side by side and look for any differences between the photos. Is there a leaf that moved or fell? Did an animal enter or exit the picture? Did a flower open up or close? Did the wind make some items move or blow about? Invite children to inspect the photos carefully and create a journal of any differences noted.

2. Invite children to select any three or four differences on a specific two-page spread in the *Look!* book. Encourage them to share (in writing or orally) the differences they note as well as the reasons for those differences. Why did the illustrator select those particular differences? What is the significance of those differences? What can you learn by noting those differences?

3. Tell youngsters that several varieties of animals have colors or shapes that help them look like something else in their environment. For some animals, this natural camouflage is extremely well developed: there are frogs that look like leaves, grasshoppers that look like rocks, birds that resemble tree trunks, and caterpillars that look like bird droppings. Explain to youngsters that animals typically camouflage themselves for one of two reasons: to protect themselves from being eaten by other animals or to disguise themselves so that they can sneak up and capture nearby prey.

    Provide children with a list of animals that "practice" camouflage. Encourage them to select books from the school or public library (the book *Clever Camouflagers* by Anthony D. Fredericks [Minnetonka, MN: NorthWord Press, 1997] is particularly good) and identify each animal and the way in which it camouflages itself. The following list (partially completed) can be used as a starting point:

Animal	Camouflage Technique
Chameleon	Can change its skin color to match surroundings
Walking stick	
Bittern	Resemble swaying grass
Ptarmigan	
Sargassum fish	
Orchid praying mantis	Looks like a flower part
Decorator crab	
Tree hopper	
Leaf fish	
Katydid	
Flounder	Colors match ocean bottom

4. Invite children to go outside and select a section of grassy area (part of a yard, lawn, or playground). Push four sharpened pencils into the soil in a one-foot square pattern. Have kids tie string around the pencils, making a miniature "boxing ring" on the ground. Invite them to get on their hands and knees and look closely inside the square. Encourage them to make notes of all the different types of animals they see inside the ring. They should note the movements, habits, or behaviors of any animals (ants, grasshoppers, caterpillars, worms) as they travel (jump, crawl, slither) through the ring. Encourage youngsters to visit their rings frequently over a period of several weeks.

CULMINATION:

Students will be invited to select one or more of the following activities and projects:

1. Have a class pet show. Invite each student to sign up for a time slot to show his or her pet. If some students do not own pets, invite them to make a presentation on a pet they would like to own, or borrow a pet from a friend or neighbor for the day.

2. Arrange for the local SPCA or Humane Society to give a presentation on pet care, adoption of pets, and birth control for pets.

3. Invite students to create a play, focusing on one of the following topics:

    a. Endangered and/or extinct animals

    b. The care and feeding of animals

    c. Animal groups

    d. Animal habitats

4. If possible, take a field trip to a zoo, park, or wildlife preserve. Invite students to write about their favorite animals.

5. Invite students to present a mini-lesson, to another class, on a specific group of animals.

6. Encourage students to keep daily or weekly journal entries on what they learned or found interesting during the unit.

7. Individual students can create an advertisement (written or oral) for their favorite animal or group of animals. Class members will be asked to describe the distinguishing features or characteristics that should be highlighted in the promotion of their selected animal(s).

8. Invite a local zoologist or biologist from a local college to visit your classroom and share information related to a specific animal or group of animals. Invite students to prepare questions beforehand to be sent to the guest speaker.

DINOSAURS

GENERALIZATIONS/PRINCIPLES:

1. Dinosaurs are ancient animals that lived many years ago.

2 Dinosaurs are extinct, yet scientists know a great deal about them from their bones.

3. There were many different kinds of dinosaurs.

CONCEPTS:

life on earth has changed over time
scientific investigation
exploring and hypothesizing

MATERIALS:

Primary Literature Selections

Lauber, Patricia. *Dinosaurs Walked Here and Other Stories Fossils Tell*. New York: Bradbury, 1987.

Lessem, Don. *Dinosaur Worlds: New Dinosaurs, New Discoveries*. Honesdale, PA: Boyds Mills Press, 1996.

Most, Bernard. *Dinosaur Questions*. San Diego, CA: Harcourt Brace, 1995.

Pringle, Laurence. *Dinosaurs: Strange and Wonderful*. Honesdale, PA: Boyds Mills Press, 1995.

Secondary Literature Selections

Aliki. *Fossils Tell of Long Ago*. New York: HarperCollins, 1990.
    A great introduction to the formation and creation of fossils, highlighted by easy-to-understand illustrations.

Barton, Byron. *Bones, Bones, Dinosaur Bones*. New York: HarperCollins, 1990.
    An ideal book for young readers. Offers a glimpse into the search for dinosaur bones, as well as how dinosaur skeletons are constructed.

Cosner, Shaaron. *Dinosaur Dinners*. New York: Watts, 1991.
    This book concentrates on the food that dinosaurs ate and offers additional information on the history and evolution of dinosaurs.

Craig, Jean. *Discovering Prehistoric Animals*. Mahwah, NJ: Troll, 1989.
    A simple, straightforward text filled with lots of down-to-earth facts about dinosaurs.

Dixon, Dougal. *Dougal Dixon's Dinosaurs*. Honesdale, PA: Boyds Mills Press, 1993.
    An exciting, up-to-the-minute compilation of everything scientists know about dinosaurs. This is one of the best reference guides around.

Hisa, Kunihiko. *How Did Dinosaurs Live?* Minneapolis, MN: Lerner, 1990.
    This book examines the lifestyles of thirty-seven different types of dinosaurs and how they lived.

Hopkins, Lee Bennett. *Dinosaurs*. San Diego, CA: Harcourt Brace, 1987.
    Eighteen delightful poems give youngsters some fresh perspectives and insights into the world of dinosaurs.

Lambert, David. *Dinosaurs*. New York: Warwick, 1989.
> A well-written book that presents general information about dinosaurs. Includes some activities on specific dinosaurs.

Lasky, Kathryn. *Dinosaur Dig*. New York: Morrow, 1990.
> Several families are involved in the search for dinosaur fossils in this description of a dig in the Montana Badlands.

Sattler, Helen. *The New Illustrated Dinosaur Dictionary*. New York: Lothrop, 1990.
> It's all here! Everything any dinosaur nut would want to know about 350 dinosaurs and other related creatures.

Sattler, Helen. *Tyrannosaurus Rex and Its Kin: The Mesozoic Monsters*. New York: Lothrop, 1989.
> The book examines the most famous of all dinosaurs and takes a look at its descendants. Colorful illustrations and a time line highlight this book.

Schlein, Miriam. *Discovering Dinosaur Babies*. New York: Four Winds, 1991.
> Lots of information about the ways in which different species of dinosaurs cared for their young.

Simon, Seymour. *New Questions and Answers About Dinosaurs*. New York: Morrow, 1990.
> Scientists are learning more about dinosaurs every day. This book presents readers with the most up-to-date information.

Audiovisual Selections (on dinosaurs)

Plants and Animals of Long Ago (Catalog No. C30165). Washington, DC: National Geographic Society (filmstrip).

Dinosaurs: Puzzles from the Past (Catalog No. C51046). Washington, DC: National Geographic Society (video).

INITIATING ACTIVITY:

Purchase three or four medium-sized watermelons and paint them white. Hide them in a "dinosaur nest" somewhere on the playground before the start of the lesson. Invite students to locate the dinosaur's nest to begin the dinosaur unit. Once the "eggs" are found, they can be cut open and shared with the group. After returning to the classroom invite students to draw illustrations of imaginary creatures that might have laid those eggs. (Provide opportunities for students to share their illustrations, and any accompanying text, in a variety of interactive experiences.)

GENERAL ACTIVITIES (related to the entire thematic unit):

1. Prior to the lessons use string to measure out the height and length of various dinosaurs. You may wish to use some of the following measurements:

Dinosaur	Length	Height
Tyrannosaurus rex	32 ft.	14 ft.
Brachiosaurus	67 ft.	27 ft.
Stegosaurus	28 ft.	13 ft.
Plateosaurus	20 ft.	7 ft.
Camptosaurus	18 ft.	8 ft.
Velociraptor	8 ft.	3 ft.
Protoceratops	8 ft.	3 ft.

Line the class up by height and choose the student in the center of the line to be "average." Trace this person on heavy butcher paper to get a pattern. Go out on the playground and roll out the string for a dinosaur. Have the students guess how many bodies long and high that dinosaur is. Record the estimates and then use the pattern to obtain actual measurements. Do this for all the dinosaurs. Invite students to compare the sizes.

2. Invite students to develop different menus for various types of dinosaurs. What plants or meats must each dinosaur eat to stay healthy? How much food should a particular dinosaur eat each day? Students may wish to create a "Dinosaur Menu," using menus from local restaurants as examples.

3. Encourage students to work in small groups to create a large wall mural showing life when the dinosaurs existed. The mural can be drawn on heavy butcher paper and decorated with paints, crayons, construction paper, or other art materials selected by the students. Be sure students know that humans appeared on the face of the earth about 60 million years after the dinosaurs died out; consequently, there should be no humans in the murals!

4. Make arrangements with the "specials" teachers to become involved in the unit, too. Let the music teacher sing dinosaur songs and possibly do a dinosaur musical for the school. Invite the art teacher to make dinosaur T-shirts using stencils and paint. Ask the gym teacher to practice dinosaur movements in games. Invite the librarian to read dinosaur stories.

5. Invite students to write to a dinosaur pen pal, explaining how life is different during the present time in comparison with the life their dinosaur pen pal had.

6. Encourage students to make graphs and charts that record the heights and sizes of various dinosaurs. Bar graphs, line graphs, and the like can all be developed from information students collect from several different resources.

7. Invite a professor from a local college to make a short presentation on dinosaurs. Encourage students to prepare a list of questions beforehand to ask the visiting speaker.

8. Using known poems and songs, create frames and invite students to turn them into dinosaur poems and songs. For example, use "Brown Bear, Brown Bear" and turn it into "Dinosaur, Dinosaur, what did you see?" Students may wish to combine all the songs and poems into a class collection.

9. Invite students to poll other students in the school about their favorite dinosaurs. The information (on favorite dinosaurs) can be collected and displayed on large wall charts.

PRIMARY LITERATURE SELECTIONS:

Title: Dinosaurs: Strange and Wonderful

Author: Laurence Pringle

Bibliographic Information: Honesdale, PA: Boyds Mills Press, 1995

Summary: The illustrations jump out at you in this all-inclusive and delightful introduction to dinosaurs, both large and small. An engaging text provides youngsters with a complete and thorough overview of the age of dinosaurs.

1. Ask students whether it would be easier for a large dinosaur or a small dinosaur to survive. What special types of survival techniques would a small dinosaur need to compete with its bigger cousins? Invite students to record their information in a "Dinosaur Response Journal." Encourage students to create charts that graph the relative heights and sizes of various dinosaurs with animals of today.

2. Invite students to create a testimonial on the benefits of herbivores versus carnivores. Their journal entries can focus on the attributes of various dinosaurs and why some attributes might be more desirable than others.

3. Encourage students to create skeletons of some of the illustrated dinosaurs, using pipe cleaners. Each student may wish to include a complete description of his or her model, outlining its special features. Invite students to display their models around the classroom.

4. Invite students to write and illustrate stories about going back in time to observe the age of dinosaurs. Remind students that dinosaurs died out long before humans appeared on the earth.

Title: Dinosaurs Walked Here and Other Stories Fossils Tell

Author: Patricia Lauber

Bibliographic Information: New York: Bradbury, 1987

Summary: In this book youngsters discover the mystery of dinosaurs and the clues they left behind—bones, teeth, and footprints. This book explains how fossils are formed and all that scientists can learn from them.

1. Provide small groups of children with a pile of chicken bones (the bones can be boiled in a solution of water and vinegar and dried thoroughly). Invite each group to arrange the bones in their original configuration. Encourage students to discuss any problems they have in putting a chicken skeleton back together, even though most of them know what a chicken looks like. Talk about the difficulties scientists have in putting dinosaur skeletons back together, particularly because no human has ever seen a live dinosaur.

2. Invite several students to pretend to be dinosaurs. As that creature, invite them to describe their bodies, outlining their size, configuration, dimensions, skeletal structure, and other important features. Invite each one to explain why his or her (dinosaur) body is different from those of other dinosaurs. (It may be necessary to precede this activity with one in which each student describes his or her own body.)

3. Encourage students to create their own dinosaur fossils. Provide small groups of students with pie plates half filled with wet sand. Place several chicken bones in the sand. Put circular strips of cardboard around the bones; mix and pour plaster of paris into the makeshift molds. After the plaster of paris has dried, encourage students to examine their "fossils" to note any similarities to dinosaur fossils.

4. Invite students to create their own dinosaur books. Encourage each student to trace an outline of a dinosaur on a sheet of construction paper and cut it out. Students may then trace that shape on another piece of construction paper, as well as several sheets of newsprint, and cut them out. All the sheets can be put together (with the construction paper sheets on the front and back) and stapled together. Ask students to write about their favorite dinosaur on the pages of their dinosaur book.

5. Locate a photograph or illustration of a dinosaur skeleton. Have students count the number of bones in a leg, in the chest, or in other sections of the dinosaur body. Encourage them to compare their count with the number of bones in a similar section in their bodies (you may wish to provide a human skeleton illustration, too). Encourage students to prepare graphs and charts of the similarities and differences.

Title: Dinosaur Worlds: New Dinosaurs, New Discoveries

Author: Don Lessem

Bibliographic Information: Honesdale, PA: Boyds Mills Press, 1996

Summary: This is the ultimate dinosaur book. Filled with an incredible array of facts, discoveries, and exciting new information by the founder of The Dinosaur Society, this is the perfect reference tool for every dino-lover.

1. Invite each student to create an illustration of the *ideal* dinosaur. What would be its physical features? What size would it need to be to survive? What about its shape or color? Encourage students to keep these illustrations and compare them with illustrations in this and other books.

2. Invite students to become reporters who have been transported back to the time of the dinosaurs. Encourage them to prepare a newspaper article on an event that happened between two or more dinosaurs as they foraged in a swamp of long ago.

3. Encourage students to create an original dinosaur dictionary. Invite them to collect dinosaur-related words from various books and resources and compile those words into a dictionary (cut into the shape of a dinosaur).

4. Use a long roll of butcher paper or newsprint and cover one wall of your classroom or a section of hallway outside your room. Invite students to create a time line (with illustrations) of the emergence and disappearance of various dinosaurs.

5. Invite students to create a "Dinosaur Observation Manual," a guide to watching and observing dinosaurs (just in case anyone happens to sight an unusual creature in the backyard).

Title: Dinosaur Questions

Author: Bernard Most

Bibliographic Information: San Diego, CA: Harcourt Brace Jovanovich, 1995

Summary: What colors were the dinosaurs? What did dinosaurs eat? How smart were dinosaurs? Which dinosaur was the biggest? An array of questions that kids normally ask about dinosaurs, and the accompanying answers, are presented in this engaging and light introduction to the world of dinosaurs.

1. Invite students to write paragraphs on some of the most distinguishing features of dinosaurs. Which features would they most like to have in a pet? If they owned a dinosaur, what feature would be most useful? How would students want to use a favorite dinosaur if they could? Encourage students to defend their choices.

2. Ask students to write a story about what their town or neighborhood would be like if it were filled with dinosaurs. How would the people have to adjust? What would they have to do differently?

3. Encourage students to create training manuals on the care and feeding of dinosaurs. What special instructions should go into the manuals with regard to diet, habitat, care, and training of pet dinosaurs? Invite students to share and discuss their ideas.

4   Invite small groups of students each to choose a favorite dinosaur. Encourage group members to take a familiar or popular song and rewrite the lyrics using dinosaur words. For example (to the tune of "I've Been Working on the Railroad"):

> *I've been watching Stegosaurus*
> *All the livelong day*
> *I've been watching Stegosaurus*
> *Just to see what he would say*
> *Can't you hear him munchin', crunchin',*
> *Rise up and start to eat a tree.*
> *Don't you ever want to meet him*
> *'Cause he will make you flee.*

CULMINATION:

Students will be invited to select one or more of the following activities and projects:

1. Students may wish to create a dinosaur alphabet book, using words and terms learned throughout the unit. For example:

    A = Allosaurus
    B = Bones in Montana
    C = Cold-blooded
        etc.

2. Invite students to write and perform a dinosaur play. The play could involve a meeting between two or more dinosaurs or an imaginative scene in which a lost dinosaur shows up in the students' home town.

3. Ask students to create a time line on a large sheet of butcher paper. The periods in which the dinosaurs lived (Mesozoic, Triassic, Jurassic, and Cretaceous) can be recorded along the bottom of the paper. Encourage students to draw illustrations of some of the dinosaurs encountered in their readings and fasten each illustration in its proper place on the mural.

4. Invite students to correspond with another class in another state (addresses can be obtained from current issues of *Learning Magazine* and *Teaching K-8 Magazine*). Encourage students to discuss their beliefs as to why the dinosaurs died out and ask their pen pals to either agree or disagree with this stand.

5. Invite a local paleontologist from a nearby college to visit your classroom and share his or her reasoning on the disappearance of the dinosaurs. Help students to prepare questions to be sent beforehand to the guest speaker.

6   Provide students with empty shoe boxes, various pieces of colored construction paper, glue, scissors, and other art materials. Using these materials, students (individually or in small groups) design dioramas of selected prehistoric scenes.

7. Invite each student take on the role of a selected dinosaur. Encourage students to record a day in the life of a dinosaur as seen through the eyes of each one's selected dinosaur. What do they eat? What do they do? What do they encounter?

8. Invite students to read *Dinosaurs and Their Young* by Russell Freedman (New York: Holiday, 1983). That book discusses the family life of hadrosaurs and some of their enemies. Afterwards, engage students in a discussion of any comparisons between the family life of dinosaurs and that of other wild (or domesticated) animals.

9. If possible, contact your district's high school and ask to borrow any fossils they may have for display. Show these to students and invite them to create their own fossils. Provide each student with a quantity of modeling clay and a variety of leaves. Flatten out the clay and place a selected leaf on top of the clay. Use a rolling pin to press the leaf into the clay. Carefully remove the leaves from the clay and then discuss the impressions made in the clay. How are these similar to or different from those made by ancient living things?

10. Help students to brainstorm for all the adjectives they can think of to describe dinosaurs. Afterwards, encourage them to brainstorm for an antonym for each of the adjectives. Invite them to select several adjectives and their antonyms and create an "Attribute Chart" (see the following sample). Encourage students to select several dinosaurs and rate each according to how it measures up on the chart.

Tyrannosaurus rex

Huge..X ....Small
Meat-eater..X ....Plant-eater
Mean..X.............................Kind
Sharp teeth..X.....................No teeth
Black..X ....White

RAINFORESTS

GENERALIZATIONS/PRINCIPLES:

1. The rainforest is a valuable ecosystem.

2. Rainforests around the world are endangered.

3. There is an amazing variety of plant and animal life in the rainforest.

4. Students can be actively engaged in preserving the world's rainforests.

CONCEPTS:

environmental preservation
ecological diversity
biological interrelationships
life cycles

MATERIALS:

Primary Literature Selections

Cherry, Lynne. *The Great Kapok Tree*. San Diego, CA: Gulliver Books, 1990.

Fredericks, Anthony D. *Exploring the Rainforest: Science Activities for Kids*. Golden, CO: Fulcrum, 1996.

Pratt, Kristin Joy. *A Walk Through the Rainforest*. Nevada City, CA: Dawn Publications, 1992.

Yolen, Jane. *Welcome to the Green House*. New York: G. P. Putnam's Sons, 1993.

Secondary Literature Selections

Asimov, Isaac. *Why Are the Rain Forests Vanishing?* Milwaukee, WI: Gareth Stevens, 1992.
    The plight of the world's rainforests and the threats to their survival are detailed in this fascinating book.

Baker, Lucy. *Life in the Rainforests*. New York: Franklin Watts, 1990.
    Readers will explore the rich variety of plant and animal life that inhabits the many layers of a tropical rainforest.

Chinery, Michael. *Rainforest Animals*. New York: Random House, 1992.
    Some of the world's most unusual animals can be found in a tropical rainforest, as well as in the pages of this fascinating book.

Dorros, Arthur. *Rain Forest Secrets*. New York: Scholastic, 1990.
    Lots to discover, lots to investigate, and lots to learn about the rainforest in this delightful book.

Dunphy, Madeleine. *At Home in the Rain Forest*. New York: Hyperion, 1994.
    Amazing animals and equally amazing plants are detailed in this fascinating book. An easy read.

Fredericks, Anthony D. *Clever Camouflagers*. Minocqua, WI: NorthWord Press, 1997.
    The world's most amazing lizard, an insect that looks like a leaf, and a rainforest frog that looks like a plant are a few of the incredible animals populating this delightful book.

George, Jean C. *One Day in the Tropical Rain Forest*. New York: HarperCollins, 1990.
> The struggle over land in the Amazon rainforest is told from the viewpoint of a young Indian boy.

Gibbons, Gail. *Nature's Green Umbrella*. New York: Morrow, 1991.
> Readers will examine the mysteries and marvels of the rainforest—unusual animals, fascinating plants, and an ecosystem unlike anywhere else on earth.

Hare, Tony. *Rainforest Destruction*. New York: Franklin Watts, 1990.
> What's happening to the rainforests of the world? Why are they threatened? Why are they being eliminated? The answers to these and other questions can be found in this informative book.

Landau, Elaine. *Tropical Rain Forests Around the World*. New York: Franklin Watts, 1991.
> The various chapters of this book acquaint readers with the variety of animal life, the diversity of plant life, and the significance of the rainforest in all our lives.

Macdonald, Fiona. *Rain Forest*. Austin, TX: Raintree/Steck-Vaughn, 1994.
> A colorful and informative journey through the different layers of the rainforest. Lots of information and loads of illustrations highlight this superb book.

Silver, Donald. *Why Save the Rain Forest?* New York: Julian Messner, 1993.
> This book tells of the many dangers facing the rainforest and the ways we can all work together to preserve this valuable environment.

Taylor, Barbara. *Rain Forest*. New York: Dorling Kindersley, 1992.
> A wonderfully photographed book describing some of the most unusual inhabitants of the rainforest, including a flying lizard and a poisonous frog.

Willow, Diane. *At Home in the Rain Forest*. Watertown, MA: Charlesbridge, 1991.
> In this book readers take a trip from the top of the highest trees in the rainforest down through the various levels. As they do, they meet all sorts of unusual and strange species.

INITIATING ACTIVITY:

Invite students to create a terrarium, a miniature controlled environment containing plants and animals in an artificial situation that closely imitates the natural living conditions of rainforest organisms. Here are some directions:

Materials:

glass container (an old aquarium [purchased at a pet store or garage sale], a large pickle jar, or even a two-liter soda bottle can be used)

small pebbles or rocks

bits of charcoal (wood charcoal from a fire or aquarium charcoal from a local pet store work equally well)

soil or potting soil

plants, rocks, pieces of wood

small land animals

Directions:

    a.   Be sure the container is thoroughly cleansed (be sure no soap or detergent residue is left behind).

b. Sprinkle the bottom of the container with a layer of small pebbles mixed with bits of charcoal. Follow with a layer of soil about twice as deep as the pebble/charcoal mixture. Soil from outside or potting soil (obtained from any garden center) will suffice.

c. Sprinkle the ground with just enough water to make it moist (too much will stimulate the growth of molds).

d. Place several plants, such as mosses, ferns, lichens, small tree seedlings, and liverworts, in the soil. Grass seed may be sprinkled in one section of the terrarium.

e. Place several large rocks and decaying pieces of wood or tree branches in the terrarium, too.

f. You may wish to introduce small land animals, such as snails, earthworms, turtles, frogs, or salamanders, to the terrarium. Be sure there is sufficient food and water for the animals living there.

g. Place a loosely fitting sheet of glass over the top of the terrarium (to permit the humidity level to build up). Make sure that some air can enter the terrarium and be certain it is kept out of direct sunlight.

GENERAL ACTIVITIES:

1. To survive, many rainforest animals need to camouflage themselves from their predators. They do this by closely matching their body colors to the colors of the environment in which they live. The following activity helps demonstrate this ability:

Materials:

100 green toothpicks (available at a party store or large grocery store)
100 red toothpicks
watch or stopwatch

Directions:

a. Invite students to work in pairs. Students can ask their partner to mix up all 200 toothpicks and to spread them out over a designated area of grass (a section of the playground or the outfield of the high school baseball field). The area should be approximately 25 square yards.

b. Invite partners to time each other to see how many toothpicks they can pick up in one minute, in two minutes, and in three minutes.

After several trials, students probably noticed that they were able to locate and pick up more red toothpicks than green toothpicks. That's because the green toothpicks were more similar in color (they were camouflaged) to the green color of the surrounding environment (the grass) than were the red ones. An excellent resource is *Clever Camouflagers* (see "Secondary Literature Selections").

2. The following activity will illustrate how rapidly nutrients are depleted from rainforest soil. Add ¼ teaspoon of blue tempera paint (dry) to ½ cup of dry dirt and mix thoroughly. Place a coffee filter in a funnel and set the funnel in a large jar. Put the dirt into the filter in the funnel. Pour water into the funnel and note the color running into the jar. Keep adding water and note how quickly the color fades.

3. Look in the local phone book for the nearest recycling center (paper, aluminum, or glass). Make arrangements to take students to the center and observe the operation. It may be helpful to ask students to generate a list of possible questions before the visit. Students should be aware that recycling helps preserve the environment as well as plant and animal life (kids may be interested to learn that 60,000 trees are needed for just one run of the Sunday *New York Times*).

   After the visit, invite students to discuss the need for additional recycling efforts in their community or city. Is a letter-writing campaign necessary to have city officials mandate recycling? How can local citizens get involved in recycling efforts? What can kids do to promote recycling in the local area?

4. The Rainforest Action Network (450 Sansome St., Suite 700, San Francisco, CA 94111 [1-415-398-4404]) produces a series of "Fact Sheets" offering updated information on the destruction and preservation of the world's rainforests. These sheets are free for the asking. Invite students to write for one or more. Here are just a few of the dozens available:

   "Native Peoples of Tropical Rainforests" (#13C)—This sheet provides valuable information about the indigenous peoples of the rainforest.

   "Tropical Rainforest Animals" (#13D)—Using a question-and-answer format, this sheet offers a variety of interesting facts about the different animals of this region.

   "Seven Things You Can Do" (#1C)—Provides seven worthwhile activities for families to do right now to help preserve the rainforests of the world.

   "Species Extinction and the Rainforests" (#3B)—Offers up-to-date information on several animal species in danger of extinction.

   "Rates of Rainforest Loss" (#4B)—Contains amazing information on the escalation of rainforest destruction currently taking place.

   "The Clean-Up Kids" (#13E)—Provides a listing of environmental groups around the country involving or started by kids. This would be a wonderful way to connect with students in all parts of the United States.

5. Keep families up to date on rainforest products and encourage them not to buy products that come from endangered plants or animals. For current information on products families shouldn't purchase, have students contact TRAFFIC at the World Wildlife Fund (1250 24th St. NW, Washington, DC 20037 [1-202-293-4800]); ask for a free copy of the "Buyer Beware" booklet.

6. Invite students to adopt a nearby stream or pond. They can work to clean up a section of the water, plant new trees along the shore, or report any pollution in the area. This long-term project can help them appreciate some of the efforts being expended in preserving large sections of the rainforest. They may want to write to The Izaak Walton League of America (1401 Wilson Blvd., Level B, Arlington, VA 22209) and ask for a copy of the free booklet "Save Our Streams."

7. Students may wish to plant some trees. By planting trees, students are helping contribute to the world's oxygen supply. Inform them that approximately 50 percent of the world's oxygen comes from the rainforest. By planting and caring for trees in the local community, they are helping reduce the carbon dioxide in the air while adding beauty to the environment. Here are some organizations that can help them in their tree planting efforts:

National Arbor Day Foundation
Arbor Lodge 100
Nebraska City, NE 68410

American Forestry Association
Global ReLeaf Program
P.O. Box 2000
Washington, DC 20013

Tree People
12601 Mulholland Dr.
Beverly Hills, CA 90210

PRIMARY LITERATURE SELECTIONS:

Title: The Great Kapok Tree

Author: Lynne Cherry

Bibliographic Information: San Diego, CA: Gulliver Books, 1990

Summary: A young man enters the rainforest to cut down a Kapok tree, but before he knows it the heat makes him tired and weak. The man sits down to rest and falls asleep. While he sleeps, the animals of the forest whisper in his ear not to cut down the Kapok tree; each animal has a different reason. Upon awakening, the man realizes the importance of the Kapok tree.

1. There are several environmental organizations in the United States working to preserve the rainforests of the world. Invite children to write to these groups and ask for information, newsletters, brochures, and facts about the world's rainforests and the efforts to protect those valuable areas. Here are some groups to contact:

Children's Rainforest
P.O. Box 936
Lewiston, ME 04240

Rainforest Action Network
450 Sansome St.
Suite 700
San Francisco, CA 94111

Rainforest Alliance
65 Bleeker St.
New York, NY 10012-2420

Rainforest Preservation Foundation
P.O. Box 820308
Ft. Worth, TX 76182

Save the Rainforest
604 Jamie St.
Dodgeville, WI 53533

2. Create a cardboard Kapok tree. Tie a bag around the trunk of the tree. Place pencils, erasers, crayons, and scissors in the bag. Invite students to go to the tree and borrow supplies from the tree's bag whenever they need to. Then one day tie the tree's bag closed and tell the students they are not allowed to borrow from the tree. Encourage the students to discuss their feelings about this sudden change.

3. Compare heights of the Kapok trees in the rainforest with the heights of trees commonly found in your community. The following is one way students can measure the heights of various trees in their neighborhood. Each child should have two rulers and a length of string. Go outside on a sunny day and locate a nearby tree. Stand a twelve-inch ruler on the ground (see fig. 4.2 on page 68) and measure the length of the ruler's shadow. Have each child take a length of string and measure the length of the shadow of a nearby tree. Help children use the following formula to compute the exact height of the tree:

$$\frac{\text{height of ruler}}{\text{length of ruler's shadow}} \quad X \quad \frac{\text{height of tree}}{\text{length of tree's shadow}}$$

For example:
Height of ruler = 12″
Length of ruler's shadow = 24″
Length of tree's shadow = 720″

$$\frac{12}{24} \quad X \quad \frac{x}{720}$$

24x = 8640 (12 x 720)
x = 360″ (30 feet)
The tree is 30 feet tall.

4. Obtain names of companies that make and/or produce life jackets (the information may be obtained from your local public library or from the local Coast Guard Auxiliary). Invite students to write to these companies asking for information on how life jackets are manufactured.

Fig. 4.2.

5.   Encourage students to create a large map of Brazil on a bulletin board or on a sheet of newsprint that has been taped to the wall. Invite them to color in the areas of Brazil that are rainforests. Ask each student to select one of the animals illustrated on the inside jacket of the book, draw and color it with colored pencils, and attach it to the rainforest area of the map.

6.   Invite students to rewrite the ending of the story and tell what would have happened if the man *had* cut down the tree. One way this can be done is in the form of letters written by the animals that used to live in the tree. Students can tell what happens to the animals now that their home is gone.

7.   Encourage students to imagine that they are one of the creatures in the story. Ask them to create posters that say "Save Our Home." They may wish to include a full-color drawing of their creature and write a convincing ad for saving the Kapok tree.

Title: Exploring the Rainforest:
Science Activities for Kids

Author: Anthony D. Fredericks

Bibliographic Information: Golden, CO: Fulcrum, 1996

Summary: Through a variety of practical science activities and experiments, students can investigate the layers of the rainforest, learn how the rainforest touches their lives, understand why it should not disappear, and discover what they can do to protect the rainforests of the world. A "must-have" book for any rainforest study!

1. The enormous amounts of rain that fall on rainforests each year are part of a regular meteorological process known as the *rain cycle*. Students may wish to create their own homemade water cycle to see this entire process in action. Here's how they can do it:

Materials:

large glass or plastic bowl

small container (a teacup works well)

small weight (two or three quarters, for example)

plastic wrap

rubber bands

water

Directions:

   a. Pour about 1 cup of water into the large bowl.

   b. Place the cup in the center of the large bowl (you may need to weigh it down so it doesn't float).

   c. Cover the top of the large bowl with a sheet of plastic wrap. Secure the plastic wrap in place with one or more rubber bands.

   d. Place the weight in the center of the plastic wrap so that it causes a slight indentation in the plastic wrap (see fig. 4.3 on page 70).

   e. Place the bowl outside on a sunny day and observe what happens inside.

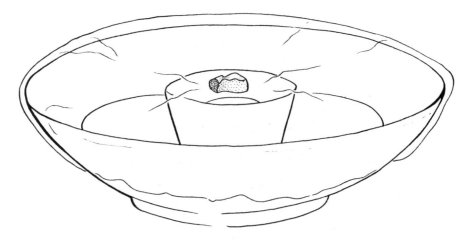

Fig. 4.3.

After the water begins to warm in the sun, it will evaporate. This water vapor condenses on the underside of the plastic wrap, forming small droplets of water. Because of the slope of the plastic wrap, these droplets will roll down the underside of the wrap and drip into the teacup.

This process will continue for some time (depending on the air temperature, the amount of sunlight, and the time of day). What students see inside the large bowl is the same process that occurs in the rainforest (obviously, on a smaller scale).

2. The following activity will help students measure the amount of rain that falls in their part of the world. The instrument they create will help them accumulate rainfall data over an extended period of time—a week, a month, a year.

Materials:

tall jar (an olive jar works best)

ruler

felt-tip pen

funnel

Directions:

a. Use a ruler and a felt-tip pen to mark off ¼" intervals up the side of the olive jar.

b. Place a funnel in the jar and place it outside in a secure location (the funnel will help collect the rain water as well as prevent some evaporation from taking place).

c. Use a chart or graph and record the amount of rain your area gets in a week or in a month. Keep an ongoing record.

d. Students may wish to compare their findings with those reported in the local newspaper.

	My Town/City	The Rainforest
One day	_____	1"
One week	_____	7"
One month	_____	30"
One year	_____	365"

3. Students may wish to grow some rainforest plants right in their own homes. Invite them to visit a large supermarket, garden shop, or nursery and look for one of more of the following rainforest plants:

African violet	Fiddle-leaf fig
Begonia	Orchid
Bird's-nest fern	Philodendron
Bromeliad	Prayer plant
Christmas cactus	Rubber plant
Corn plant	Snake plant
Croton	Umbrella tree
Dumb cane	Zebra plant

Inform students that the plants they grow at home will be somewhat smaller than the plants normally found throughout the rainforest.

Title: A Walk Through the Rainforest

Author: Kristin Joy Pratt

Bibliographic Information: Nevada City, CA: Dawn Publications, 1992

Summary: In this delightfully illustrated book, readers travel through the rainforest, exploring the lush vegetation and unusual animals that inhabit this threatened ecosystem. The beautiful drawings and entertaining prose provide a rich source of fascinating rainforest facts for any child.

1. Create a rainforest environment in the classroom. Cover the walls with paper and let students paint scenes of the rainforest, using vibrant colors. Individual animals can be painted directly on the paper, or created out of papier-mâché or cardboard, and suspended from the ceiling with strings. Make some of the trees and plants in relief by constructing them out of cardboard and attaching them so they stand out from the wall.

2. Invite students to assume the role of a creature in the book. Encourage each student to write a thank-you note to humans for their efforts in preserving the creature's environment.

3. Invite students to write to the National Wildlife Federation (Educational Publications, 1400 16th St. NW, Washington, DC 20036) and request a free copy of "You Can Do It!," a sixteen-page pamphlet giving tips on how children can help clean up the environment.

4. For a $10.00 donation, CARE will plant thirty trees in a rural community in Latin America and teach farmers there the best planting techniques. To raise money for this, you may wish to have your class create a play dramatizing an environmental issue. Invite parents and other community members and ask for donations for the cause.

5. Create an Ecology Club. Interested students can initiate school and community projects aimed at improving the environment (see *50 Things Kids Can Do to Save the Earth*, Earthworks Group/Andrews and McMeel, 1990 for potential ideas). Invite local senior citizens to join the club.

6. The rainforest is filled with hundreds of varieties of frogs. Students may be interested in raising their own frogs in the classroom. If so, contact Holcombs Educational Materials (3205 Harvard Ave., Cleveland, OH 44105). They sell a kit that includes a container, food, instructions, and a coupon for live tadpoles. As the frogs grow, invite students to maintain individual diaries on the life cycle of the frogs.

Title: Welcome to the Green House

Author: Jane Yolen

Bibliographic Information: New York: G. P. Putnam's Sons, 1993

Summary: A poetic exploration of all the layers of the rainforest and the plants and animals that inhabit this magical ecosystem. Readers will delight in this lyrical journey into one of the world's most mysterious and intriguing environments.

1. Invite students to make a collage of all the animals listed in the book. They may wish to cut out photographs and illustrations from a collection of old magazines or environmental catalogs. The collages can be posted throughout the room or throughout the school.

2. Get permission to plant a tree on the school grounds. Take a field trip to a local nursery to learn about the types of trees available for your area. Have students help with the planting and care of the tree. They can keep a class journal, writing about the planting, care, and growth of the tree and how the tree changes through the seasons. They may also want to develop a tree "baby book," taking pictures of its first year of growth and describing its first spring, its first leaf, and so on.

3. A bromeliad is a rainforest plant in the pineapple family. Students may wish to grow their own bromeliads (pineapples) in the classroom. Obtain a full pineapple from the grocery store. Cut off the crown of the pineapple (the top part with the green leaves), leaving about one or two inches of fruit attached. Dry the top for 36 hours and root it in a large container of potting soil. Keep the soil evenly moist (but not too wet) and place the container in a warm location (about 72°F is ideal). Invite students to develop a video, journal, or notebook on the pineapple's growth.

4. The rainforest is filled with an enormous variety of birds. Students may wish to create a series of bird feeders and compare the birds in their part of the country with those that inhabit the rainforest. Here are some simple feeders students can build:

a. Cut the plastic cover for a coffee can in half. Nail the can (sideways) to a board and place outside. Fill the can with birdseed and place the cover over the bottom half of the opening.

b. Cut an orange in half. Scoop out the insides. Tie four pieces of string to four holes punched around the side of the orange half. Fill with birdseed and hang in a tree.

c. Cut a coconut in half and place it outside. Fill halfway with birdseed.

CULMINATION:

The following activity can be used to help students appreciate the role of rainforests in their daily lives: Invite students to look for some of the following rainforest fruits, vegetables, and plants in the aisles, display counters, and produce section of a local grocery store. How many can they locate?

Chocolate:	found in cocoa, cookies, cakes, drinks, candies, ice cream
Coffee:	the most popular beverage in the world
Banana:	the most popular fruit eaten in the United States
Pineapple:	now grown around the world in many tropical areas, including Hawaii
Avocado:	grown in California; used in guacamole, a popular Mexican dish
Rice:	a staple food for many people around the world
Corn:	grown all over the world as a food product for humans and livestock
Sweet potato:	a staple of tropical rainforest inhabitants for hundreds of years
Manioc:	used to make tapioca; a food staple for more than 300 million people around the world
Sugarcane:	used primarily as a food flavoring
Orange:	most oranges eaten in the United States come from California, Florida, and Brazil
Mung bean:	a low-calorie vegetable often used in salads
Guavas:	a popular tropical fruit
Mango:	a tropical fruit frequently found in fruit salads
Papaya:	a popular tropical fruit
Peanut:	most peanuts used in the United States come from Georgia or Africa
Cinnamon:	a food flavoring taken from the bark of the cinnamon tree
Cardamom:	a popular spice used in cooking
Clove:	used as a flavoring for foods
Cashew nut:	a popular nut
Tomato:	a popular fruit grown in gardens throughout the United States
Tea:	originated in the rainforests of Southeast Asia
Grapefruit:	a popular breakfast food and drink
Kiwi fruit:	originally known as Chinese gooseberry; now cultivated in California and New Zealand
Brazil nut:	a popular nut found in canned nut mixes

Mini-Units

BEARS

Kids love bears! Polar bears, grizzly bears, koala bears, and, of course, the ever present teddy bear. Stories and tales about bears have been around ever since humans began spinning tales around a campfire; so, too, are legends and superstitions about bears prevalent. The following books and activities provide students with a wide range of "bear-y" good experiences.

Literature Resources

Brimmer, Larry. *Animals That Hibernate*. New York: Watts, 1991.

Chinery, Michael. *Questions and Answers About Polar Animals*. New York: Kingfisher, 1994.

Fair, Jeff. *Bears for Kids*. Minocqua, WI: NorthWord Press, 1991.

Gill, Shelley. *Alaska's Three Bears*. New York: Paws IV, 1990.

Lesser, Carolyn. *Great Crystal Bear*. San Diego, CA: Harcourt Brace, 1996.

Penny, Malcolm. *Bears*. New York: Bookwright Press, 1990.

Petty, Kate. *Bears*. New York: Gloucester Press, 1991.

Sackett, Elisabeth. *Danger on the Arctic Ice*. Boston: Little, Brown, 1991.

1. The National Geographic Society (P.O. Box 96580, Washington, DC 20077-9964 [1-800-343-6610]) produces several wonderful videos, including "Polar Bear Alert" (Catalog No. 51290), "Giant Bears of Kodiak Island" (Catalog No. 51654), "The Grizzlies" (Catalog No. 51300), and "Secrets of the Wild Panda" (Catalog No. 51997). If possible, obtain one or more videos and show them to students. Discuss with students any differences between the events of the videos and those described in the books listed previously. How accurate were the videos in depicting the life of a specific bear? What information was left out? What information should have been included?

2.   Suggest that students write letters to the Office of Endangered Species, U.S. Fish and Wildlife Service, Department of the Interior, Washington, DC 20240, to obtain information on the current status of endangered species of bears. When the information is received, invite students to create special posters to inform the public about the status of specific species.

3.   Invite students to create a series of bar graphs illustrating the life span of different species of bears. Which species has the longest life span? The shortest? Does a bear's life span change when it is confined in a zoo or wildlife animal park? Students may wish to contact a zoologist or biologist at a nearby college to obtain answers.

4.   Invite students to form small groups and research various bear legends and tales in different countries or cultures. Students may wish to duplicate stories and gather them together in a bound book (e.g., "Bear Legends of Native Americans"). Some students may wish to investigate various bear constellations (e.g., Ursa Major) and report their findings to the class.

BEES

Several varieties of bees are found throughout the world. The two most common in the United States include the honeybee and the bumblebee. Bees live together in colonies (often in hives) and do special dances that communicate messages to each other. They gather pollen and nectar from flowers which, when combined, make honey. Many bees produce honey in their natural habitats, whereas commercial honey is produced in apiaries, where a beekeeper harvests honey to sell.

Literature Resources

Bailey, Jill. *The Life Cycle of a Bee*. New York: Bookwright Press, 1990.

Heller, Ruth. *The Reason for a Flower*. New York: G. P. Putnam's Sons, 1983.

Micucci, Charles. *The Life and Times of the Honeybee*. New York: Ticknor, 1995.

Mound, Laurence. *Insect*. New York: Knopf, 1990.

Polacco, Patricia. *The Bee Tree*. New York: Philomel, 1993.

Selsam, Millicent. *Backyard Insects*. New York: Scholastic, 1988.

Snedden, Robert. *What Is an Insect?* Boston: Little, Brown, 1993.

1.   Students may wish to create their own homemade beehives. Here's how they can do it:

Materials:

large drinking straws
masking tape
modeling clay
string

Directions:

Invite selected students to gather together about 25 drinking straws. Ask them to put some modeling clay in one end of each straw to plug it and then mix up the straws so that the plugged ends are facing in both directions. Ask students to tape all the straws together into a bundle. Using string or tape, students can fasten this bundle (horizontally) underneath a window sill, a rain gutter, or the eaves of their house. **This may require adult permission and assistance.** Each bundle should be placed in a sunny location. After some time bees may begin to move into their new "homes" and take up residence. *Note:* This activity works best in the early spring. Some varieties of bees are very particular about where they live, and may choose to ignore these "hives." (See fig. 4.4.)

2.   If possible, invite an apiarist, or beekeeper, to come to the class and explain how bees make honey, what a beekeeper does, and what kind of equipment is used. If feasible, visit an apiary and allow students to see a beekeeping operation first-hand.

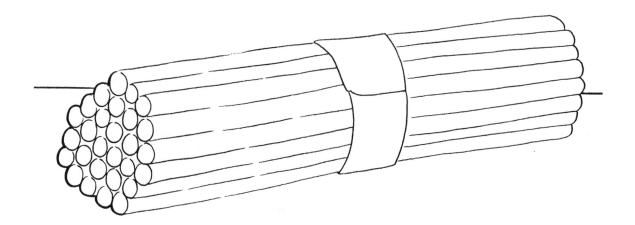

Fig. 4.4.

3.   Students may enjoy preparing the following snack:

Honey Bees

> 2 cups peanut butter
> 4 tablespoons honey
> 1⅓ cup nonfat dry milk
> 8 tablespoons toasted wheat germ
> unsweetened cocoa powder
> sliced almonds

In a mixing bowl, mix peanut butter and honey. Stir in dry milk and wheat germ until well mixed. Lay waxed paper on a baking sheet. Using 1 tablespoon at a time, shape peanut butter mixture into ovals to look like bees. Put on baking sheet. Dip a toothpick in cocoa powder and press lightly across the top of the bees to make stripes. Stick on almonds for wings. Chill for 30 minutes. Makes 20 honeybees.

4.   If possible, obtain a honeycomb. Share with students the fact that, in most cases, the bees build this structure out of wax and then fill it with honey. If honeycombs are not available, bring in some jars of raw honey. Allow children to taste the honey and the beeswax (be aware of any allergies). Provide pieces of toast or crackers for the honey.

5.   Invite students to listen to a recording of Rimsky-Korsakov's "Flight of the Bumblebee." Encourage students to interpret the music through a self-created dance or dramatic production.

WHALES

Kids love whales! It may be because they are the largest creatures in the world, because they can stay underwater for long periods of time, or because they have been the stars of movies such as *Free Willy*. Whatever the reason, it is important that students learn that whales are not fish, but rather are air-breathing, warm-blooded mammals (just like humans). Most species of whales are noted for their extremely long migration patterns, often traveling thousands of miles to reach breeding or feeding grounds (depending on the season).

But several species of whales are also on the endangered species list. A hundred years ago there used to be millions of whales throughout the world. However, because they have been over-hunted for their meat, blubber, hides, and bones, many varieties are now on the verge of dying out.

Literature Resources

Arnold, Caroline. *Killer Whale*. New York: Morrow, 1994.

Carrick, Carol. *Whaling Days*. New York: Clarion, 1993.

Kraus, Scott, and Kenneth Mallory. *The Search for the Right Whale*. New York: Crown, 1993.

Parker, Steve. *Whales and Dolphins*. San Francisco: Sierra Club Books for Children, 1994.

Patent, Dorothy. *Humpback Whales*. New York: Holiday House, 1989.

Sheldon, Dyan. *The Whale's Song*. New York: Dial, 1990.

Simon, Seymour. *Whales*. New York: HarperCollins, 1989.

Waters, John. *Watching Whales*. New York: Cobblehill, 1991.

Wexo, John. *Whales*. Mankato, MN: Creative Education, 1989.

1. Invite students to write to one or more of the following organizations, requesting information on how many whales still exist and how children can help save the whales.

   American Cetacean Society
   P.O. Box 2639
   San Pedro, CA 90731

   The Whale Protection Fund
   1725 DeSales
   Washington, DC 20036

   Pacific Whale Foundation
   101 N. Kihei Rd.
   Kihei, HI 96753

   When the information arrives, invite students to create an advertising campaign that will alert other students or the general public about the plight of various species of whales.

2. Divide students into several groups and assign a whale to each group. Invite each group to conduct the necessary research (via library books, encyclopedias, cetacean experts, high school biology teacher, etc.) to create a tabletop diorama of that species of whale in its natural habitat. Ask students to compose a written description of their whale to accompany the diorama. Provide opportunities for students to share their dioramas with others.

3. Here's a simple activity that will demonstrate how a baleen whale obtains its food.

Materials:

sink filled with cold water
packet of dry vegetable soup
kitchen strainer

Directions:

    a. Fill a kitchen sink with cold, clear water.

    b. Open and sprinkle the packet of vegetable soup over the surface of the water (students will note that the soup does not sink, but rather floats on the surface).

    c. Invite one student to hold the kitchen strainer in one hand and skim it slowly over the surface of the water.

    d. Encourage students to note how the vegetable pieces are caught in the strainer and how the water passes through the wire mesh of the strainer.

The strainer is able to capture the various vegetable pieces in its bowl, but the water passes through. If the strainer is lifted out of the water, it will contain a wide variety of food.

Baleen whales sift their food in much the same way as students did with the strainer. However, their food does not float on the surface, but rather swims through the water. The baleen combs allow a whale to swim through its dinner, strain the water from the plant or animal life, and eat what remains on its baleen. This is a very efficient form of eating as long as there is a sufficient quantity of food in the water. For example, one blue whale needs to eat about four tons of krill every *day* to survive. That's a lot of food to strain from the water!

4. This activity will help students appreciate the lengths of various types of whales throughout the world.

Materials:

Ball of yarn
Scissors
Yardstick.

Directions:

    a. Measure the height of selected students. Cut pieces of yarn according to those heights. Lay the strings of yarn outside (on the sidewalk, back yard, or driveway).

    b. Measure and cut other pieces of yarn according to the lengths of the whales listed below:

Porpoise	8 ft.
Dolphin	8 ft.
Pilot whale	22 ft.
Killer whale	30 ft.
Grey whale	45 ft.
Humpback whale	50 ft.
Right whale	60 ft.
Sperm whale	60 ft.
Blue whale	100 ft.

   c. Lay all the various pieces of yarn side by side. How do various students compare with the lengths of common whales around the world? Students may want to chart or graph the comparisons.

FOOD CHAINS AND FOOD WEBS

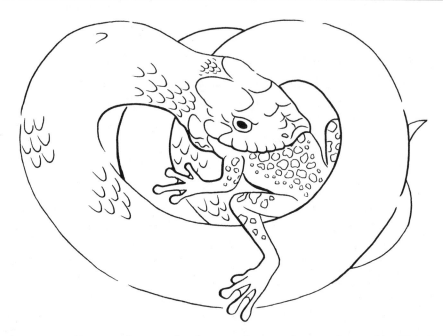

    A frog eats a mosquito, a snake eats the frog, and an eagle eats the snake. This is an example of just one of the many food chains in nature. Each organism in an environment is dependent upon one or more other organisms for its survival. The elimination of one species of organism from an environment may have a significant impact on other species, too. Students can begin to understand some of these life processes through the following books and activities.

Literature Resources

Aeseng, Nancy. *Prey Animals*. Minneapolis, MN: Lerner, 1987.

Banks, Martin. *Endangered Wildlife*. New York: Rourke Enterprises, 1988.

Lauber, Patricia. *Who Eats What?* New York: HarperCollins, 1995.

Mabey, Richard. *Oak and Company*. New York: Greenwillow Books, 1983.

Pringle, Laurence. *Fire in the Forest: A Cycle of Growth and Renewal*. New York: Atheneum, 1995.

   1. Divide the class in half. One half can be predators and the other half can be prey. A predator is matched up with a prey. The pair is to construct a book on the life of a predator trying to catch its prey and the prey's attempt at escape. Illustrations should also be included.

   2. Have the class hold a discussion on what types of animals this world could do without. What animals would they prefer to be extinct? The class can have a debate on the suggestions offered.

3. Obtain a copy of the sound filmstrip "Cycles in Nature" (National Geographic Society, Washington, DC 20036; Catalog No. C30332). This filmstrip describes how plants and animals form food webs throughout nature. Take time afterward to discuss some of the ramifications of those webs for humans. How are humans involved in the various webs of nature?

4. Ask several professors from a local college to visit your class and describe some of the webs and chains of nature. If possible, set up a panel discussion involving two or more experts from a biology department. The presentation can be videotaped for viewing in succeeding years.

5. Students may enjoy observing how different kinds of animals grow and mature. The following specialized containers (and the accompanying animals and creatures) can all be obtained through the mail from Delta Education, P.O. Box 950, Hudson, N.H. 03051 (800-442-5444):

   a. Aquaria/terraria (Catalog No. 57-200-6256)—includes coupon for goldfish, tadpole, hermit crab, or chameleon, $24.95.

   b. The Bug House (Catalog No. 57-020-8086)—$5.65.

   c. Critter City (Catalog No. 57-031-6557)—$24.95.

   d. Fruit Flies, Mealworms, & Butterflies Mini-Kit (Catalog No. 57-740-0096)—includes coupon for living organisms, $89.95.

   e. Butterfly Garden (Catalog No. 57-716-0010)—includes coupon for 25 larvae, $44.95.

   f. Giant Ant Farm (Catalog No. 57-010-2310)—includes coupon for ants, $19.95.

   g. Grow A Frog (Catalog No. 57-110-0296)—includes a coupon for tadpoles, $14.95.

6. Work with the school nurse or physical education teacher to present some information on the life cycles of humans. What types of cycles do humans go through during their lifetimes? How do those cycles compare with some of the cycles in the animal kingdom?

WHY DINOSAURS BECAME EXTINCT

Many different theories have been offered on why the dinosaurs became extinct. Some of the more popular ones include a sudden change in the earth's climate, a loss of food, and a collision between an enormous meteor and the earth. Although scientists do not agree on *the* reason for the extinction of dinosaurs, students will enjoy discussing their own hypotheses and suggestions.

Literature Resources

Barton, Byron. *What Happened to the Dinosaurs*. New York: Crowell, 1989.

Branley, Franklyn. *Dinosaurs, Asteroids, and Superstars: Why the Dinosaurs Disappeared.* New York: Crowell, 1982.

Branley, Franklyn. *What Happened to the Dinosaurs?* New York: Crowell, 1989.

Cobb, Vicki. *The Monsters Who Died: A Mystery About Dinosaurs.* New York: Coward-McCann, 1983.

Elting, Mary, and Ann Goodman. *Dinosaur Mysteries.* New York: Platt and Munk, 1980.

Simon, Seymour. *New Questions and Answers About Dinosaurs.* New York: Morrow, 1990.

1. Invite students to correspond with a class in another state (addresses can be obtained from current issues of *Learning Magazine* and *Teaching K-8 Magazine*). Have students discuss their beliefs as to why the dinosaurs died out and ask their pen pals to either agree or disagree with this stand.

2. Encourage each student to select a dinosaur and write a letter to that dinosaur explaining why the student would or would not like it to come back.

3. If possible, contact the speech or drama department at your local high school or college. Ask if some students would like to try out their debating skills in your classroom by selecting different theories on the disappearance of the dinosaurs and arguing them in your class. If possible, make a videotape of the debate to share with other classes.

4. Invite a local paleontologist from a nearby college to visit your classroom and share reasons for the disappearance of the dinosaurs. Have students prepare questions to be sent beforehand to the guest speaker.

5. Obtain a copy of the video "Dinosaurs: Puzzles from the Past" (National Geographic Society, Washington, DC 20036, Catalog No. C51046). Discuss with students how information in the film is similar to or different from that discovered in the books listed earlier in this unit.

OTHER ANCIENT ANIMALS

Dinosaurs certainly weren't the only animals that lived long ago. Mammoths, mastodons, pterodactyls, and other strange creatures were also part of the history of the earth. Although most appeared after the dinosaurs died out, they are still a source of fascination for many scientists.

Literature Resources

Craig, Jean. *Discovering Prehistoric Animals*. Mahwah, NJ: Troll, 1989.

Knight, David. *"Dinosaurs" That Swam and Flew*. New York: Prentice-Hall, 1985.

Matthews, Rupert. *Ice Age Animals*. New York: Bookwright Press, 1990.

Peters, David. *A Gallery of Dinosaurs and Other Early Reptiles*. New York: Knopf, 1989.

Sattler, Helen. *Pterosaurs, the Flying Reptiles*. New York: Lothrop, 1985.

Selsam, Millicent. *Sea Monsters of Long Ago*. New York: Four Winds, 1977.

Wright, Robin. *Dinosaurs and Other Prehistoric Animals*. Mahwah, NJ: Troll, 1991.

1. Many prehistoric creatures have features similar to animals of today (for example, the mammoth shares characteristics with the elephant). Invite students to construct a large bulletin board display. On one half of the bulletin board, post pictures and illustrations of ancient animals. The other half of the bulletin board displays illustrations and photos of today's animals. Yarn can be used to link the prehistoric animals with the existing animals they most resemble.

2. Challenge students to create Venn diagrams to compare a prehistoric animal with its more current cousin.

3. Invite students to create several big books. The front and back covers of each can be cut from stiff cardboard into the shape of a selected prehistoric animal. Sheets of paper can also be cut into the same pattern as the covers and stapled between them. Each book acts as a record of important data about the selected animal. The completed books can eventually be donated to the school library, or be part of a visiting book collection that goes to various classrooms.

4. Invite students to brainstorm for adjectives that could be used to describe various ancient animals. List the adjectives on the board. Next, ask students to select an antonym for each adjective listed. Have students identify several adjectives and their antonyms and create an "Attribute Chart" (see the following sample). Ask students to select several ancient animals and rate each according to how it measures up on the chart.

Mammoth

```
Huge..X...........................................Small
Meat-eater...............................X....Plant-eater
Sharp teeth................X....................No teeth
Ferocious.....................................X...Gentle
```

TREES AND FORESTS

For many years there was a belief that this country's supplies of trees was inexhaustible. Over the past 200 years, much of the forested land in this country was cleared for lumber or farming. Only recently have we begun to understand that wholesale destruction of forests has serious consequences for plants, animals, and people. The following books and activities can help students become more aware of the value of trees and the need to preserve this nation's forest land.

Literature Resources

Anholt, Laurence. *The Forgotten Forest*. Boston: Little, Brown, 1992.

Burnie, David. *Tree*. New York: Knopf, 1988.

Collard, Sneed. *Green Giants*. Minocqua, WI: NorthWord Press, 1994.

Gackenbach, Dick. *Mighty Tree*. San Diego, CA: Harcourt Brace, 1992.

Gamlin, Linda. *Trees*. New York: Dorling Kindersley, 1993.

Lambert, David. *Forests*. Mahwah, NJ: Troll, 1990.

Locker, Thomas. *Sky Tree*. New York: HarperCollins, 1995.

Luenn, Nancy. *Song for the Ancient Forest*. New York: Atheneum, 1993.

Markle, Sandra. *Outside and Inside Trees*. New York: Bradbury, 1993.

Reed-Jones, Carol. *The Tree in the Ancient Forest*. Nevada City, CA: Dawn Publications, 1995.

1.   Trees for Life (1103 Jefferson, Wichita, KS 67203) is an organization that uses its profits to plant fruit trees in underdeveloped countries. For a fee of 50 cents per student, the organization will send you seeds, individual cartons for planting, and a teacher notebook. The type of tree they send will depend on the state in which you live, because they only send trees that are native to your region. Students will enjoy watching their seeds sprout and finally grow into a tree.

2.   Invite each student to select a tree on the school grounds and to adopt that tree for the length of the school year. Photos can be taken of each tree, bark rubbings can be made, and observations of animal or plant life in and around the tree can be recorded. Encourage students to observe their adoptees on a regular basis (once a week, for example) and to maintain a journal of their observations, predictions, experiments, etc. throughout the school year. If the tree is very young, a student may wish to create a "baby album" for his or her tree.

3.   Discuss the importance of recycling newspapers as a significant way of saving trees. Explain that approximately one four-foot stack of newspapers equals the wood from one tree. Designate one corner of your room or hallway as a newspaper recycling center. Encourage students to begin saving newspapers and stacking them in the designated area. Once a week, measure the stack of newspapers and record the measurement on a chart, placing a figure of a tree on the chart each time four feet of newspapers are collected.

4.   Help students write to the National Arbor Day Foundation (100 Arbor Avenue, Nebraska City, NE 68410) and request a copy of "The Conservation Trees" brochure. This brochure explains how trees help the environment. Challenge students to draft a similar document that would apply to the trees in your particular area of the country.

5.   Invite an employee of a local garden center or nursery to visit the classroom and discuss the types of trees that are native to your area of the country. What are some planting techniques? How should trees be cared for? Why are some trees easier to grow than others? Invite students to gather the responses to those questions, as well as their own, into an informative brochure or leaflet that could be distributed at the garden center or nursery.

PLANTS: PROCESSES

The plant process most of us are familiar with is *photosynthesis*, the means whereby a plant makes its own food. It does so by trapping sunlight and changing it to a form of chemical energy. That chemical energy is combined with carbon dioxide in the air to make a special kind of sugar, which is transported to all parts of the plant. Much of the oxygen we breathe is released by plants through photosynthesis. *Transpiration* is the process by which a plant moves water throughout its system. Plants typically lose water through cells in their leaves. This loss of water pulls up more water from the roots. *Respiration* is the process whereby plants use oxygen to break down sugar into carbon dioxide and water. This action also releases energy from the sugar—energy the plant's cells need to do their work. Another process of plants is *fertilization*, or when a sperm cell joins with an egg cell to form a seed. Each seed has a seed coat, an embryo, and stored food.

Literature Resources

Ardley, Neil. *The Science Book of Things That Grow*. New York: Harcourt Brace, 1991.

Fredericks, Anthony D. *Simple Nature Experiments with Everyday Materials*. New York: Sterling, 1995.

Johnson, Sylvia. *How Leaves Change*. Minneapolis, MN: Lerner, 1986.

Rafferty, Kevin. *Kids Gardening: A Kid's Guide to Messing Around in the Dirt*. Palo Alto, CA: Klutz Press, 1989.

Riehecky, Janet. *What Plants Give Us: The Gift of Life*. Chicago: Childrens Press, 1990.

1.   Obtain two similar potted plants (of equal vigor and height). Invite students to select 20 random leaves on a plant. Ask students to smear a thin layer of petroleum jelly on the tops of 10 leaves and the bottoms of 10 other leaves (on the same plant). Place both plants on a window sill and water and fertilize as necessary. After several days ask students to observe the two plants and note any differences. What happened to the leaves with petroleum jelly on the top? What happened to the leaves with petroleum jelly on the bottom? What can this tell us about some of the processes of plants?

2.   Obtain two similar potted plants (of equal vigor and height). Water and fertilize the plants as necessary. Have one student place a large, clear cellophane bag over the top of one plant, securing it around the pot with a rubber band (the bag should be as airtight as possible around the plant). Place the plants on a window sill. After several days, encourage students to note what happens inside the bagged plant. Students may wish to remove the bag from that plant and measure the amount of water that is transpired by the plant (every two days, for example). Be sure to keep both plants adequately watered.

3.   Invite students to consult some library books to determine how seeds travel. Encourage students to construct a large chart with the words "WATER," "WIND," "ANIMALS," and "OTHER" across the top. Challenge students to record the names of plants in one or more of the categories on the chart. They may want to specifically look at plants such as the milkweed, dandelion, coconut, thistle, and sugar maple. What devices do some seeds have that help them in being transported to new areas?

4.   Here's an experiment that will help students learn about what seeds need to begin growing.

Materials:

36 radish seeds

6 plastic sandwich bags

paper towels (cut in half)

water

candle wax

marker

Directions:

Have students moisten pieces of paper towel and place them in the bottom of sandwich bags as directed below. Drop 6 radish seeds in each bag (leave the bags open). Label each bag with a number and then finish setting up each bag as follows:

Bag #1: paper towel, water, no light (put in a drawer or closet), room temperature.

Bag #2: paper towel, water, light, room temperature.

Bag #3: paper towel, no water, light, room temperature.

Bag #4: no paper towel (seeds floating in water), light, room temperature.

Bag #5: paper towel, water, no light, keep in refrigerator or freezer.

Bag #6: paper towel, no water, no light, room temperature, seeds covered by candle wax (done beforehand by an adult).

Invite students to record the date and time they began this activity and check each of the bags twice daily for any changes.

Eventually, students will note that the seeds in Bag #1 and Bag #2 begin to germinate. There may be some minor change in the seeds in Bag #4. Discuss with them the fact that seeds need favorable temperature, adequate moisture, and oxygen to germinate. Light is not needed for germination.

KILLER PLANTS

When most students think of carnivores, they typically think of animals such as tigers, lions, sharks, and perhaps an occasional snake or two. But they may be surprised to learn that there are more than 400 species of plants that feast on animals (primarily insects). Although there are no known man-eating plants in the world, there is an intriguing assortment of enough carnivorous and other dangerous plants to whet anyone's appetite.

Literature Resources

Coil, Suzanne. *Poisonous Plants*. New York: Watts, 1991.

Doyle, Mycol. *Killer Plants*. Los Angeles: Lowell House Juvenile, 1993.

Lerner, Carol. *Pitcher Plants: The Elegant Insect Traps*. New York: Morrow, 1983.

Nielsen, Nancy. *Carnivorous Plants*. New York: Watts, 1992.

Overbeck, Cynthia. *Carnivorous Plants*. Minneapolis, MN: Lerner, 1982.

Wexler, Jerome. *Secrets of the Venus Fly Trap*. New York: Dodd, 1981.

1. Students may be interested in obtaining additional information about carnivorous plants. Invite them to write to the International Carnivorous Plant Society (The Fullerton Arboretum, California State University, Fullerton, CA 92634) and request a sample copy (or subscription information about the *Carnivorous Plant Newsletter.*

2. Students may wish to grow their own carnivorous plants at home or in the classroom. Many garden centers and nurseries carry carnivorous plants for sale. If they do not, invite your students to write to Peter Pauls Nurseries (4665 Chapin Road, Canandaigua, NY 14424-8713 [1-716-394-7397]) and ask for the latest catalog. This mail-order nursery specializes in carnivorous plants and supplies. For example, Terrarium Kit 8-A consists of two venus fly trap bulbs, one sundew plant, one butterwort plant, a one-quart plastic terrarium, and soil. At this writing the kit sells for $13.95. Other mail-order nurseries include Lee's Botanical Gardens (12731 SW 14th Street, Miami, FL 33184); Orgel's Orchids (Route 2, Box 90, Miami, FL 33187); and Southern Carnivores (5600 Hiram Road, Powder Springs, GA 30073).

3. If possible, students may wish to visit (or write for information to) arboretums that have carnivorous plants displays on a regular basis. Here are a few of the best known (you may be able to find others listed in your local telephone book or through a nearby nursery):

Atlanta Botanical Garden, Atlanta, GA

California State University, Fullerton, CA

Los Angeles County Arboretum, Arcadia, CA

Longwood Gardens, Kennett Square, PA

Missouri Botanical Gardens, St. Louis, MO

New York Botanical Garden, Bronx, NY

University of North Carolina, Chapel Hill, NC

THE HUMAN BODY

Thematic Units

THE HUMAN BODY

GENERALIZATIONS/PRINCIPLES:

1. The human body is an amazing and intricate structure.

2. The human body consists of several systems.

3. The human body is controlled by the brain.

CONCEPTS:

growth and development
interrelationships
cause and effect

MATERIALS:

Primary Literature Selections

Cole, Joanna. *The Magic School Bus Inside the Human Body*. New York: Scholastic, 1989.

Ontario Science Centre. *Foodworks*. Reading, MA: Addison-Wesley, 1987.

Parker, Steve. *Brain Surgery for Beginners and Other Major Operations for Minors*. Brookfield, CT: Millbrook Press, 1995.

Parker, Steve. *What If...The Human Body*. Brookfield, CT: Copper Beech Books, 1995.

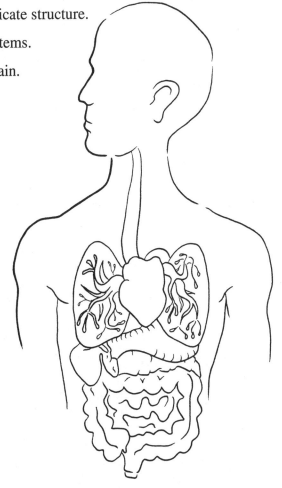

Secondary Literature Selections

Allison, Linda. *Blood and Guts: A Working Guide to Your Own Insides*. Boston: Little, Brown, 1976.
This is an imaginative and fascinating look inside the human body. Included are experiments and projects kids can do with their own bodies.

Bennett, David. *What Am I Made Of?* New York: Aladdin Books, 1990.
A primary-level book that briefly covers the human body and some of its systems.

Bishop, Pamela. *Exploring Your Skeleton: Funny Bones and Not-So-Funny Bones*. New York: Watts, 1991.
Humorous illustrations highlight this very valuable guide to the human skeletal system and how it works.

Brown, Laurene. *Dinosaurs Alive and Well: A Guide to Good Health*. Boston: Little, Brown, 1990.
Cartoon dinosaurs are used to provide young readers with valuable and important information about healthy habits.

Brown, Robert. *Our Bodies*. Milwaukee, WI: Gareth Stevens, 1990.
Lots of illustrations guide the reader to a broad understanding of human anatomy.

Bruun, Ruth Dowling, and Bertel Bruun. *The Brain: What It Is, What It Does*. New York: Greenwillow, 1989.
How the human brain operates, what it looks like, and how it compares with animal brains are just a few of the many topics in this enlightening book.

Crocker, Mark. *The Body Atlas*. New York: Oxford University Press, 1991.
This book features all the primary systems of the human body, including reproductive, skeletal, circulatory, nervous, and digestive. Lots of charts and diagrams.

Markle, Sandra. *Outside and Inside You*. New York: Bradbury Press, 1991.
Lots of color photographs provide readers with a close-up examination of human functional anatomy.

Pringle, Laurence. *Everybody Has a Bellybutton: Your Life Before You Were Born*. Honesdale, PA: Boyds Mills Press, 1997.
An outstanding introduction to life before birth by an award-winning science author. A must-have for young readers.

Royston, Angela. *The Human Body and How It Works*. New York: Random House, 1990.
Provides young readers with an overall picture of the design and function of the human body. A good first book.

Audiovisual Selections

The Incredible Human Machine (Catalog No. 50873). Washington, DC: National Geographic Society (video).

The Invisible World (Catalog No. 51595). Washington, DC: National Geographic Society (video).

INITIATING ACTIVITY:

Form students into groups of two. Have one student in each group lie down on a large sheet of newsprint. Ask the other student in the pair to draw an outline of the partner's body on the paper. Reverse the roles. Then invite students to illustrate each outline with organs, bones, and other anatomical features—as many as they can recall. Afterward, take time to discuss similarities and or differences between the illustrations. *Note:* As the unit progresses, invite students to add data and illustrations of internal organs to their body outlines, as they are learned throughout the unit. Body drawings can be posted throughout the classroom.

GENERAL ACTIVITIES:

1. People come in different sizes and shapes, yet many body parts are related to each other. For example, invite students to measure their arms from their wrists to their elbows. Have them record the size and ask if they know what other part of the body is the same size. Once the students have made several predictions, explain that the foot is the same size as that bone. Invite them to measure the inside of a foot, from the very end of the heel to the end of the big toe. They will also discover that the distance around a closed fist (use a piece of string to measure) equals the length of the foot, as well as the distance from wrist to elbow. Here are some other equivalents students may wish to test. (*Note:* Because youngsters are still growing and developing, there may be more variation in these equivalents than would be the case with adults.)

   a. The distance between the shoulder and the elbow and the elbow and the wrist is about the same.

   b. The distance between the eyes to the top of the head is equal to the distance between the eyes and the tip of the chin.

   c. A person's height is about 6 to $7\frac{1}{2}$ times the length of the head (from tip of chin to top of head).

   d. The bottom of the ears line up with the base of the nose.

   e. The eyebrows are on the same level as the tops of the ears.

   f. The width of the mouth (from corner to corner) is the same as the distance between the middle of one eyeball to the middle of the other eyeball.

   g. The width of the nose (at its base) is the same as the width of an eye.

   h. The distance between the eyes (over the bridge of the nose) is the same as the width of one eye.

2. We use the five bodily senses in our everyday lives: touch, taste, hearing, sight, and smell. Put several objects in a paper bag and invite students to put their hands in the bag to identify the items. For taste, blindfold several students and ask them taste a piece of apple and a piece of potato. Do they know which is which? For hearing, invite students to close their eyes and listen to a tape of nature sounds. What do they hear? For sight, ask them to look at a picture of Vincent Van Gogh's painting of "The Starry Night." Invite them to write descriptions of what they see. For smell, blindfold selected students and have them smell several selected foods or scents. You may wish to set up some simulations in which students go through part of the day without using one of their senses (e.g., sight—blindfold; touch—several thick cotton gloves; hearing—cotton balls placed in the ears). Ask selected students to relate any difficulties they have with diminished senses.

3. Invite the school nurse or a local doctor to visit the class and talk to students about the importance of good health. Prior to the speaker's arrival, have students compile a list of questions they would like to ask. Set up a video camera and videotape the speaker's presentation for review at a later date. Encourage students to compare the information the speaker(s) shares with data from other sources.

4.   Invite students to create an imaginative newspaper with "reporters" providing information from within the human body. Students may wish to divide the newspaper into sections similar to the daily newspaper (for example: Sports—slalom down the alimentary canal; Fashion—designing the perfect heart; Architecture—the skeletal system; and Horoscope—"Parts of your body will continue to multiply today while other parts will be lost. Fear not, for you will enjoy good health").

5.   Show students a picture of Michelangelo's sculpture, "Pieta," to give them an example of muscle structure in the human body. Invite students to look through magazines and find several pictures of the human body. Invite students to discuss the musculature of the human body and its relation to good health. If possible, invite several athletes (from the local high school) to the class to discuss the muscles they use in their respective sports and how they exercise those muscles for maximum performance. (*Note:* Some students will be amazed to discover that their grandmother has the same number of muscles as an Olympic wrestler.)

6.   Assign each of several groups a specific human disease. Challenge each group to locate as much outside information as possible about the causes of and cures for each selected illness. Invite groups to assemble their data in the form of brochures or leaflets that can be distributed throughout the school. Local health organizations can be contacted for some preliminary data.

PRIMARY LITERATURE SELECTIONS:

Title: Brain Surgery for Beginners and Other Major Operations for Minors

Author: Steve Parker

Bibliographic Information: Brookfield, CT: Millbrook Press, 1995

Summary: This light-hearted book, filled with amusing and descriptive illustrations, looks at all aspects of the human body from the vantage point of the brain. Facts and figures are cleverly presented and designed to help kids learn all about the most important "machine" in the world.

1.   Visit a local butcher shop and obtain a calf's brain (the shape of a calf's brain is similar to that of a human's). Lay sheets of newsprint on top of a table and place the calf's brain in the middle. Using a sharp kitchen knife, cut into the brain (you may wish to do the cutting while children refer to the illustrations of various brain parts in *Brain Surgery*).

   As you are cutting, take time to discuss the similarities between the calf's brain and the human brain. What external or internal features are identical? Does a calf's brain perform the same functions as a human brain? What is a human brain able to do that a calf's brain cannot?

During the cutting process, youngsters may wish to take a series of photographs. Later, these photos can be mounted in a scrapbook along with accompanying comments or descriptions. Children may wish to refer to *Brain Surgery* for labels and relevant information on selected features. Additional comparisons can be made between the calf's brain and photographs of the human brain found in encyclopedias.

2. Children may be interested in selecting one or more of the following experiments to learn more about their own bodies.

    a. Roll some clay into a ball about the size of a marble. Stick a wooden match into the ball. Invite youngsters to place this device on their wrist (match sticking up). They may need to move it around until they find a spot with a strong beat. Encourage them to record the number of beats in 15 seconds and multiply by 4 to obtain their heartbeat rate per minute. How do you account for any differences between children?

    b. Inform children that the human tongue has four different types of taste buds (sour, bitter, salty, and sweet). Students can map out portions of their tongues as follows: Obtain several clean cotton-tipped swabs (four for each student). Invite youngsters to dip each of four swabs into the following solutions and then touch those tips to various portions of their tongues.

        • lemon juice (sour)
        • salt water (salty)
        • sugar water or corn syrup (sweet)
        • tonic water (bitter)

    Youngsters may wish to draw an oversize illustration of a human tongue and plot the location of the four major types of taste buds.

    c. Mix together $\frac{1}{2}$ cup of water and 2 teaspoons of cornstarch. Stir well. Cut some paper toweling into several 2″ x 2″ squares and dip them in the liquid. Set them aside to dry. Work with youngsters and paint one of their palms with iodine (this should be done only by an adult). Encourage youngsters to engage in vigorous physical activity for a while (they should build up a sweat). Place one of the paper-towel squares on the iodine-covered palm. They will notice the sweat glands on that palm showing up as dark spots. Youngsters will also see that sweat glands seem to be concentrated in selected areas of the skin.

Title: Foodworks
Author: Ontario Science Centre
Bibliographic Information: Reading, MA: Addison-Wesley, 1987
Summary: A magnificent book that looks at what we eat, how we eat it, and what happens to food after it has been eaten. Humorous illustrations, a light-hearted text, and more than 100 science activities and fascinating facts about food make this book the ideal complement to any study of the human body.

1. In each of three small plastic cups, pour 3 tablespoons of milk. In the first cup put 2 tablespoons of water. Cover the cup with a sheet of plastic wrap, using a rubber band to hold the wrap in place. In the second cup, put 2 tablespoons of a weak acid such as lemon juice or vinegar, and cover as for the first. In the third cup put 2 tablespoons of an enzyme, such as a meat tenderizer, and cover as for the first. After one or two hours, invite youngsters to observe the changes that have occurred in each cup. The changes that occurred in cups 2 and 3 are similar to the digestive process in the human stomach.

2. Invite students to write a list of all the foods they eat for three days. At the end of the three day period, encourage students to categorize their foods into the major food groups. Invite them to prepare an essay on whether they ate a balanced diet during that time period. Students may wish to suggest other foods that could have been eaten to provide a more balanced diet.

3. Invite students to design a food collage of nutritious foods by cutting pictures out of from magazines and posting them onto poster board. Invite students to label each item according to what food group it belongs to.

4. Invite students to make an oversize two-dimensional model of the human food canal (they may wish to review the illustration on page 14 of *Foodworks*). Have students cut out pictures of food items from several old magazines. Invite them to affix each of the food items on various portions of the model, describing the events that lead to the food's arrival at that particular spot in the digestive system.

5. Blow up a balloon and explain that the balloon, like the human stomach, expands when filled. Measure out 23 feet of yarn or string for each student. Explain that the small intestine in an adult's body is this length when stretched out.

6. Ask students to imagine themselves as a piece of food traveling down the digestive tract. Lead them through a visual imagery exercise in which they mentally travel from the mouth through the stomach and down into the lower parts of the digestive tract. Invite students to write about their voyages through the digestive system and some of the sights and sounds they experienced.

7. Invite students to take a food scale into the school cafeteria at lunch time. Encourage various students to weigh their lunches and chart the results. Invite students to develop graphs or charts of the foods according to weight and determine the relationship of food weight to body weight. In other words, does the weight of the food have something to do with the weight of the person or is something else involved (calories)?

Title: The Magic School Bus Inside the Human Body

Author: Joanna Cole

Bibliographic Information: New York: Scholastic, 1989

Summary: This remarkable book (part of a series) provides young readers with an engaging, thoroughly detailed, and delightful journey through the human body. Rich illustrations, humorous text, and an attention to the interest level of youngsters highlight this magical book.

1. If possible, visit a local video store and obtain a copy of the movie *Fantastic Voyage* (in which a group of scientists is miniaturized and injected into a scientist's bloodstream to repair damage to his brain). After viewing the film, ask students to create their own original skit depicting a journey deep into the human brain. What adventures will they have and what dangers will they encounter?

2. Invite children to select one or more of the following topics and discuss their creative insights. They may wish to write a brief report on their personal interpretation, too. Obviously, there are no right or wrong answers to these investigations; however, youngsters should feel free to use the data and information in the book to arrive at some conclusions or suppositions.

    a. Discuss or write a story from the viewpoint of a body organ, such as the heart, lungs, or stomach.

    b. Prepare a time line or storyboard on "A Day in the Life of My _____ *(body organ)."*

    c. "My favorite body part"

    d. If I could look inside my body I would like to see ....

3. Select one or more of the following field trips to share with children. Depending on the size and location of your local community, visits to other sites (with accompanying interviews) may also be possible. Check with your local health organization, hospital, doctor referral service, or visiting nurses association. They will be glad to refer you to additional groups, organizations, and specialists.

   a.   If possible, obtain permission to visit a local rehabilitation center or chiropractor. Encourage students to talk with the personnel about the structure and function of the human skeleton and muscle system. The data that students collect can be assembled into a scrapbook or notebook.

   b.   If possible, visit a nearby blood bank and encourage youngsters to talk with one of the technicians or nurses. Invite them to find out how blood is collected, measured, stored, and preserved. What precautions do the workers have to follow? How much blood is collected in a day, a week, or a month? How is that blood used?

4.   Invite the biology teacher from the local high school to visit your classroom. Ask that individual to bring several examples of preserved animals used for dissection purposes. The teacher can explain and demonstrate the different systems in various kinds of animals. Ask that teacher to describe the similarities and differences between animal body systems and human systems.

Title: What If...The Human Body

Author: Steve Parker

Bibliographic Information: Brookfield, CT: Copper Beech Books, 1995

Summary: This is a clever and engaging book filled with delightful and imaginative illustrations. The author asks a series of intriguing "What if" questions (e.g., "What if we had no skin?," "What if the body had no stomach?") and provides enlightening, and often humorous, responses. A terrific classroom addition.

1.   You may wish to obtain an anamod of the human brain for classroom display (an *anamod* is a three-dimensional model constructed from flat pieces of cardboard). One can be obtained from Delta Education, P.O. Box M, Nashua, NH 03061, 800-258-1302 (Catalog No. 57-010-1474). At this writing it is priced at $11.95. After students have had an opportunity to observe the anamod (or a similar illustration), challenge them to create their own three-dimensional model from pieces of stiff cardboard.

2.   Ask a local hospital or doctor for an x-ray of a broken bone. Show students the x-ray and invite them to imagine how the bone should look when it is whole. Students may wish to create an imaginative story about an individual and how his or her bone got broken.

3.   Invite youngsters to write to one or more of the following organizations and request some relevant literature on the human body and its care. Plan time to discuss the information with children and encourage them to assemble the data into a notebook or scrapbook.

American Speech-Language-Hearing Association
   10801 Rockville Pike
   Rockville, MD 20852

(They have some descriptive literature on the care of eyes and ears.)

National Institutes of Health
   Building 1, Room 2B19
   Bethesda, MD 20892

(Request information and brochures on the diseases of the lungs and kidneys.)

National Clearinghouse for Alcohol and Drug Information
   P.O. Box 2345
   Rockville, MD 20852

(They have a free catalog of materials available to share with children.)

National AIDS Information Clearinghouse
   P.O. Box 6003
   Rockville, MD 20849

(Write and obtain the "AIDS Prevention Guide," which has ideas on how to talk about this disease and accurate answers to common questions.)

National Institute of Child Health and Human Development
   National Institutes of Health
   Building 31, Room 2A32
   9000 Rockville Pike
   Bethesda, MD 20892

(Write and obtain a listing of the brochures and information sheets on mental health for children.)

4. Invite students to collect a series of amazing facts and information about the human body. The information can be obtained from both the primary and secondary literature resources listed in this unit, as well as from other books in the school library. Invite them to assemble the information into descriptive and informative booklets to be displayed in the school library. The booklets can be organized by body systems. For example, here are some amazing facts about the body's largest organ, the skin, to get students started:

   a. A square inch of skin on the back of a human hand contains 144 inches of blood vessels, 800 pain sensors, 40 hairs, 400 sweat glands, and 204 feet of nerves.

   b. The life span of a strand of human hair (on the head) is between two and four years.

   c. The thickness of the human skin ranges from $\frac{1}{100}$ inch on the eyelid to about $\frac{1}{5}$ inch on the back.

   d. Human skin completely replaces itself about every 28 days.

   e. The weight of all the skin (on an adult) is about twice the weight of the brain (an average brain weighs 3 pounds).

CULMINATION:

Students can be invited to select one or more of the following activities and projects:

1. If possible, make arrangements to visit the emergency room of a local hospital. Help students to prepare questions to ask emergency room technicians, nurses, or doctors about some of the typical cases they treat during the course of a week. Upon returning to the classroom, invite students to prepare a descriptive brochure on what they learned.

2. Invite a representative of a local wellness center to visit the classroom and share information and data on the importance of establishing and maintaining a healthy lifestyle.

3. Invite students (in small groups) to put together a picture book on the human body for use in lower grades. What information should be included and how should that information be presented to younger students?

4. Challenge students to put together a "Book of Body Records." Included in this book could be "records" of various members of the class. For example: Who has the longest thumb? Who has the shortest big toe? Who has the thinnest wrist? Invite students to create as many different categories as they can and add to the book over a period of time.

5. Provide students with modeling clay and invite them to create replicas of various body organs. These can be set up on a display table or placed in a large bakery box (the type used for large sheet cakes) and covered with plastic wrap.

6. Just for fun, have students look through maps and atlases for place names of various towns, counties, or other geographical features that contain the names of body parts (e.g., *Arm*our, S.D., *Leg*gett, CA).

7. Invite students to write the most interesting fact they learned about the human body on a piece of construction paper (cut in the shape of a body part). Place them around the room.

Mini-Units

STAYING HEALTHY

Here's an interesting question to ask students: Why is it important to stay healthy? Although the answer may be obvious to us as adults, you may discover that many students have some difficulty in responding to that particular question. Too often we take our health for granted until we experience a disease, illness, or other medical emergency. What is most important for students is the fact that their individual health is something that should concern them on a regular basis. In fact, the attitudes and practices children develop early in their lives will have a profound effect on their health as adults.

Literature Resources

Berger, Melvin. *Germs Make Me Sick.* New York: HarperCollins, 1985.

Berger, Melvin. *Why I Cough, Sneeze, Shiver, Hiccup and Yawn.* New York: Crowell, 1983.

Brown, Laura, and Marc Brown. *Dinosaurs Alive and Well.* Boston: Little, Brown, 1990.

Cherry, Lynn. *Who's Sick Today?* New York: Dutton, 1988.

Kuklin, Susan. *When I See My Doctor.* New York: Bradbury, 1988.

Nourse, Alan. *Your Immune System.* New York: Watts, 1989.

Settel, Joanne, and Nancy Baggett. *Why Does My Nose Run? And Other Questions Kids Ask About Their Bodies.* New York: Atheneum, 1985.

1. Many family doctors, hospitals, and health clinics have a variety of brochures and other printed information on health and nutrition, you may want to pick these up for your students. Take some time to share and talk about the information in these printed materials.

2. The three major health needs for growing children are a nutritious diet, regular exercise, and sufficient sleep. Invite students to make a personal notebook divided into three sections. In the first section, ask each student to record the foods he or she eats

(even snacks) during the course of a week. Students may want to divide a sheet of paper into the four major food groups (vegetable-fruit group, bread-cereal group, meat-poultry-fish-bean group, and milk-cheese group) and record the types and amounts of each eaten during the week. In the next section, each youngster records the type and duration of various physical activities he or she participates in during the week. In the third section, each student records the number of hours of sleep he or she gets during each night of the selected week. Invite students to share their notebooks with a family doctor for comments and suggestions.

3. Take time to talk with students about the dangers of alcohol, tobacco, and drugs. The attitudes children have about these substances are formed very early in childhood and it is vitally important that these subjects be included in any lessons on staying healthy. Important information and materials can be obtained from your local hospital, health clinic, or family doctor (or write or call the National Clearinghouse for Alcohol and Drug Information, P.O. Box 2345, Rockville, MD 20852; 800-729-6686 for a free catalog of their materials).

4. Invite students to write to the Center for Science in the Public Interest (1875 Connecticut Ave. NW, Suite 300, Washington, DC 20009) and request information about one or more of the following:

   • a three-dimensional Healthy Eating Pyramid that rates more than 200 foods.

   • the "Junk Food Jail" poster.

   • the "Kids Against Junk Food" organization.

BODY SUPPORT AND MOVEMENT

The bones and muscles of the human body have always fascinated youngsters. Whether students are participating in some sort of physical activity or sport, performing some chore around the house, or simply getting from place to place, the muscles and bones of their bodies are always involved. Bones are also important scientifically, because scientists can determine a great deal of information about ancient peoples by examining bones. The age, sex, weight, height, mode of death, and general health while alive can all be determined through an examination of bones, even those thousands of years old.

Literature Resources

Baldwin, Dorothy, and Claire Lister. *The Structure of You and Your Body.* New York: Bookwright, 1984.

Cole, Joanna. *Your Insides.* New York: Putnam, 1992.

Cumbaa, Stephen. *Bones Book.* New York: Workman, 1991.

Elting, Mary. *The Answer Book About You.* New York: Putnam, 1984.

Grant, Lesley. *Discover Bones.* Reading, MA: Addison-Wesley, 1991.

Parker, Steve. *Skeleton.* New York: Knopf, 1988.

Royston, Angela. *What's Inside My Body.* New York: Dorling Kindersley, 1991.

Showers, Paul. *You Can't Make a Move Without Your Muscles.* (New York: Crowell, 1982.

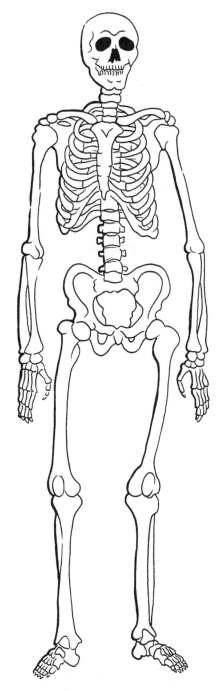

1. Seek permission to visit a local physical rehabilitation center or chiropractor. Encourage students to talk with the personnel about the structure and function of the human skeleton and muscle system. What are some of the ways in which we can protect our bones and muscles? What are some beneficial exercises and good dietary habits? What happens to people who suffer diseases or injuries to their bones or muscles? On your return to the classroom, invite students to collect the information into a brochure to be shared with other classes.

2.   Obtain a whole chicken and boil it for one or two hours. With students watching, carefully remove all the meat and observe the structure of the skeleton. Invite students to draw illustrations of the chicken's skeleton. After the skeleton has cooled, work with selected students to remove bone sections from the skeleton. Encourage students to note the joints and how they are held together with ligaments (tissues that connect bone to bone). Invite students to compare the structure of a chicken skeleton with that of a human skeleton.

3.   The human skeleton continues to grow until sometime between the ages of 16 and 22. Invite students to record the heights of their respective family members. This can be done once each month. Encourage students to make predictions about each family member's height for the forthcoming month. Which persons in the family are continuing to grow? Who has stopped growing? Students may wish to create a special chart or graph of family members' heights over time. Friends and other relatives can be added to the chart, too.

GROWING AND CHANGING

Growth begins at birth and continues until a person is between 16 and 22 years of age (girls usually reach their full adult height by the age of 16; boys reach their full height by about age 20). Although we may think of growth as a very natural and normal part of each child's development, it is actually a very complex process that is determined by diet, hormones, and heredity. Having a balanced and nutritious diet affects the amount of growth a child will experience over the developmental years. Lack of some nutrients can affect a child's eventual height. Hormones secreted by the **pituitary gland** (a small gland at the base of the brain) are also responsible for growth. Students can appreciate some of the processes taking place in their bodies with the literature and activities listed here.

Literature Resources

Aliki. *I'm Growing*. New York: HarperCollins, 1992.

Caselli, Giovanni. *The Human Body*. New York: Grosset, 1987.

Daly, Kathleen. *Body Words: A Dictionary of the Human Body, How It Works, and Some of the Things That Affect Its Health*. New York: Doubleday, 1980.

Evans, David, and Claudette Williams. *Me and My Body*. New York: Dorling Kindersley, 1992.

Patterson, Claire. *It's OK to Be You: A Frank and Funny Guide to Growing Up*. Berkeley, CA: Tricycle Press, 1994.

Stein, Sara. *The Body Book*. New York: Workman, 1992.

1. When born, a baby's head is about one-fourth the length of its entire body. As a baby grows, the head becomes smaller in comparison to the rest of the body. Invite each student to select several photographs of various family members at different ages. Encourage students to measure the length of each family member's head as well as the length of each person's whole body. What kinds of proportions are noted? What is the proportion of the head to the body in infancy, childhood, teenage years, young adult, and the adult stages? Are there some trends in selected families?

2. Invite students to look through several old magazines for photographs of young animals. Encourage students to note the proportion of body parts in young animals in comparison with the adults. For example, a young horse has legs that seem to be too long, but an adult horse's legs are just right in proportion to other parts of the body. What other young animals have body parts that seem considerably different from the adult's.

3. Invite a family doctor or a local health clinic worker to visit your classroom. Ask that individual to provide information on the suggested heights and weights of children at different ages. Students should be reminded that these measurements are only averages, and may be different from the height and weight of selected individuals in the class. Invite your guest to talk about the diet, sleep, and exercise students need to maintain proper growth and development.

4. Students may enjoy putting together a collection of "Body Records"—an assembly of amazing growth and development facts experienced by most individuals. Here are a few to get you started; others can be collected by reading the resources listed earlier or through additional library work.

    *   It takes a human being about $4\frac{1}{2}$ months to replace a fingernail from the quick to the tip.
    *   A newborn baby's brain is about 90 percent of its grown-up size.
    *   By the age of 60, most people have lost 50 percent of their taste buds and 40 percent of their ability to smell.
    *   Humans are born with 350 bones, but because bones fuse as one matures, adults wind up with exactly 206 bones.

RESPIRATION AND EXCRETION

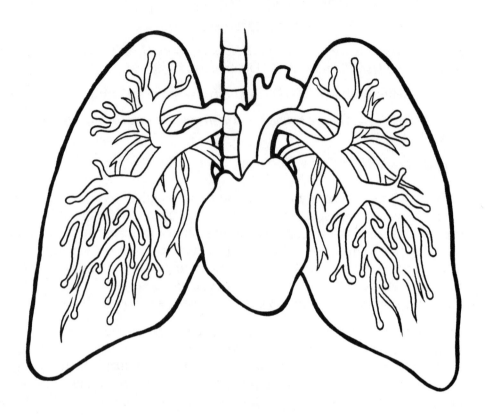

Respiration is the process whereby the human body takes in air and uses the oxygen from that air. Our body cells need this oxygen to function, but it is equally important that they be able to get rid of the wastes, such as water, salts, sugars, nitrogen, and carbon dioxide that the body cannot use. This is done through the excretory system. Students can begin to understand and appreciate these two body systems by selecting some of the books and activities listed here.

Literature Resources

Baldwin, Dorothy, and Claire Lister. *The Structure of You and Your Body*. New York: Bookwright, 1984.

Elting, Mary. *The Answer Book About You*. New York: Putnam's, 1984.

Kramer, Stephen. *Getting Oxygen: What to Do If You're Cell Twenty-Two*. New York: Crowell, 1986.

London, Jonathan. *The Lion Who Had Asthma*. Morton Grove, IL: Albert Whitman, 1992.

Miller, Jonathan. *The Human Body*. New York: Viking, 1983.

Parker, Steve. *The Body Atlas*. New York: Dorling Kindersley, 1993.

Western, Joan, and Ronald Wilson. *The Human Body*. Mahwah, NJ: Troll, 1991.

1. Breathing is an action we take for granted. Students may be interested in learning about some of the things they breathe into their bodies. Invite students each to take several 3″ x 5″ index cards and tape or tie them to various places in and outside of the classroom (for example, on the side of the teacher's desk, on the ceiling, outside just above the classroom door, on a branch of a nearby tree). On each card smear a thin layer of petroleum jelly. After several days, note the amount of pollutants on each card. Which card had the most? Why? How do students feel about breathing in those pollutants? Students may wish to check the cards over a span of two or three weeks.

2. Most humans need approximately eight glasses of water a day to properly maintain the excretory system. Although some water is obtained from vegetables, soups, and milk products, most individuals need to drink regular amounts of tap water, too. Invite each student to construct a chart listing the names of all family members. Encourage students to ask each family member to report to the student the exact amount of water or number of glasses of water he or she drinks each day. Maintain those records for two or three weeks. Invite students to discuss with family members the importance of a constant water supply for the body.

3. Students may wish to write to or call the National Institute of Health (Building 31, Room 2B19, Bethesda, MD 20892; 301-496-8855) to request information or literature on diseases of the lungs and kidneys, as well as research being conducted to prevent or reduce the dangers of those diseases. The information obtained can be shared with all class members.

6 EARTH SCIENCE

Thematic Units

THE FOUR SEASONS

GENERALIZATIONS/PRINCIPLES:

1. The earth goes through an annual cycle of four seasons: summer, autumn, winter, and spring.

2. Each season has distinctive characteristics, patterns, and circumstances.

3. Each season is predictable.

CONCEPTS:

continuity and cycles
cause and effect
change

MATERIALS:

Primary Literature Selections

Drake, Jane, and Ann Love. *The Kid's Summer Handbook*. New York: Ticknor, 1994.

Hirschi, Ron. *Winter*. New York: Cobblehill, 1990.

Markle, Sandra. *Exploring Autumn*. New York: Atheneum, 1991.

Simon, Seymour. *Spring Across America*. New York: Hyperion, 1996.

Secondary Literature Selections

Asimov, Isaac. *Why Do We Have Different Seasons?* Milwaukee, WI: Gareth Stevens, 1991.
> A well-respected science writer offers clear answers to kids' questions about seasonal changes.

Berger, Melvin. *Seasons*. New York: Doubleday, 1990.
> Simple and straightforward explanations highlight this book about how the earth's movement determines days and seasons.

Branley, Franklyn. *Sunshine Makes the Seasons*. New York: HarperCollins, 1985.
> Clear illustrations explain how and why the seasons change with the earth's journey around the sun.

Garland, Sherry. *The Summer Sands*. San Diego, CA: Harcourt Brace, 1995.
> Two youngsters work hand in hand with adults to rebuild sand dunes destroyed by a winter storm.

Gibbons, Gail. *The Reasons for the Seasons*. New York: Holiday House, 1995.
> In a clear and convincing style, the author illustrates why and how the seasons occur.

Greeley, Valerie. *The Acorn's Story*. New York: Macmillan, 1994.
> The growth and development of an acorn into an oak tree is detailed through the seasons and through the years.

Highwater, Jamake. *Songs for the Seasons*. New York: Lothrop, 1995.
> A well-respected author describes the many ways in which plants and animals respond to the seasons.

Markle, Sandra. *Exploring Winter*. New York: Atheneum, 1983.
> This book is a potpourri of information on the creation of weather instruments, how animals survive winter, and winter home gardening.

Muller, Gerda. *Circle of Seasons*. New York: Dutton, 1995.
> A delightful and wonderful examination of all the seasons of the year.

Owen, Roy. *The Ibis and the Egret*. New York: Philomel, 1993.
> An ibis and an egret share what they like about each of the seasons.

Sansfield, Steve. *Snow*. New York: Philomel, 1995.
> This intriguing book offers young readers a magical description of winter's first snow.

Smith, William, and Carol Ra. *The Sun Is Up*. Honesdale, PA: Boyds Mills Press, 1996.
> A marvelous collection of poetry celebrating all the seasons of the year.

Yolen, Jane. *Ring of Earth: A Child's Book of Seasons*. San Diego, CA: Harcourt Brace, 1986.
> The praises of the seasons are told by a variety of animals in this delightful collection of poetry.

INITIATING ACTIVITY:

The following activity is designed to help children understand the reasons for seasonal changes. Because the causes for seasonal changes are often misunderstood by children (and adults), this demonstration will help them appreciate the books, activities, and information shared throughout this thematic unit.

Introduction

In a large area of the United States, individuals experience four seasons: winter, spring, summer, and fall. They experience changes in weather, temperature, and daylight hours. This is due to the earth's rotation, tilt of $23\frac{1}{2}$ degrees, and its revolution around the sun. In an attempt to better understand certain phenomena, human beings have created models to help them understand the world in which they live. One model is the globe with its $23\frac{1}{2}$-degree tilt, equator, Tropic of Cancer, and Tropic of Capricorn. This model will be used to demonstrate the seasons of the year.

Organization and Material

A large object is needed to represent the sun. This may be a large beach ball or a large circle cut out of construction paper or oaktag. The "sun" will be placed in the center of the room and the individual carrying the globe will move in a elliptical fashion around the sun. As the globe is moved around the sun, the north pole should always point toward the north star. A flashlight may be inserted in the center of the sun to show where the direct rays of the sun are striking the earth at various times. (See fig. 6.1.)

Labels containing the words "winter," "spring," "summer," and "fall" should be placed in the appropriate areas of the classroom corresponding to the seasons being demonstrated.

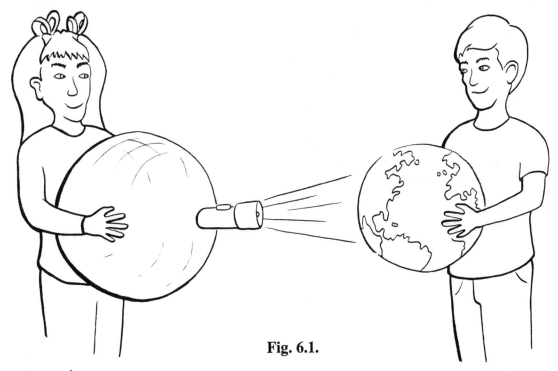

Fig. 6.1.

Procedure

1. Use a compass to orient students to the directions. Place a star in the ceiling above the wall in the northerly direction. Explain that the north pole of the globe must point in the direction of the north star as it revolves around the sun.

2. Place the sun in the center of the room. Invite a student to hold the sun, with a flashlight in its center, if possible. Review the rotation of the earth and the concept of day and night.

3. Invite a second student to hold the globe. If it is not fixed with a 23½-degree tilt, explain the necessity of holding it tilted and pointed in the northerly direction.

4. Ask the student to walk the globe around the sun, making one complete revolution. Ask other students to explain what they observed.

5. After the discussion, have students place, at the appropriate locations, the labels "winter," "spring," "summer," and "fall." Invite the second student to make the revolution of the earth a second time, with the students noticing where the sun shines directly. Ask students why there are lines on the globe at the equator, Tropic of Cancer, and Tropic of Capricorn.

Explanation

As Earth continues its journey around the sun, we experience a change in the duration of sunlight, changes in temperature, and other modifications. These changes occur primarily because Earth is tilted 23½ degrees from a line perpendicular to the plane of its orbit. This tilt causes individuals living in the northern hemisphere to experience less sunlight during a certain time each year and experience winter. While the northern hemisphere is experiencing winter, the southern hemisphere is having summer. This situation is reversed six months later.

As Earth orbits the sun, the sun appears at different positions in the sky at a designated time of the day. At noon, for example, the sun is much higher in the sky on June 21 in the northern hemisphere than it is on December 21. Thus, the direct rays of the sun are striking the northern hemisphere and for a longer time, because that part of Earth is exposed to direct sunshine for more hours on June 21 than on December 21; hence it warms the earth and there are fewer hours for it to cool. When the sun is directly overhead, at its zenith, at the equator, equal degrees of latitude north and south of the equator are receiving the same amount of sunlight. This is the beginning of spring in one of the hemispheres and fall in the other. The determining factor is the direction of Earth's rotation. Scientists have conveniently labeled the four seasons: winter, spring, summer, and fall. The beginning of each season is determined not by the weather in a particular location, but by where the sun will be directly overhead at noon at a particular location on Earth.

GENERAL ACTIVITIES:

1. Invite students to construct a bulletin board. Create a tree out of construction paper or felt. Invite students to create objects (snowflakes, birds, ornaments, brown leaves, etc.) from pieces of construction paper, each of which can be placed on the tree to designate a particular season. Encourage students to write the name of the corresponding season on the back of each piece.

2. Invite students to construct a bar graph. Encourage students to interview students in other classes to determine what their favorite season is. The results can be tabulated on the graph (for example, snowballs cut from construction paper can designate a certain number of people who like winter; robins can designate a certain number of people who enjoy spring the most). If each object represents five people, students will be able to construct a most interesting and revealing chart.

3. Divide the class into four groups. Assign each group one wall of the classroom. Invite each group to create a large, oversized mural of facts, pictures, collages, illustrations, etc. for one assigned season of the year. Each group can be responsible for adding to its mural for a designated period of time. Provide opportunities for students to share their murals and reasons why certain objects were placed on the wall.

4.   Invite students to make a circular collage (see below) to be hung in the room. Encourage them to cut out pictures from old magazines and arrange them according to the seasons. The purpose of the circular pattern is to illustrate that the seasons are continuous.

5.   Invite each student to create his or her own book on the seasons. Each student can incorporate what he or she has learned in class, as well as information obtained from other resources, into the book. Each child should be allowed to illustrate his or her own book and share the finished product with the rest of the class.

PRIMARY LITERATURE SELECTIONS:

Title: Winter

Author: Ron Hirschi

Bibliographic Information: New York: Cobblehill, 1990

Summary: Incredible photography and spare prose highlight this examination of winter. Young readers will be fascinated by the rich and compelling information portrayed and explained in this book. Part of a series including Spring, Fall, and Summer.

1. Invite students to tell a story about a great adventure they had in the snow one day. They could tell about making a giant snowman, making a fort, etc. If you live in a warm climate, invite students to imagine what they might do in the snow.

2. Invite students to write a series of journal entries from a snowman's perspective. Encourage them to pretend that they are a snowman or snowwoman. Invite them to write what they look like, what they are feeling, and what they like to do all day.

3. Invite students to make a snowperson out of styrofoam balls. Materials you might need include construction paper, glitter, glue, buttons, felt-tip markers, small sticks, toothpicks, felt, yarn and fabric. Finished snowpeople can be displayed on a ledge or window sill.

4. Ask students to create an imaginary story about what they would do if they woke up one morning and saw that what they thought was snow was really something else (you may wish to share the book *Cloudy with a Chance of Meatballs* by Judi Barrett [New York: Aladdin Books, 1978] with students first). Encourage students to write about things that look like snow, such as mashed potatoes or ice cream.

Title: Spring Across America

Author: Seymour Simon

Bibliographic Information: New York: Hyperion, 1996

Summary: A richly photographed book, this wonderful introduction to spring (by a celebrated science author) describes how this season arrives throughout the United States. A delightful resource for every classroom (part of a series).

1. After a brief discussion about spring, invite students to write a poem about how spring makes them feel, what they like to do in the spring, or what the weather is like. After they are done, ask selected individuals to share their poems with the class.

2. Encourage each student to imagine that he or she is a flower preparing to bloom. Invite each child to write a paragraph describing what he or she is doing as the blooming process begins. How do they feel? What is happening around them? What changes are they experiencing? Students may wish to post their paragraphs on the bulletin board.

3. Invite students to create signs or posters announcing the coming of spring.

4. Bring in different kinds of seeds and talk about them (use the information on the back of each seed packet). Invite students to make a chart illustrating the various seeds and to create some illustrations of what they think each seed will become when fully grown. Encourage students to plant their seeds in small containers set on the window sill of the classroom and monitor their growth.

5. If practical in your area, take students on a nature walk around the school. Invite students to record everything they see that has to do with spring. For example: birds chirping, flowers that are in bloom, etc. Encourage students to make a collage using pictures from old magazines, each representing an item or object specifically located on the class trip.

Title: The Kid's Summer Handbook

Author: Jane Drake and Ann Love

Bibliographic Information: New York: Ticknor, 1994

Summary: This book provides youngsters with a potpourri of exciting, creative, and energizing summer activities that will delight, amaze, and stimulate. The emphasis is on doing summer in imaginative and rewarding ways.

1. Lemonade stands are popular in the summer. Invite students to set up a lemonade stand in the cafeteria. Encourage them to discuss how the stand will be operated, how the supplies will be purchased, how the money will be handled, and so forth. Plan time to talk about what will be done with the proceeds.

2. Encourage students to write a story about where in the world they would want to go during summer vacation. Invite students to write about how they would go about getting there, how much money they would take, how long they would stay, and what they would do once they got there.

3. Invite students to make a large list on poster board titled "Summer is ..." Encourage each student to contribute several words, phrases, pictures cut from old magazines, individual illustrations and the like to the list. *Note:* You may decide to create separate lists for each of the seasons.

4. Introduce students to some of the weather reports in the daily newspaper (or videotape a weather report from a local television station). Take time to discuss all the different symbols used in describing the weather. Later, invite students to write their own weather report for an ideal summer day. Encourage them to make symbols for their weather conditions, such as sun for hot, raindrops for rain, etc. Post these around the room.

5. Invite students to make a pie graph interviewing children and adults throughout the school about their favorite summertime activities. Tally the results and create a pie chart indicating which activities are most popular. Add up all the students' results and color in the pie according to those results, using different colors.

Title: Exploring Autumn

Author: Sandra Markle

Bibliographic Information: New York: Atheneum, 1991

Summary: This book provides young readers with a wealth of facts and ideas about the events of autumn, as well as suggestions for experiments, crafts, games, and other related seasonal activities. This book will be used throughout the entire year, not just in the fall (part of a series by the same author).

1. Show students some pictures of what trees look like in the fall. Invite them each to draw a picture of a tree. Encourage them to cut out leaves from construction paper (in fall colors) and post them on the large picture.

2. Invite students to write in their journals about their first day of school in the fall. Encourage them to express their feelings, record events that happened, note their surroundings, etc. Provide opportunities for students to share their experiences.

3. Invite students to paint a picture using fall colors and relate it to a fall scene. Later, invite children to use winter colors and relate it to a winter scene. Begin a discussion on each picture and the feelings students have about the different seasons.

4. If possible, have students collect leaves that have fallen or that can easily be removed from trees. Invite students to press the leaves between two sheets of construction paper and piles of heavy books. (An inexpensive leaf press can be ordered from Delta Education, P.O. Box 950, Hudson, NH 03051 [Catalog No. 57-160-4580]. At this writing it is priced at $11.95.) Afterward, invite students to put the leaves in a large scrapbook. Descriptions of each leaf can also be included.

5. Squirrels collect acorns in the fall to prepare for winter. Invite some students to take inventory of the food they have in their homes and figure out how long the food would last if there was a blizzard and they couldn't get out to get more food. Would they be prepared like the squirrels?

CULMINATION:

Students can be invited to select one or more of the following activities and projects:

1. Invite a park ranger come in to speak to the class about his or her job and how the season of the year affects the requirements of the job.

2. Invite students to go on a scavenger hunt for nature items associated with the season just studied.

3. If possible, take a field trip to a specific location near the school (a local park, for example). Ask students to note any changes in the scenery or conditions as a result of the season of the year. Provide selected students with cameras to take photographs of the area. The photographs can be arranged in an attractive scrapbook.

4. Invite the class to create its own "Big Book" on a season just studied. Included could be a class-generated story as well as individual illustrations from each student.

5. Invite students to create shoe box dioramas of various seasonal scenes. Divide the class into several small groups. Ask each group to collect various natural objects from around the school or their respective neighborhoods. Items can include leaves, twigs, flowers, feathers, and the like—anything that may represent a part of a selected season. Invite each group to arrange the collected objects in a three-dimensional display inside a shoe box. Be sure to display the dioramas on a ledge or shelf.

6. The National Geographic Society (Educational Services, Washington, DC 20036) produces a sound filmstrip series on the seasons. Entitled "The Seasons" (Catalog No. C03765), it describes the cycle of the seasons and seasonal changes that occur in living things. Invite students to view these audiovisual presentations and prepare critical reviews of them for possible publication in the local newspaper.

7. Your students may be interested in reading or listening to traditional stories and folktales from various cultures and countries. Contact your school librarian for suggestions. The following will get you started: *Little Sister and the Month Brothers* by Beatrice Schenk de Regniers (New York: Lothrop, 1994); *The Old Man and His Birds* by Mirra Ginsburg (New York: Greenwillow, 1994); and *The Seasons and Someone* by Virginia Kroll (San Diego, CA: Harcourt Brace, 1994).

WEATHER

GENERALIZATIONS/PRINCIPLES:

1. There are many different types of weather.

2. Several different instruments are used to measure and record weather.

3. People who study weather and its effects are known as meteorologists.

4. Some weather is predictable; some is not.

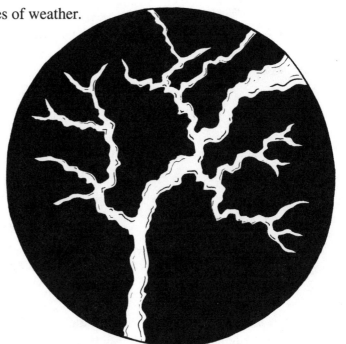

CONCEPTS:

change is constant
commonality and variation
scientific investigation

MATERIALS:

Primary Literature Selections

Aardema, Verna. *Bringing the Rain to Kapiti Plain*. New York: Dial, 1981.

Barrett, Judy. *Cloudy with a Chance of Meatballs*. New York: Aladdin Books, 1978.

Gibbons, Gail. *Weather Forecasting*. New York: Four Winds, 1987.

Simon, Seymour. *Storms*. New York: Mulberry, 1989.

Secondary Literature Selections

DeWitt, Linda. *What Will the Weather Be?* New York: HarperCollins, 1991.
     This brief book is a wonderful introduction to meteorologists, the instruments they use, what they measure, and weather patterns and changes.

Gibbons, Gail. *Weather Words and What They Mean*. New York: Holiday House, 1990.
     A terrific book that introduces young readers to common meteorological terms and their definitions.

Leslie, Clare. *Nature All Year Long*. New York: Greenwillow, 1991.
     Provides readers with a month-by-month seasonal guide to changes in plant and animal behavior.

Markle, Sandra. *A Rainy Day*. New York: Orchard, 1993.
     An illustrated explanation of why it rains, what happens when it does, and where the rain goes.

Martin, Bill, and John Archambault. *Listen to the Rain*. New York: Henry Holt, 1988.
     A playful and creative introduction to the sounds of rain.

McMillan, Bruce. *The Weather Sky*. New York: Farrar, 1991.
     This book presents a year's worth of sky changes, along with color photographs and descriptive illustrations.

McVey, Vicki. *The Sierra Club Book of Weatherwisdom*. San Francisco: Sierra Club, 1991.
    Basic weather principles and experiments, in tandem with weather customs and traditions, highlight this book.

Otto, Carol. *That Sky, That Rain*. New York: Crowell, 1990.
    An introduction to the water cycle, with an emphasis on the creation of rain.

Polacco, Patricia. *Thunder Cake*. New York: Philomel, 1990.
    Approaching storms frighten a young girl until her grandmother shows her how to bake a thunder cake.

Serfozo, Mary. *Rain Talk*. New York: McElderry Books, 1990.
    During a summer rainstorm, a small girl notices the way the rain affects her senses.

Steele, Philip. *Rain: Causes and Effects*. New York: Watts, 1991.
    An excellent introduction to rain and its effects on humans. Includes several simple experiments.

Wyatt, Valerie. *Weatherwatch*. Reading, MA: Addison-Wesley, 1990.
    A book packed with weather lore, weather facts, weather data, and loads of experiments.

INITIATING ACTIVITY:

Help children create their own homemade weather station. The following instruments will help them learn about the weather and some of the ways in which meteorologists measure various aspects of the weather.

1. *Thermometer:* Use a nail to dig out a hole in the center of a small cork. Fill a bottle to the brim with colored water and push the cork into the neck of the bottle. Push a straw into the hole in the center of the cork. (See fig. 6.2.) Mark the line the water rises to in the straw with a felt-tip pen. Note the temperature on a regular thermometer and mark that on a narrow strip of paper glued next to the straw. Take measurements through several days, noting the temperature on a regular thermometer and marking that at the spot where the water rises in the straw on the strip of paper. After several readings, youngsters will have a fairly accurate thermometer. Liquids expand when heated (water rises in the straw) and contract when cooled (water lowers in the straw).

Fig. 6.2.

2. ***Barometer:*** Stretch a balloon over the top of a wide-mouth jar and secure it with a rubber band. Glue a straw horizontally on top of the stretched balloon, starting from the center of the balloon (the straw should extend beyond the edge of the jar). Attach a pin to the end of the straw. Place another straw in a spool and attach an index card to the end of that straw. Place this device next to the jar so that the pin is close to and points to the index card. (See fig. 6.3.)

    When air pressure increases, the pressure inside the bottle is less than that of the outside air. Therefore, the balloon rubber is pushed down, and the pointer end of the straw moves up (that spot can be marked on the index card). When the air pressure goes down, the air inside the jar presses harder than the outside air. The rubber is pushed up and tightens, and the pointer moves down. Point out to children that when the pointer moves down, bad weather is probably on the way, because air pressure falls when a storm is approaching. When the pointer rises, that's usually a sign that good weather is on the way.

Fig. 6.3.

3. *Anemometer:* Cut out two strips of cardboard approximately 2″ x 16″. Make a slit in the middle of each one so that they fit together to make an "X." Cut four small paper cups so that they are all about 1″ high. Staple the bottom of one cup to each arm of the "X." Use a felt-tipped marker to color one of the cups. Make a hole in the center of the "X" with a needle.

Stick the eye of a needle into the eraser of a pencil and place the pencil into a spool (jam some paper around the sides of the spool hole so that the pencil stays erect). Glue the spool to a large block of wood. Place the "X" on the tip of the needle so that it twirls around freely. (See fig. 6.4.) Blow on the cups to make sure they spin around freely (the size of the hole may have to be adjusted a bit). Invite youngsters to place their anemometer outside on a breezy day and count the number of times the colored cup spins past a certain point. That will give them a rough idea of wind speed. (Meteorologists use a device similar to this one, but the revolutions are counted electronically.) Later, you may wish to introduce youngsters to the Beaufort Scale, a widely used scale to judge the speed of wind.

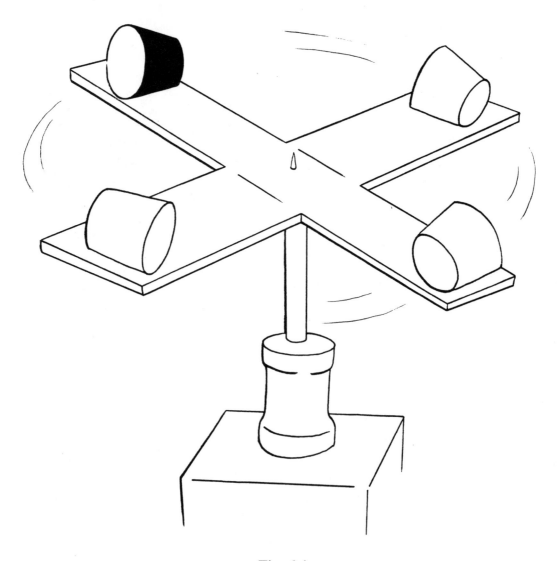

Fig. 6.4.

Children may wish to set up their makeshift weather station outside and take regular readings. These measurements can be matched with those reported in the daily newspaper. Comparisons between the readings obtained by children and those reported in the daily paper can be discussed. Children should record their readings over a period of several days or weeks in a journal or appropriate notebook.

GENERAL ACTIVITIES:

1. Temperature Experiment: Have your students, working in pairs, do the following experiment.

   a. Get two clear cups and two thermometers.

   b. Put a thermometer in each cup.

   c. Fill one cup halfway with water. Fill the other cup halfway with dirt.

   d. Keep the cups in a cool spot in the classroom for 30 minutes. Read each temperature and record and label it.

   e. Move the cups to a sunny spot outside. Wait 1 hour.

   f. Read each temperature and record it.

   g. Subtract the inside temperature from the outside temperature to find each change in temperature. Record this also.

2. Invite a local meteorologist to visit your classroom to talk about his or her job. Brief your students beforehand so they can generate questions for the guest. Follow up the visit by inviting students to share their thoughts on the topic of being a meteorologist.

3. Invite students to gather newspaper and magazine articles about weather or to bring in information from daily weather forecasts from local newspapers or television news shows. Articles can be filed in shoe boxes and shared in a "Weather News" area. Encourage students to examine all of the clippings and compile a list comparing and contrasting the different forecasts.

4. Discuss why weather is different in different places. How can we find out the weather in the United States? What symbols could we use to record and report the weather on a map? Use the map in your local newspaper to find out this information. For homework, have students find out about the weather patterns in the United States. Make weather symbols from pieces of construction paper and position them on a map of the United States to denote the weather forecast for that particular day. Change these as the conditions in selected areas change.

5. Designate a "Weatherperson of the Day" to predict the next day's weather. Invite that student to write his or her prediction on a card and put it on the bulletin board, to be uncovered the next morning. Be sure to talk about the current weather conditions and how they might affect the weather the following day.

6.   Challenge students to complete a temperature chart. Encourage students to work in groups of two or three as follows:

   a.   Place a thermometer outside in a shady area.

   b.   Note the temperature in the morning, noontime, and afternoon on each of several days.

   c.   Put three dots on a graph to indicate the temperatures measured for that day. Connect the dots to illustrate the rise and fall in daily temperature.

   d.   Keep an ongoing record of daily temperatures over a span of several weeks (the temperature charts can be posted on a bulletin board or collected into a scrapbook).

7.   Invite students to make weather word cutouts. Begin by cutting out shapes of clouds, the sun, raindrops, and snowflakes. On each shape, write one or more appropriate weather-related words. Display the weather words on a bulletin board and add new cutout words as they are learned.

PRIMARY LITERATURE SELECTIONS:

Title: Cloudy with a Chance of Meatballs

Author: Judy Barrett

Bibliographic Information: New York: Aladdin Books, 1978

Summary: Life is delicious in the town of Chewandswallow, where it rains soup and juice, snows mashed potatoes, and blows storms of hamburgers every day. Then one day the weather takes a turn for the worse and the people must make some difficult decisions. A perfect book for any weather unit. Facts about food make this book the ideal complement to any study of the human body.

1. Before reading *Cloudy with a Chance of Meatballs*, have students form their chairs in a circle. Go around the circle and encourage each student to create a wild and wacky form of weather (e.g., "The sun was like a melted lump of butter," "Rain came down like spraying soda pop," and "The snow was like huge mountains of mashed potatoes."). Write the statements on sheets of construction paper and post on the bulletin board.

2. After listening to several sample statements (in the preceding activity), invite each student to select one and write a tall tale in his or her journal. These tales may be illustrated and posted if desired.

3. Invite students to create a chart of the weather phrases in the book and corresponding weather phrases in actual use.

4. Students may wish to create their own version of the story using possible weather words found in the story. A suggested beginning could be: "One morning, I woke to see _____ falling outside my window." Stories may be illustrated and a book cover designed.

5. Invite youngsters to reread the book and "shop" from the sky. They may wish to prepare shopping lists of food words selected from the story and arrange them into food groups or according to how those products are located in the local supermarket. Food words can each be written on separate index cards and then placed inside brown lunch bags according to individual categories.

    Invite youngsters to assemble the food words into various menus for family members. Are they able to put together a series of balanced meals for several days or an entire week? Are they able to provide for all the dietary needs of family members?

Title: Bringing the Rain to Kapiti Plain

Author: Verna Aardema

Bibliographic Information: New York: Dial, 1981

Summary: A wonderful African folk tale with a rhythmic pattern and an engaging story line. This story involves Ki-pat, a herdsman who watches his cows go hungry and thirsty because there is no rain to make the grass grow. He watches a large cloud overhead and devises an ingenious way to make the rain come using a special arrow and a special feather.

1. Invite students to talk about rain and how it makes them feel. They may wish to complete the following sentence stems orally or in writing:

    Rain tastes like _____

    Rain smells like _____

    Rain looks like _____

    Rain sounds like _____

    Rain feels like _____

2. The following activity provides youngsters with a chance to see what a raindrop looks like:

    Invite children to fill a cake pan (9″ x 15″) with about 2 inches of sifted all-purpose flour. At the start of a rainstorm, encourage kids to stand outside for a few moments and collect approximately 30 to 50 raindrops in the flour. (This will have to be done quickly and at the beginning of a rainstorm. Just a few moments in the rain will be sufficient.) Have them bring their pans inside and allow the pans to sit overnight.

    The next day, encourage children to gently sift through the flour and gather up all the congealed raindrops they can. Have them organize the drops on a flat surface (a counter or table). They will note that raindrops come in two basic sizes, large and small (large raindrops fall from higher clouds and thus gather more moisture than small raindrops). Children will also note that the drops will be in a state of either expansion or contraction, depending on when they hit the pan of flour (as a drop falls, it expands and contracts in a natural molecular action).

    Children may wish to preserve their raindrops. This can be done by spraying the drops with a commercial varnish or carefully dipping them into it. When dry, youngsters will be able to manipulate the drops in a variety of activities.

3. Students may enjoy making their own rain. You will need a large glass jar, very hot tap water, 10 to 12 ice cubes, a foil pie pan, and a flashlight. Directions: Fill the jar with very hot tap water. Fill the pie pan with ice cubes. Put it on top of the jar. Turn out the lights. Shine a flashlight into the jar. Have students note what happens inside the jar. After completing the experiment, students can write down what happened and illustrate it step by step.

4. Invite students to check an almanac for the yearly rainfall in your area. Then they can locate several cities in the United States and find the normal annual precipitation. Encourage them to compare the rainfall in several cities with that in your town or city. That information can be plotted on a large chart. Invite students to note any similarities or differences.

5. After reading the story to children, invite them to create their own folktale about the setting or events in their town. Encourage them to use the rhythmic pattern in the book. Following are two examples that children can modify according to their own locale:

> *This is the great Missouri plain,*
> *All soggy and wet and filled with rain—*
> *With wading birds and crying frogs,*
> *And echoing insects in all the bogs.*

> *This is the small California town,*
> *Flanked by fields of thistledown—*
> *A powerful place of long ago,*
> *Before the gold began to slow.*

Encourage students to continue with their own cumulative tales about their specific part of the world. Provide opportunities for individuals to share their tales.

Title: Weather Forecasting

Author: Gail Gibbons

Bibliographic Information: New York: Four Winds, 1987

Summary: The weather is always changing. Meteorologists are needed to help us understand the weather, its patterns, and what it means in our daily lives. This book is a simple yet thorough introduction to the importance and significance of weather forecasting.

1. Students may enjoy observing and recording the weather patterns that occur in your area of the country. Be sure students have an opportunity to record weather conditions over a long period of time (two to three months, if possible). You may wish to create your own "Weather Notebook" so that students can keep track of rainfall, cloud conditions, temperature, humidity, barometric pressure, and the like. A Weather Watching Kit (Catalog No. 5J-738-2253) is available from Delta Education, P.O. Box 950, Hudson, NH 03051. Also available from the same company are two classroom weather charts: Chalkboard Weather Station (Catalog No. 57-230-1639) and Weather Chart (Catalog No. 57-230-1640).

2. Invite each student to imagine that he or she is a particular form of weather (a raindrop, a gust of wind, a snowflake, etc.). Encourage students to write about the life cycle from the perspective of that particular form of weather. What are some of the things it observes? What distances are traveled? How long is the life span?

3. Obtain a copy of *USA Today*. Show students the color weather map on the back of the first section. Invite students to note the various designations used to record weather information. Encourage students to read through the weather section and note the predictions for their area of the country. Invite students to create a special weather map similar to the *USA Today* map, but specifically tailored to their geographic region (as opposed to the entire country).

4. Invite students to watch the local television weather report each evening. Encourage them to record the predictions for the weather for each day. Then, each following day, invite students to record the actual weather. Discuss with them any differences or similarities between the predictions and the actual daily weather. Invite students to graph and chart their information. How accurate (over an extended period of time) are the forecasters in predicting weather?

6. If possible, invite selected students to take photographs of various cloud patterns. When the photos are developed, ask students to arrange them into an attractive display for the entire class. Students may wish to include descriptions of each cloud type and what it means in terms of impending weather.

Title: Storms
Author: Seymour Simon
Bibliographic Information: New York: Mulberry, 1989
Summary: A wonderfully photographed book filled with incredible information and fascinating facts about
storms—how they form, different types, and the effects they
have on various parts of the earth. Youngsters will turn to
this book again and again.

1. Many sayings and predictions about the weather have been handed down from one generation to the next. Following are two sayings or admonitions that have been passed down through the years:

   • "Red sky at morning, sailor take warning. Red sky at night, sailor's delight."

   • "A January fog will freeze a hog."

   Invite students to look through other books and assemble a collection of traditional weather sayings. How accurate are those sayings? How do those sayings compare with actual meteorological events?

2. Because people did not always understand the weather, they have had many beliefs about the conditions or situations that cause weather patterns. Following are a few that people have had down through the ages:

   • Sea fog was once thought to be the breath of an underwater monster.

   • In Germany, some people believed that a cat washes itself just before a rain shower.

   • The Aztecs believed that the sun god could be kept strong and bright only through the use of human sacrifices.

   • The Norse peoples thought that weather was created by the god Thor, who raced across the sky in a chariot pulled by two giant goats.

   Invite students to research other beliefs about the weather. They may wish to collect their data from trade books, encyclopedias, or conversations with weather experts. Encourage them to put together a collection of these beliefs into a notebook or journal.

3. Many strange things have fallen from the sky as a result of unusual weather patterns. Students may want to research some of these unusual events and assemble them together into a notebook of "Weird and Wacky Weather." Here are a few to get them started:

   • On October 14, 1755, red snow fell on the Alps.

   • In June 1940, a shower of silver coins fell on the town of Gorky, Russia.

   • On June 16, 1939, it rained frogs at Trowbridge, England.

4. When severe weather is predicted for a specific area of the country (e.g., a hurricane along the Gulf coast, a tornado in the Plains states, severe thunderstorms in the Midwest), invite students to track the history of that storm. They may wish to consult the daily newspaper, a weekly news magazine, television or radio broadcasts, or first-hand accounts from meteorologists or television weather forecasters. The life story of a storm can be put together into a album that includes a variety of photos and news stories.

CULMINATION:

Students are invited to select one or more of the following activities and projects:

1. As a class, students may wish to create a weather dictionary containing all the weather words they have learned from the unit. They may wish to include an illustration for each definition or find pictures from magazines or newspapers to illustrate the words.

2. Divide the class into various groups. Invite each group to assemble a collection of amazing weather data or weather facts. For example:

    • Lightning strikes the earth as frequently as 100 times every second.

    • In 1953, hailstones as big as golf balls fell in Alberta, Canada.

    • In a blizzard, winds often reach speeds of 186 mph.

    • The wettest place in the world is a spot on the island of Kauai in the state of Hawaii. It rains more than 450 inches every year (that's more than 37 feet) on one mountain top.

    • The fastest tornado had a recorded speed of 280 mph.

3. Many local television weather forecasters make visits to elementary classrooms as a regular part of their jobs. Contact your local television station and inquire about scheduling a visit from the local weatherperson. Be sure students have an opportunity to prepare some questions prior to the visit.

4. Encourage students to create their own fables or folktales about specific weather patterns or events. They may wish to share these stories in a collection to be donated to the school library, or a videotape that can be circulated to other classrooms in the school.

THE CHANGING EARTH

GENERALIZATIONS/PRINCIPLES:

1. The surface of the earth is constantly changing.

2. Changes in the earth affect people living on the surface.

3. There are different types of forces which affect the earth.

CONCEPTS:

change is constant
change over time
cause and effect

MATERIALS:

Primary Literature Selections

Hooper, Meredith. *The Pebble in My Pocket*. New York: Viking, 1996.

Lauber, Patricia. *Volcano: The Eruption and Healing of Mt. St. Helens*. New York: Bradbury, 1986.

Newton, David. *Earthquakes*. New York: Watts, 1993.

Simon, Seymour. *Volcanoes*. New York: Morrow, 1988.

Secondary Literature Selections

Bain, Iain. *Mountains and Earth Movements*. New York: Watts, 1984.
> What are the effects of erosion, weathering, faulting, folding, and continental drift on the creation of mountains? This book describes all of them in detail.

Farndon, John. *How the Earth Works: 100 Ways Parents and Kids Can Share the Secrets of the Earth*. New York: Readers Digest, 1992.
> Lots and lots of experiments and projects designed to help kids learn about the earth.

Hiscock, Bruce. *The Big Rock*. New York: Atheneum, 1988.
> The story of a single rock in the Adirondack Mountains and the weathering, erosion, and mountain building that created it.

Lasky, Kathryn. *Surtsey: The Newest Place on Earth.* New York: Hyperion, 1992.
Lyrical prose and spectacular photographs recount the story of this newest volcanic island, created off the coast of Iceland in 1963.

Loeschnig, Louis. *Simple Earth Science Experiments with Everyday Materials.* New York: Sterling, 1996.
Dozens of explorations, discoveries, and experiments designed to help youngsters learn more about their planet.

Sattler, Helen. *Our Patchwork Planet.* New York: Lothrop, 1995.
This book provides the reader with an interesting excursion through present-day tectonic theory.

Taylor, Barbara. *Mountains and Volcanoes.* New York: Kingfisher, 1993.
A wonderfully illustrated text highlighted by informative details and stories about mountains and volcanoes.

Watt, Fiona. *Earthquakes and Volcanoes.* London: Usborne, 1993.
Lots of illustrations and a detailed text make this a fascinating book.

Zoehfeld, Kathleen. *How Mountains Are Made.* New York: HarperCollins, 1995.
Mountain formation is described through the eyes of four children.

Audiovisual Selections

The Forces of Nature (Catalog No. C31012). Washington, DC: National Geographic Society (filmstrip).

Our Ever Changing Earth (Catalog No. C30730). Washington, DC: National Geographic Society (filmstrip).

INITIATING ACTIVITY:

Invite students to share their thoughts and feelings about living through a violent earthquake (such as the one that occurred in Los Angeles on January 17, 1994, or any recent one) or a volcanic eruption. Invite each student to record his or her thoughts in a personal journal. Students may elect to share their thoughts and feelings in small- or large-group settings. Afterward, encourage students to select one or more of the following activities to do by themselves or with one or more partners:

1. Create a "graffiti wall" that records personal feelings about the aftermath of an earthquake or volcanic eruption. Students may post a long sheet of newsprint on one wall of the classroom and invite classmates and others to record their thoughts, feelings, and ideas.

2. Create a short skit about a make-believe earthquake or volcano in their neighborhood. What events happen in the neighborhood? How do the local residents react to those events? Does a memorable incident happen nearby?

3. Invite students to create a mock news broadcast about an imaginary earthquake or volcano. Selected students can each take on the roles of newscaster, interviewer, local citizens and interested bystanders and recreate the events that occurred in their neighborhood.

4. Create a collage (using photos cut out of the newspaper or selected news magazines) that replicates the major events of a recent earthquake or volcano. Encourage students to share their finished products with the class and arrange them into an appropriate display in the classroom (bulletin board, poster, collage, etc.). Students may wish to include appropriate captions for selected photos using ideas from their individual journals.

5. Invite students to interview adults in their neighborhood concerning the adults' feelings and emotions about an earthquake or volcano. What would they do? How would they feel? How do the emotions expressed by adults differ from those recorded in students' journals? Students may wish to discuss any similarities or differences.

6. Invite students to use playhouses and other models to create a make-believe town located on a fault line. Allow students to assemble a town on a large sheet cake (see "Cakequake! An Earth-Shaking Experience," by Garry Hardy and Marvin Tolman, in *Science and Children* vol. 29, no. 1 [September 1991], pp. 18–21). Invite students to make a videotape of the effects of their earthquake.

GENERAL ACTIVITIES:

1. Ask students to look through the daily newspapers for articles regarding changes in the earth (volcanic eruptions, earthquakes,etc.). Encourage them to create a bulletin board to display the articles under the heading, "The Changing Earth."

2. Invite students to create a dictionary booklet entitled "My Earth Book." Students may wish to create a page for each letter of the alphabet (for example: A = Abyss; B = Biosphere; C = Chasm; D = Dangerous).

3. Share one or more videos from the following list. After viewing a selected film, invite students to create a review of the film to be included in an ongoing unit newspaper called: *Earth Watch* (specific activities for each film are also suggested).

    a. "This Changing Planet" (Catalog No. 30352) available through National Geographic Society, Washington, DC. Explains how the earth is constantly changing its surface through weather, erosion, earthquakes, and volcanoes. After viewing, invite students to choose one of the ways described in the movie and draw an illustration regarding the event, using appropriate captions.

    b. "The Violent Earth" (Catalog No. 51234) available through National Geographic Society, Washington, DC. The video tours active volcanoes throughout the world. After viewing, encourage students to make a replica of a volcano from modeling clay or papier-mâché. Challenge students to model their volcanoes after one or more of those in the film.

4. Invite students to maintain an "Earthquake Journal" that includes an ongoing chart of the Richter Scale readings for aftershocks that occur in the days and weeks following an earthquake; photographs or illustrations of the damage observed in various neighborhoods; interviews with adults and other students; and lists of earthquake-related books located in the local library.

PRIMARY LITERATURE SELECTIONS:

Title: Earthquakes

Authors: David Newton

Bibliographic Information: New York: Watts, 1993

Summary: This book contains information about earthquakes and how they affect our world. What causes earthquakes? How do earthquakes destroy the land? How do scientists measure and predict earthquakes?

1. Show the film "The Great San Francisco Earthquake," produced by PBS Video (1988) or the video "Our Dynamic Earth," produced by the National Geographic Society (Catalog No. C51162). Invite students to discuss the similarities between the events portrayed in the film(s) and those described in Newton's book. Encourage students to create a Venn diagram illustrating the similarities and differences.

2. Invite students to write their own personal newspaper articles about a recent earthquake. Afterward, encourage students to form small groups and discuss their articles and how those pieces compare with the descriptions given in the book.

3. Invite students to construct a model of the different layers of the earth by painting a huge ball on a piece of poster board. The inside of the ball can be painted in three colors according to the three layers of the earth (the core, the mantle, and the crust). Students may then wish to use a globe of the world to plot selected countries on their illustrations. They may also wish to plot the locations of some of the major earthquakes that have occurred during the past 25 to 50 years.

4. Encourage students to work in small groups and research other books about earthquakes (see the Secondary Literature Selections for this unit). Each group may wish to prepare a brief summary on its findings and present the discoveries to the rest of the class. Invite each group to prepare a fact book about the collected data and present their finished products to the school library.

5. Assign selected students to work in small groups to construct their own makeshift seismographs. Each group will need a ball of clay, a pencil, a string approximately one foot long, tape, and a white piece of paper. Tie the string to the eraser end of the pencil and punch the tip of the pencil through a clay ball until just the lead point is sticking out of the clay. (See fig. 6.5 on page 136.) One student in each group tapes a sheet of white paper to a desk. One group member stages an earthquake by shaking the desk, while another group member holds the string up steady above the desk so that just the tip of the pencil is barely touching the paper. Invite students to observe how their makeshift seismograph records the waves of the simulated earthquake. Encourage students to compare the recordings they obtained with those found in various library books.

6. Provide each of several small groups of students with a shallow pan of water and a marble. Invite individual students each to drop a marble into the pan and describe the ripples that are sent out. Encourage students to compare the waves in their pans with those that might be sent out from the epicenter of an earthquake. Students may also wish to compare their ripples with waves in the ocean. What similarities do they notice? Invite students to record their observations in an appropriate journal.

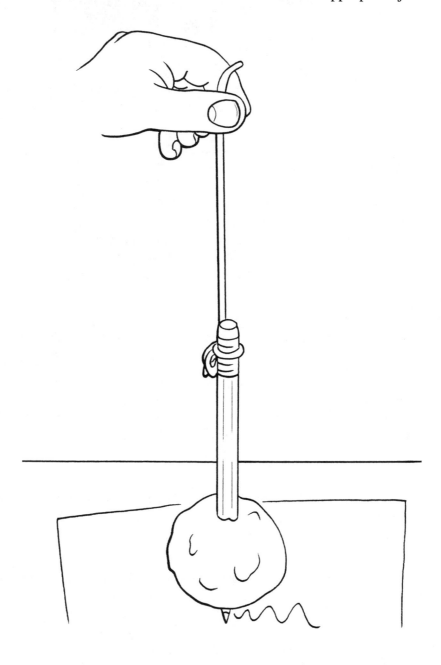

Fig. 6.5.

Title: Volcano: The Eruption and
Healing of Mount St. Helens

Author: Patricia Lauber

Bibliographic Information: New York: Bradbury, 1986

Summary: The events leading up to and following the eruption
of Mt. St. Helens in Washington are described in rich detail.
The author also describes how the surrounding environment
began to rebuild itself.

1. Before reading the book with students, provide them with photographs of Mount St. Helens as it was before the eruption. Invite students to imagine what the mountain must have looked like after the eruption and encourage each one to draw an illustration of how they think the mountain looked after the eruption. Later, invite students to compare their predictions with the actual photos in the book. What differences do they note?

2. Invite each student to imagine that he or she is a volcano. Have students write their own biographies in their journals based on this perspective. Encourage students to write about why they erupted, what they felt prior to and following the eruption, what triggered the eruption, how the eruption affected the environment in the immediate vicinity, and so on. Afterward, students may wish to create illustrations of themselves (as volcanoes) to share with the class.

3. Invite students to research other books about volcanoes. Students may wish to choose a volcano (e.g., Mount Fuji) to compare and contrast with Mount St. Helens.

4. Invite small groups of students to write fictional stories about how they were affected when Mount St. Helens erupted. What were some of the effects of the volcano's eruption on their daily lives? How did they survive? What did they do afterward? Provide opportunities for students to share their creations with the class.

5. Demonstrate the gas pressure that builds up inside of volcanoes by shaking a bottle of warm soda and then taking the cap off (use caution). Invite students to compare what they observe with the eruption of Mount St. Helens. Students may wish to discuss how the soda compares with the magma of Mount St. Helens.

6. Divide the class into groups of scientists. Invite each group to chart the specific eruptions of Mount St. Helens on a piece of poster board. Students may wish to include the date of the eruption, what caused the eruption, what type of eruption it was, and what the effects were. Invite each group to give a presentation of its findings.

7. Generate a class discussion on how the eruption of Mount St. Helens affected the food chain for the surrounding area. Encourage students to discuss such aspects as: How did the avalanches and mud slides affect the food chain? What are some of the ways

that the vegetation was able to rejuvenate after the eruption? Why were some animals able to escape harm from the eruption? Invite students to create individual journals to record their discussions.

8. Invite students to compare and contrast the environment immediately following the eruption to the environment two years after the eruption. Encourage students to take on the roles of news reporters and interview the plants and animals in the region about the processes they experienced during this transition phase.

Title: Volcanoes

Author: Seymour Simon

Bibliographic Information: New York: Morrow, 1988

Summary: Using clear and concise language, the author explains how volcanoes are formed, how they erupt, different types of lava, and how volcanoes affect the earth. Full-color photographs are included throughout the text.

1. Bring in samples of volcanic ash and/or lava and show them to students (these can be obtained through science supply companies such as Hubbard Scientific, P.O. Box 104, Northbrook, IL 60065, 800-323-8368; The Institute for Earth Education, P.O. Box 288, Warrenville, IL 60555, 509-395-2299; or Scott Resources, P.O. Box 2121F, Fort Collins, CO 80522, 800-289-9299). Ask students to discuss the feel of these substances in comparison with the descriptions in the book.

2. Invite students to record the names of each of the four different kinds of volcanoes on four separate sheets of oaktag. Encourage them to draw illustrations of selected volcanoes (from around the world) on the appropriate sheet of oaktag. Students may wish to consult other references (see the Secondary Literature Selections for this unit).

3. Challenge students to construct comparative charts of volcanoes according to different climatic regions of the world (e.g., how many active volcanoes are located in tropical regions versus how many active volcanoes are located in polar regions?). Is there a relationship between climate and the location of volcanoes?

4. Invite students to make charts of the dormancy periods of selected volcanoes. For example, which volcanoes have remained dormant the longest? Which volcanoes have had the most recent eruptions? Where are the most dormant volcanoes located? Where are the most active volcanoes located?

5. Ask students to compare the photographs in this book with volcano photos in other books. What similarities are there? What kinds of differences do they note? How can students account for the differences in photos of the same volcanoes? Encourage students to record their inferences in journals.

6. Invite students to speculate on what happens when a bottle of soda pop is vigorously shaken. How is that action similar to the action of a volcano? Are there other actions similar to those that take place inside a volcano?

7. Invite students to watch a video of a volcano erupting (e.g., "The Violent Earth," National Geographic Society, Washington, DC 20036; Catalog No. 51234). Afterward, encourage students to pretend that they are at the site of one of the eruptions. Invite them to put together an on-the-spot newscast (videotape) recording their reactions during the eruption.

8. Invite students to conduct some library research on famous volcanoes in history (e.g., Krakatoa, Mt. Fuji, Vesuvius, etc.). Collected data can be assembled into a large class book or presented via a specially prepared videotape.

9. Some students may be interested in investigating the myths and legends of volcanoes throughout history. How do those stories and tales compare with what modern science knows about volcanoes today?

Title: The Pebble in My Pocket

Author: Meredith Hooper

Bibliographic Information: New York: Viking, 1996

Summary: This incredible book traces the life history of a small pebble from the beginning of the earth's formation, 4.5 billion years ago, to the present day. A richly illustrated and magnificent book.

1. Invite students to create a time line from the events in the book. Encourage students to plot approximate dates on the time line. Provide opportunities for students to share their results.

2. Soak pieces of sandstone in water overnight. Place a piece of saturated sandstone in a plastic bag and seal tightly. Put the bag in the freezer overnight. Invite students to observe the results. (Water expands as it freezes, causing the rock to split. The same type of weathering occurs in nature, breaking large rocks into smaller ones.)

3. Mix three tablespoons of sand with three tablespoons of white glue (you may need to adjust the mixture depending on the type of sand—it should have the consistency of wet concrete). Form the mixture into two or three "rocks" and allow them to dry in a low (250°F) oven for several hours. Place the "rocks" in a tumbler or sturdy cup filled with water. Cover the cup with a tight-fitting lid. Invite students to shake the cup vigorously for several minutes and note the results. (The "rocks" will be worn down by the eroding power of the water.)

4. Invite students to look for various types of erosion in and around their homes. Some examples to look for include coins that are smooth from handling, shoes with the heels worn down, old car tires with no tread, and a plate or countertop with the design or finish worn away. Invite students to compare these forms of erosion with those that occur in nature (wind and water erosion).

CULMINATION:

Students will be invited to select one or more of the following activities and projects:

1. College students from a local university can be invited to share specially prepared lessons on the changing earth. Additionally, students majoring in geology at the university can be invited to share their expertise with the class. Invite students to interview the college students.

2. Students can be invited to initiate an "Earth Watch Newspaper"—a collection of stories about violent activities taking place on the earth's surface over a designated period of time. Periodic reports may be made to the class.

3. Individual students can be challenged to create an advertisement (written or oral) for a volcano. Class members will be asked to describe the features that would be most necessary in the promotion (i.e., the sale) of an active volcano.

4. Invite students to create a play or readers' theater adaptation of a story concerning the steps to be taken in case of a natural disaster. Encourage students to consult with the local Red Cross center for information necessary to prepare the presentation.

5. Have students work in small groups to create "before" and "after" dioramas of the local area prior to and immediately after an imaginary earthquake. Other groups of students may be invited to create "before" and "after" dioramas of selected volcanic eruptions, floods, or other natural disasters as a result of their readings. Encourage students to discuss their feelings about these events.

6. Invite students to create semantic webs of important information introduced in the unit and post the webs throughout the room. Encourage students to make two separate webs: "Natural Earth Changes" and "Changes Created by Humans." Plan time to discuss any similarities or differences.

OCEANS

GENERALIZATIONS/PRINCIPLES:

1. The oceans of the world are rich and diverse.

2. There is an amazing variety of flora and fauna in the ocean.

3. Oceans are endangered.

CONCEPTS:

conservation

diversity

interrelationships

MATERIALS:

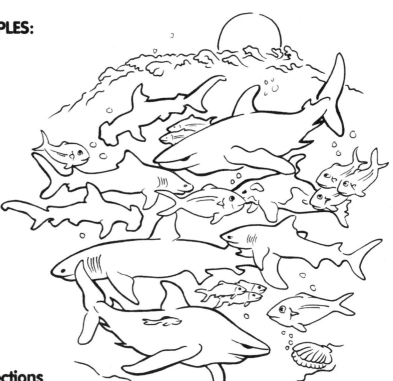

Primary Literature Selections

Fredericks, Anthony D. *Exploring the Oceans: Science Activities for Kids*. Golden, CO: Fulcrum, 1998.

Macquitty, Miranda. *Ocean*. New York: Knopf, 1995.

Pratt, Kristin Joy. *A Swim Through the Sea*. Nevada City, CA: Dawn Publications, 1994.

Silver, Donald M. *One Small Square: Seashore*. New York: W. H. Freeman, 1993.

Secondary Literature Selections

Burnie, David. *Seashore*. New York: Dorling Kindersley, 1994.
    A richly photographed and detailed examination of life at the seashore.

Chinery, Michael. *Questions and Answers About Seashore Animals*. New York: Kingfisher, 1994.
    More than two dozen questions and answers about some common and not-so-common seashore animals.

Fredericks, Anthony D. *Surprising Swimmers*. Minocqua, WI: NorthWord Press, 1996.
    Birds that fly underwater, snakes with one lung, and snails that travel on "homemade" rafts are just a few of the incredible animals in this delightful book.

Guiberson, Brenda. *Into the Sea*. New York: Henry Holt, 1996.
    A richly illustrated book details the trials and travels of a sea turtle during his first year of life.

Hare, Tony. *Polluting the Sea*. New York: Gloucester Press, 1991.
    A useful source for projects, this information-packed book examines the damage caused by oil spills and other pollutants.

Hopkins, Lee Bennett. *The Sea Is Calling Me*. San Diego, CA: Harcourt Brace, 1986.
    A collection of 21 poems about the sea.

Lazier, Christine. *Seashore Life*. Ossining, NY: Young Discovery Library, 1991.
    An accurate overview of seashore life, presented in a direct and factual format.

Pallota, Jerry. *The Ocean Alphabet Book*. Watertown, MA: Charlesbridge, 1989.
    An introduction to various ocean creatures, one for each letter of the alphabet.

Pringle, Laurence. *Coral Reefs: Earth's Undersea Treasures*. New York: Simon & Schuster, 1995.
    With this intriguing and informative book readers examine the wonders of the world's coral reefs including the threats to their survival.

Rinard, Judith. *Along a Rocky Shore*. Washington, DC: National Geographic Society, 1990.
    Illustrated with crisp photographs, this book introduces the reader to life along the rocky sea coast.

Wu, Herbert. *Life in the Oceans*. Boston: Little, Brown, 1991.
    Stunning photographs highlight this examination of the wide variety of ocean life throughout the world.

INITIATING ACTIVITY:

Provide students with a list of oceanic occupations similar to the ones shown here. Invite them to conduct some library research on one or more chosen occupations with specific reference to job requirements, training and education, amount of time spent at sea, and occupational dangers. Provide opportunities for students to share their research with others.

Commercial fishers—catch ocean creatures to sell to markets.

Marine geologists—study rocks and the formation of the ocean floor.

Marine biologists—study the animals and plants of the ocean.

Divers—assist in finding sunken treasures, repairing underwater equipment, gathering information for research, and so on.

Oceanographers—study and explore the ocean.

Offshore drillers—explore beneath the ocean floor for deposits of petroleum and natural gas to be used for various forms of energy.

Mariculturists—raise or farm fish and other sea life for food and/or restocking the ocean.

Marine ichthyologists—study fish, their habitats, the food they eat, and their relationship to their environment.

Marine ecologists—study the relationships between sea creatures and their environment.

Captain/crew of ship—work on a commercial freight, fishing, cruise ship.

Navigators—use directions to determine a ship's course at sea.

Encourage students to report their findings to others or to prepare a short report entitled "A Week in the Life of a _____."

Students may wish to contact any one of the following organizations or obtain any of the listed publications to learn more about marine science careers:

American Association of Zoo Keepers
635 SW Gage Blvd.
Topeka, KS 66606

American Zoo and Aquarium Association
Oglebay Park
Wheeling, WV 26003

Environmental Opportunities
P.O. Box 1437
Keene, NH 03431

Goodwin, Harold, "Today's Youth in Tomorrow's Seas." Available from Oregon State University School of Oceanography Corvallis, OR 97331

International Marine Animal Trainers Association
1720 South Shores Rd.
San Diego, CA 92109

International Wildlife Rehabilitation Council
4437 Central Place, B-4
Suison, CA 94585

"Marine Careers" (videotape). University of Delaware, Marine Communications Office, Newark, DE 19716 (302-831-8083)

National Marine Educators Association
P.O. Box 5215
Pacific Grove, CA 93950

Sea Grant. For information on regional offices, contact Sea Grant National Office NOAA, Sea Grant, R-ORI, SSMB-1 Room 5214
1335 E-W Highway
Silver Spring, MD 20910-3226.

Any college or university with a marine science program will be able to provide students with important and valuable information on careers in marine science.

GENERAL ACTIVITIES:

1. Invite youngsters to keep a watch on the local news or local newspaper for reports of ocean pollution from around the world. They may wish to focus on events related to grounded tankers, but other types of pollution can be tracked as well. Allow students to hang up a large wall map of the world. For each incident of ocean pollution, invite youngsters to write a brief summary (date, nature of occurrence, place, resolution, etc.) on a 3″ x 5″ index card. Post each card around the wall map and connect the card with the actual location on the map using a length of yarn (the yarn can be taped or pinned to the wall).

2. Invite students to visit a local grocery store and take along a list similar to the one following. This list represents several varieties of fish that are commonly found in most supermarkets throughout North America and that are sold as food. Encourage students to check off each type of fish as it is located in the store. They may want to visit the fresh fish department, the frozen fish section, and the canned food section.

☐ herring   ☐ salmon
☐ shrimp   ☐ tuna
☐ orange roughy   ☐ crab
☐ lobster   ☐ scallops
☐ catfish   ☐ cod
☐ haddock   ☐ flounder
☐ perch   ☐ clams
☐ whiting   ☐ halibut
☐ monkfish   ☐ grouper
☐ scrod   ☐ oysters
☐ anchovies   ☐ sardines
☐ whitefish   ☐ mussels
☐ mackerel   ☐ octopus
☐ pollock

3. Here's an activity that gives students an opportunity to create a homemade ocean in a bottle.

Materials:

empty one-liter soda bottle (with a screw-on top)

salad oil

water

blue food coloring

Directions:

Fill an empty one-liter soda bottle one-third of the way up with salad oil. Fill the rest of the bottle (all the way to the brim) with water dyed with a few drops of blue food coloring. Put the top on securely and lay the bottle on its side. Slowly and gently tip the bottle back and forth.

The oil in the bottle will begin to roll and move just like the waves in the ocean. Students will have created a miniature ocean in a bottle.

4. Invite students to contact several of the following groups and ask for information on the work they do and the types of printed materials they have available for students:

American Littoral Society
Sandy Hook
Highlands, NJ 07732
201-291-0055

American Oceans Campaign
725 Arizona Ave., Suite 102
Santa Monica, CA 90401
310-576-6162

Center for Marine Conservation
1725 DeSales St., NW, Suite 500
Washington, DC 20036
202-429-5609

Cetacean Society International
P.O. Box 953
Georgetown, CT 06829
203-544-8617

Coastal Conservation Association
4801 Woodway, Suite 220 West
Houston, TX 77056
713-626-4222

The Coral Reef Alliance
809 Delaware St.
Berkeley, CA 94710
510-528-2492

International Marine Mammal Project
Earth Island Institute
300 Broadway, Suite 28
San Francisco, CA 94133
1-800-DOLPHIN

International Oceanographic Foundation
4600 Rickenbacker Causeway
Virginia Key, Miami, FL 33149
305-361-4888

International Wildlife Coalition (IWC) and **The Whale Adoption Project**
70 E. Falmouth Highway
East Falmouth, MA 02536
508-548-8328

Marine Environmental Research Institute
772 West End Ave.
New York, NY 10025
212-864-6285

Marine Technology Center
1828 L St., NW, Suite 906
Washington, DC 20036-5104
202-775-5966

National Coalition for Marine Conservation
3 W. Market St.
Leesburg, VA 20176
703-777-0037

National Wildlife Federation
8925 Leesburg Pike
Vienna, VA 22184-0001
703-790-4000

Ocean Voice International
P.O. Box 37026
3332 McCarthy Rd.
Ottawa, Ontario, Canada K1V 0W0
613-990-8819

PRIMARY LITERATURE SELECTIONS:

Title: One Small Square: Seashore
Author: Donald M. Silver
Bibliographic Information: New York: W. H. Freeman, 1993
Summary: In this book, readers meet a dazzling collection of creatures and watch how they interact with each other and with other elements of their environment, including plants, rocks, soil, and the weather. There is a lot to discover at the seashore and this book offers young adventurers incredible an array of information.

1. The following activity will alert children to the speed at which a seaside community can become fouled by oil. Provide students with four sealable sandwich bags. Label the bags "A," "B," "C," and "D." Fill each bag with one-third of water and one-third of used motor oil. Invite students to place a hard-boiled egg in each bag. Seal the bags. Invite students to remove the eggs from each of the bags (they should wear kitchen gloves or some sort of disposable gloves) according to the following schedule:

   From Bag "A"—after 15 minutes
   From Bag "B"—after 30 minutes
   From Bag "C"—after 60 minutes
   From Bag "D"—after 120 minutes

   Have students peel each of the hard-boiled eggs and note the amount of oil that has seeped through the shell and onto the actual egg. Which egg has the most pollution? How rapidly did the pollution seep into each egg? Provide time afterward to discuss the rapidity with which these eggs became polluted and the implications for spilled oil polluting a beach or shoreline.

2. Waves constantly pound on the shoreline. This is a process that has been going on for millions of years. As a result, rocks are broken down through continuous wave action. Here's a fun activity that demonstrates this process.

Materials:

white glue

playground sand

water

small coffee can (with lid)

cookie sheet

Directions:

    a.   Mix together 6 tablespoons of white glue with 6 tablespoons of sand in a bowl.

    b.   Using the tablespoon, place small lumps of the mixture on a cookie sheet.

    c.   Place the cookie sheet in a low oven (250°F) and bake the "rocks" for three to four hours.

    d.   Remove the rocks and allow them to cool.

    e.   Put three or four rocks into a coffee can with some water and place the lid securely on top.

    f.   Shake for 4 to 5 minutes and remove the lid.

The rocks will have begun to wear down. Some of the rocks will be worn down into sand. The action of the waves inside the coffee can causes the rocks to wear against each other. As a result, they break down into smaller and smaller pieces. On a beach or shoreline, this process takes many years, but the result is the same. Rocks become smaller by being tossed against each other by the action of the waves. Over time, rocks wear down into sand-like particles that eventually become part of the beach or shoreline.

   3.   Students can build a three-dimensional model of a shoreline or tidal area with the following activity.

Materials:

deep baking pan (a bread loaf pan is ideal)
non-stick vegetable spray
4 cups flour
1 cup salt
1½ cups warm water
acrylic or tempera paints

Directions:

    a.   Knead the flour, salt, and warm water together in a large bowl for about 10 minutes (the mixture should be stiff but pliable).

    b.   Spray the baking pan with vegetable spray.

    c.   Spread the mixture into the pan, forming it into various landforms (beach, rocky shore, sand dunes, outcroppings, cliffs). (See fig. 6.6.) If necessary, you may want to make some more of the mixture using the same recipe.

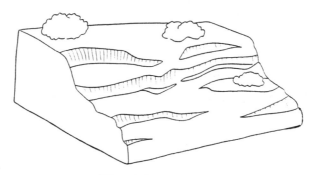

Fig. 6.6.

d. Bake in an oven set at 325°F for about one hour or more, depending on size and thickness.

e. Test the sculpture for doneness by sticking a toothpick into various spots (the sculpture should be firm to hard). If necessary, replace the sculpture in the oven to bake some more.

f. Remove the sculpture from the oven and allow to cool.

g. Carefully slide the sculpture from the baking pan (this should be done by an adult).

h. Paint the sculpture with different colors of acrylic or tempera paints (available at any art, craft, or hobby store).

i. Optional: When the paint is dry, spray the sculpture with a clear varnish to preserve it.

Title: A Swim Through the Sea

Author: Kristen Joy Pratt

Bibliographic Information: Nevada City, CA: Dawn Publications, 1994

Summary: Seamore the Seahorse explores the fascinating plants and animals of the undersea world. His alphabetic journey takes him past a flashlight fish, manatees, a porcupine fish, and a wise and wondrous whale, among others. This journey through the undersea world is a beautiful environmental awareness book, full of interesting facts and colorful illustrations.

1. Here's a great activity to help students learn about fish physiology. In fact, this activity has been practiced in Japan for more than 100 years.

Materials:

one whole fish (can be obtained from the fish department of any large supermarket)

newspaper

paper towels

newsprint (available from any art store or hobby store)

water-soluble paint (liquid tempera paint or artist's acrylic paint are both available from hobby, craft, or art stores)

artist's paintbrushes

masking tape

Directions:

     a.   Wash the fish thoroughly with soap and water to remove any mucus.

     b.   Lay the fish on a sheet of newspaper. Paint one side of the fish with the paint (any color will do). If necessary, thin the paint with a few drops of water. Stroke the fish from tail to head (this allows paint to catch under the edges of scales and spines and will improve the print, especially if you use a thin coat of paint).

     c.   Paint the fins and tail last, because they tend to dry out quickly. Do not paint the eye.

     d.   If the newspaper under the fish becomes wet with paint during the painting process, move the fish to a clean sheet of newspaper before printing. Otherwise the print will pick up leftover splotches of color.

     e.   Carefully and slowly lay a sheet of newsprint over the fish. Taking care not to move the paper, use hands and fingers to gently press the paper over the fish, including the fins and tail. Be careful not to wrinkle the paper, or a blurred or double image will result.

     f.   Slowly and carefully peel the paper off. Paint in the eye with a small brush. Tape the print to a wall and allow to dry.

     This activity is a traditional Japanese practice called *gyotaku* (pronounced ghio-ta-koo). It comes from two Japanese words (*gyo* = fish, *taku* = rubbing). This was a way Japanese fishermen recorded their catches, and it has evolved into an art form throughout the world.

     Students may want to experiment with different types of paper for this activity. Thinner papers (tissue paper, rice paper) will provide a print that shows more details of the fish, but they tend to wrinkle very easily when wet. Thicker paper (construction paper) is easier to handle, but does not provide a detailed print. *Note:* Students may need to practice this activity several times to get the technique down. Encourage them to be patient and they will discover that the more they practice, the more intricate their fish prints become.

  2.   Just like trees, fish have rings—on their scales. Here's how students can use these rings to determine the age of a fish:

Materials:

a fish

dark construction paper

hand lens or magnifying glass

Directions:

     a.   Remove 4 or 5 scales from the fish (you may want to assist students by using a fish scaler). One way to remove the scales is to use a pair of pliers to gently pull off selected scales.

     b.   Place the scales on the dark construction paper.

     c.   Use the hand lens to examine each scale.

     d.   Note the bands, or rings, on each scale.

As fish grow, they develop bands or rings on their scales. As students look at a fish scale, they'll probably notice (depending on the species) that a scale has both wide bands and thin bands. The wide bands represent summer growth when there is a lot of food for the fish to eat. The thin bands represent growth during the winter months. Also, students might notice that the wide bands are lighter in color than the thin bands. Because fish grow slower during the winter months, the bands are darker and thinner.

Because a year is made up of both summer and winter months, a full year's growth (for a fish) consists of one wide band plus one thin band (or one dark band plus one light band). To determine how old the fish was, students can simply count the total number of wide bands or rings on a scale.

3. Provide each student with two paper plates. Invite each student to cut out a circular section from one plate and glue blue cellophane over the inside of the hole to create a water effect. Encourage students to draw illustrations of kelp and seaweed, various sea creatures from the book, and other underwater items on the face of the uncut plate. They may wish to glue birdseed on the "ocean floor" to simulate sand or to use fish crackers to provide a three-dimensional effect. Invite students to staple or glue the two plates together (face to face) to create an imaginary porthole.

Title: Exploring the Oceans: Science Activities for Kids

Author: Anthony D. Fredericks

Bibliographic Information: Golden, CO: Fulcrum, 1998

Summary: This book provides readers with a delightful and intriguing collection of hands-on activities, experiments, and projects designed to alert them to the mysteries and marvels of ocean life. Packed with information and filled with an amazing assortment of data, readers will find this book an ideal addition to any ocean study.

1. Students are often amazed at the variety of food harvested from the world's oceans. You and your students may wish to put together an "Ocean Picnic" using ocean-related recipes (see the following) or others collected from family cookbooks. This feast can be part of an "Oceans Celebration." Plan to discuss the various types of food harvested from the ocean and provide students with library resources for learning more about those food items.

Ocean in a Cup

2 lg. pkgs. blueberry gelatin
4–5 small gummy fish
graham cracker crumbs

Mix gelatin according to package directions. Pour into clear plastic cups, leaving a 1″ space at top. Refrigerate until slightly set. Mix gummy fish into each cup. Refrigerate until firm. Put graham cracker crumbs on half of each "ocean" to simulate beach. Insert beverage umbrella into "sand."

Shark Eggs

6 hard-boiled eggs
4 oz. can tuna, drained
mayonnaise and pickle relish
paprika

Slice eggs in half lengthwise. Carefully scoop out yolks and put in mixing bowl. Add tuna, mayonnaise, and pickle relish to taste. Stir until blended. Fill egg centers with mixture and sprinkle with paprika.

Sea Mix

1 pkg. mini fish pretzels
1 pkg. mini fish crackers (cheese)
1 pkg. fish cookies
½ lb. Swedish gummy fish
1 can nuts
1 box raisins

Combine all ingredients. Serve in a sand pail.

2. Several organizations have brochures, leaflets, and guidebooks on ocean pollution and ways to prevent it. Encourage students to write to several of these groups requesting pertinent information. When the resources arrive, plan time to discuss with students methods and procedures by which they can help prevent or alleviate this global problem. Invite them to prepare an action plan for themselves and their friends in which they take a proactive stance against ocean pollution. The following will get them started:

    a. The New York Sea Grant Extension Program (125 Nassau Hall, SUNY, Stony Brook, NY 11794-5002 [516-632-8730]) has a 24-page booklet entitled "Earth Guide: 88 Action Tips for Cleaner Water." Copies are free.

    b. A variety of informational brochures are available from the NOAA Marine Debris Information Office, Center for Marine Conservation, 1725 DeSales St., NW, Washington, DC 20036.

    c. If students are interested in adopting an endangered animal—specifically, a whale—they can write for further information to the International Wildlife Coalition, Whale Adoption Project, 634 North Falmouth Highway, Box 388, North Falmouth, MA 02566.

    d. To join a coalition of environmentally conscious youngsters from around the country, invite students to write to the Strathmore Legacy's Eco Amigos Club, 333 Park St., West Springfield, MA 01089.

    e. Invite students to contact Keep America Beautiful (99 Park Ave., New York, NY 10016) and ask for "Pollution Pointers for Elementary Students," a list of environment improvement activities.

3. The book discusses some of the efforts to contain ocean pollution such as spreading oil. One method uses a boom (a floating line) that is placed in the water in an attempt to contain the oil spill. Students can experiment with different devices to contain their own oil spill to determine the best material to use in a boom.

    Place water in a large round pan or pie plate. Invite students to collect several different floating objects that could be used as booms. These may include a rubber band; a length of yarn, string, twine, or cotton batting; a ring of foam cut from the top of a disposable coffee cup, etc. (let students use their creative powers in inventing other types of potential booms). Place several drops of cooking oil in the middle of the water (students will note that oil and water do not mix; hence, the oil floats on top of the water). Invite students to encircle the oil with one or more different devices to determine which device or material best prevents the oil from spreading across the surface of the water.

    To further test their devices, create small ripples in the water of the pan with your finger. Invite students to note what happens to the oil on the surface. Take time to discuss the difficulties that arise in the ocean when the surf is high or the seas are rough and there is a need to contain any oil on the surface. How do the students' devices work in containing oil on a choppy sea? What are the implications for real-life rescue and anti-pollution efforts?

Title: Ocean
Author: Miranda Macquitty
Bibliographic Information: New York: Knopf, 1995
Summary: It's all here! Packed with loads of information and dozens of startling facts, this book is a wonderful overview of ocean life. A terrific resource that covers every aspect of sea life and reasons why it needs to be protected. Part of the Eyewitness Book series.

1. Here's an activity that allows students to create their own fresh water, using principles identical to those used by scientists around the world.

Materials:

water
table salt
measuring cup
measuring spoons
large bowl
small cup
plastic food wrap
small stone

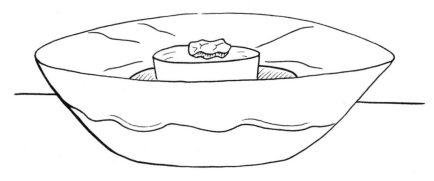

Fig. 6.7.

Directions:

a. In the large bowl, mix 3 teaspoons of salt with 2 cups of water until thoroughly dissolved. Use a spoon to carefully taste a small sample of the salt water.

b. Set the small cup in the middle of the large bowl. (You may have to weigh the cup down to keep it in position.)

c. Cover the bowl with plastic food wrap.

d. Place a small stone in the center of the plastic wrap (directly over the cup) so that there is a small depression in the food wrap. (See fig. 6.7.)

e. Set this entire apparatus in the sun for several hours.

f. After some time, beads of water will form on the underside of the plastic food wrap and drip into the small cup.

g. Remove the plastic wrap and carefully taste the water in the cup.

The salt water inside the large bowl will begin to evaporate into the air inside the bowl. It will condense as beads of water on the underside of the plastic wrap. Because the plastic wrap is shaped the way it is, the beads of water will roll down and drip into the small cup.

This activity illustrates the process in nature known as solar distillation. Distillation involves changing a liquid into a gas (evaporation) and then cooling the gas vapor (condensation) so that it can change back into a liquid. The energy from the sun is able to evaporate water, but not salt, because salt is heavier than water. Thus, the salt remains in the bowl. The distilled water can now be used for drinking purposes and the salt can be used for food seasoning purposes. This entire process (often referred to as desalination) is used in many countries in the Middle East to make fresh water from salt water.

2. Under water, pressure increases by one atmosphere for every 33 feet of depth. That means that at sea level the water pressure is about 14.7 pounds per square inch. At 33 feet below the surface of the ocean, the water pressure is two atmospheres, or twice that at sea level (2 x 14.7 = 29.4 pounds per square inch). At 66 feet below sea level the water pressure is three atmospheres (3 x 14.7 = 44.1 pounds per square inch). This activity demonstrates how water pressure increases the further down into the ocean one goes.

Materials:

medicine dropper

tall, deep, and clear container

water

Directions:

a. Fill the container with water (select a container made of glass or clear plastic so that students can see through the sides).

b. Push the medicine dropper down into the water, open end down, until it reaches the bottom.

c. Hold it there and invite students to note how some water has entered the medicine dropper.

d. Slowly raise the medicine dropper up in the container. As it rises, encourage students to notice how less and less water appears inside the medicine dropper.

Air takes up space, even inside a medicine dropper. However, as the medicine dropper is pushed deeper into the water, the more the increasing water pressure compresses the air trapped inside the medicine dropper. The further down the dropper goes in the water, the greater the pressure becomes and the more the air molecules are squished inside the dropper. As a result, more water is able to enter the dropper.

In the ocean, water pressure increases the further down one goes. At sea level, the water pressure at the surface of the water is 14.7 pounds per square inch. At the bottom of the Mariana Trench, which is 35,827 feet below sea level, the water pressure is 14,622.94 pounds per square inch.

3. Here's another activity to help students appreciate some of the difficulties of exploration at great depths.

Materials:

2 medium-size balloons

2 pieces of flexible tubing (about 6′ each); available at most drug stores or hardware stores)
rubber bands and/or waterproof tape
large container of water

Directions:

    a.   Stretch each balloon several times to loosen it.

    b.   Place a piece of flexible tubing in the neck of each balloon. Use a combination of rubber bands and/or waterproof tape to secure the neck of the balloon to the tubing (no air should escape when you blow up the balloons using the tubing).

    c.   Label the balloons "A" and "B."

    d.   Invite one student to blow up balloon "A" by blowing into the end of the flexible tubing. Invite that student to note how easy it was to fill that balloon with air.

    e.   Place balloon "B" at the bottom of a large, deep container of water (a deep sink, a barrel, a swimming pool). Invite the same student to blow it up by blowing into the end of the flexible tubing. Encourage that student to relate how difficult that is.

    Balloon "A" was easier to blow up than balloon "B." In fact, it may have been impossible to blow up balloon "B," because the water pressure on balloon "B" prevented air from getting into the balloon. The water pressure was greater than the pressure of the air the student was trying to force into the balloon.

    In the ocean, water pressure increases with depth. Students may want to experiment with balloon "B" at various depths to determine the ease or difficulty of filling the balloon with air depending on how deep it is in the water.

CULMINATION:

    Invite students to assemble an informational book on the facts and information learned throughout this unit. Included in the book can be articles clipped from various magazines, students' illustrations, favorite experiments and activities selected from different teacher resources, photographs donated by family members, fish prints, and other items that students feel would be representative of the information they learned.

    Students may elect to donate their "Ocean Book" to the school library or local public library. A special ceremony involving the librarian might be appropriate.

Mini-Units

POLLUTION

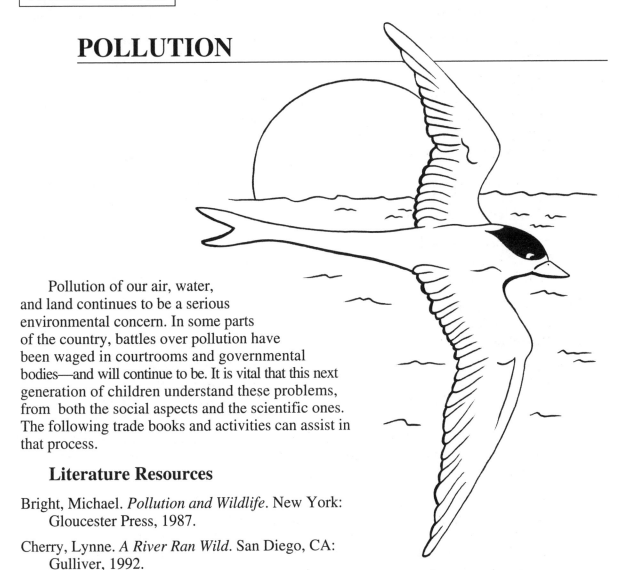

Pollution of our air, water, and land continues to be a serious environmental concern. In some parts of the country, battles over pollution have been waged in courtrooms and governmental bodies—and will continue to be. It is vital that this next generation of children understand these problems, from both the social aspects and the scientific ones. The following trade books and activities can assist in that process.

Literature Resources

Bright, Michael. *Pollution and Wildlife*. New York: Gloucester Press, 1987.

Cherry, Lynne. *A River Ran Wild*. San Diego, CA: Gulliver, 1992.

Earthworks Group. *50 Simple Things Kids Can Do to Save the Earth.* Kansas City, MO: Andrews & McMeel, 1990.

Hadingham, Evan, and Janet Hadingham. *Garbage!: Where It Comes from, Where It Goes.* New York: Simon & Schuster, 1990.

Say, Allan. *The Lost Lake*. Boston: Houghton Mifflin, 1989.

Spurgeon, Richard. *Ecology*. London: Usborne, 1988.

Van Allsburg, Chris. *Just a Dream*. Boston: Houghton Mifflin, 1990.

1. Following is a list of organizations to which you and your students may wish to write for information, brochures, leaflets, and pertinent data on pollution problems. This list can be posted on the bulletin board or sent home to parents in the form of a newsletter.

Adopt-A-Stream Foundation
P.O. Box 5558
Everett, WA 98201

Alliance for Environmental Education
211 Wilson Blvd.
Arlington, VA 22201

American Forestry Association
P.O. Box 2000
Washington, DC 20010

Center for Marine Conservation
1725 Desalles St., NW
Washington, DC 20036

Environmental Defense Fund
257 Park Ave., South
New York, NY 10010

Friends of the Earth
218 D St., SE
Washington, DC 20003

Greenpeace
1436 U St., NW
Washington, DC 20009

National Audubon Society
915 3rd Ave.
New York, NY 10022

National Geographic Society
Educational Services
17th and M Sts., NW
Washington, DC 20036

National Recycling Coalition
1101 30th St., NW
Washington, DC 20007

National Wildlife Federation
1412 16th St., NW
Washington, DC 20036

Renew America
1400 16th St., NW
Washington, DC 20036

Sierra Club
730 Polk St.
San Francisco, CA 94109

World Wildlife Fund
P.O. Box 96220
Washington, D.C. 20077

2. Arrange for a trip to a nearby garbage dump. Have the students generate questions for the speaker at the dump. Have students record the answers and then ask them to write a story on what it would be like to live in a world where everything was garbage.

3. Have students write a letter to the governor's office asking for information on the state's recycling program. Ask for information on which counties and towns also have recycling programs. Compare and contrast counties and towns that have programs with those that do not. Have students put a letter or pamphlet together about starting a recycling program. Send these out to the mayor or officials of that town.

4. Using fresh-cut celery, blue or red food coloring, and a glass of water, show your students what polluting the water can do to plants and other living things. Carefully cut off the bottom of the celery stalk. Put a few drops of food coloring into the glass of water. Ask the class to pretend the food coloring is pollution. Then put the celery into the glass. Let it sit for a few hours. Then have students write down their observations of how the pollution contaminated the plant.

5. Provide student groups with several index cards and a jar of petroleum jelly. Direct students to smear the jelly over the face of five separate cards. Have students place the cards in various locations around the school (cafeteria, office, basement, etc.). Cards should be placed inside and outside the building as well as at different heights (ground

level, head level, etc.). Periodically, over the space of several days, have students check their cards to note the amount of air pollutants covering the petroleum jelly. Have students speculate as to the effects of these pollutants over a span of several weeks, months, or years.

6. **DEMONSTRATION BY ADULT ONLY:** Place a clean white sock over the tail-pipe of a car (be sure the tailpipe is cool). Secure the sock with a rubber band. Turn on the car and allow it to run for one minute. Turn off the car and allow it to cool for several minutes. Remove the sock and invite students to note the amount of pollution on the sock. Ask them to calculate the amount of pollution pumped into the air on your daily drive to school. How much pollution do all the teachers' cars contribute each day? Each week? During the school year?

WATER

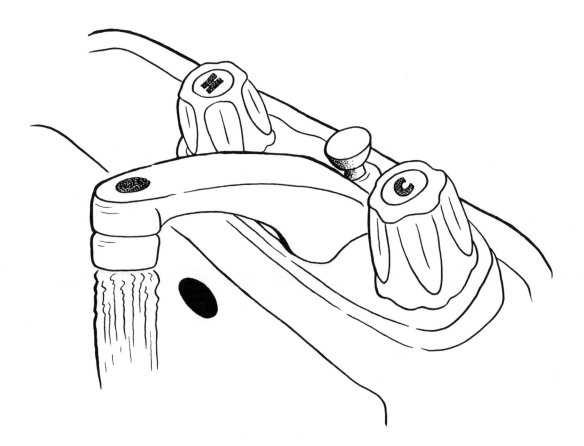

We often take water for granted. Nevertheless, it is one of the most precious commodities on the face of the earth. It is necessary for our health and survival, important in business and industry, and needed for the sustenance of life in all its forms. One of the major concerns we have with water today is its purity. Pollution of our water sources and resources is an increasingly difficult social, economic, and environmental issue. Helping students appreciate the importance of water in their lives can help them understand their role in preserving this valuable resource.

Literature Resources

Ardley, Neil. *The Science Book of Water*. New York: Harcourt Brace, 1991.

Arnold, Caroline. *Bodies of Water: Fun, Facts, and Activities*. New York: Watts, 1985.

Fredericks, Anthony D. *Simple Nature Experiments with Everyday Materials*. New York: Sterling, 1995.

Peters, Lisa. *Water's Way*. (New York: Arcade Publishing, 1991.

Taylor, Barbara. *Sink or Swim!: The Science of Water*. New York: Random House, 1990.

Taylor, Barbara. *Water at Work*. New York: Watts, 1991.

1. Invite students to make a list of all the different ways in which water is used in their homes (cooking, drinking, bathing, etc.). How many different ways do they find? Encourage students to compute the average amount of water used in the home each day. Students whose families use city water may be able to use their monthly water bill to compute a daily average.

2. Students may wish to create their own well. Obtain a large (#10) aluminum can (a coffee can works well). Place a cardboard tube (from a roll of paper towels) upright in the can. Pour a layer of gravel inside the can around the outside of the tube. Pour another equal layer of sand on top of the gravel. Pour in water until it reaches the top of the layer of sand. Invite students to notice what happens inside the tube. Explain to them that this is the same process used for obtaining well water.

3. Have students obtain several different water samples from in and around their homes (e.g., tap water, water from a standing puddle, rain water, etc.). Place several coffee filters over each of several glass jars. Then have students pour each of the water samples into a separate jar. Encourage students to note the impurities that are trapped by each of the filters. Which type of water has the most impurities?

4. Obtain some chunks of sandstone from a neighborhood building supplier or hardware store. Soak the pieces in water for a few hours. Place individual pieces of (soaked) sandstone in sealable sandwich bags and seal them tightly. Place the bags in the freezer overnight. Take them out and invite students to note what has happened inside each bag (the sandstone has split apart because water expands as it freezes). Share with students the fact that this process is identical to what occurs in nature when water seeps into the cracks and fissures in rocks. It freezes and (over time) begins to break them apart.

ROCKS AND SOIL

There are three different kinds of rocks. *Igneous rocks* form from melted minerals and can often be found near volcanoes. Granite is one type of igneous rock. *Sedimentary rocks* are usually formed under water as a result of layers of sediment pressing down on other layers of sediment. Sandstone and limestone are examples of sedimentary rocks. *Metamorphic rocks* result from great heat and pressure inside the earth's surface. Marble is an example of a metamorphic rock.

Soil is actually rocks that have been broken up into very fine pieces. Soil is usually created over many years (hundreds or thousands) and is the result of weathering, erosion, and freezing. Soil also contains air, water, and decayed matter (known as *humus*). There are three basic types of soil: clay, sandy, and loam (a rich mixture of clay, sand, and humus).

Literature Resources

Bass, Lin. *Rocks*. Racine, WI: Western, 1991.

Barkin, Joanne. *Rocks, Rocks Big and Small*. Englewood Cliffs, NJ: Silver Press, 1990.

Bourgeois, Paulette. *The Amazing Dirt Book*. Reading, MA: Addison-Wesley, 1990.

Fredericks, Anthony D. *Simple Nature Experiments with Everyday Materials*. New York: Sterling, 1995.

Hiscock, Bruce. *The Big Rock*. New York: Atheneum, 1988.

Parker, Steve. *Rocks and Minerals*. New York: Dorling Kindersley, 1993.

Selsam, Millicent. *First Look at Rocks*. New York: Walker, 1984.

1.   Provide students with several sealable plastic sandwich bags. Take a field trip through your town or neighborhood and invite students to collect as many different soil samples as possible. Upon your return to the classroom, have students gently pour each sample onto a white sheet of paper. Provide students with some tooth-picks and hand lenses (available at most toy or hobby stores). Invite students to carefully sift through each sample to determine its components. What ingredients

are found in each sample? Are the samples distinctively different, or about the same? How big or small are the particles in each sample? Which sample would be best for growing plants?

2. Invite a local gardener or employee of a local gardening center to visit your classroom to talk about soil conditions in your area. What recommendations would that person make for turning the native soil into the best possible growing medium? What special nutrients or additives should be added to the soil to begin a garden? What is distinctive about the native soil that make it appropriate or inappropriate for growing vegetables, for example?

3. Obtain some organic clay and some modeling clay from a local arts and crafts store. Invite students to note the difference in the composition of the two clays. Encourage students to make a simple piece of pottery from each sample. Place each piece of pottery in the sun. After a few days, ask students to note the difference between the two pottery pieces. What has changed? What has remained the same? You may wish to share with students the fact that pottery pieces more than 5,000 years old have been found at various archeological sites around the world.

4. **DEMONSTRATION BY ADULT ONLY:** Bring a small piece of brick to the classroom, soak it in water, and place it in a bowl. In a separate large container, mix together ½ cup of water, ½ cup of bluing (from the laundry section of the grocery store), and ½ cup of ammonia. Use a measuring cup to pour some of this mixture over the brick. Sprinkle the brick with salt and let it stand for 24 hours. The next day students will be able to see crystals forming on the surface of the brick. Continue to add some more of the water/bluing/ammonia mixture to keep the crystals growing. Explain to students that this is similar to a process in nature known as *crystallization*, a process in which crystals are formed over long periods of time (hundreds of years).

DESERTS

The desert is a magical and marvelous ecosystem. Full of life and full of adventures, it is also one of the world's most misunderstood environments. Many children believe deserts are dry life-less places, when in fact they are some of the most ecologically diverse regions on the surface of the earth. The following activities and literature will help students learn about and appreciate these magnificent places.

Literature Resources

Arnold, Caroline. *A Walk in the Desert*. Englewood Cliffs, NJ: Silver Press, 1990.

Baker, Lucy. *Life in the Deserts*. New York: Watts, 1990.

Catchpole, Clive. *The Living World: Deserts*. New York: Dial Books for Young Readers, 1984.

Hogan, Paula. *Expanding Deserts*. Milwaukee, WI: Gareth Stevens, 1991.

Siebert, Diane. *Mojave*. New York: HarperCollins, 1988.

Silver, Donald. *One Small Square: Cactus Desert*. New York: W. H. Freeman, 1995.

Twist, Clint. *Deserts*. New York: Dillon Press, 1991.

Wallace, Marianne. *America's Deserts*. Golden, CO: Fulcrum, 1996.

Yolen, Jane. *Welcome to the Sea of Sand*. New York: G. P. Putnam's Sons, 1996.

1. Students may enjoy creating their own desert terrarium. The following directions will help them design a fully functioning terrarium:

    a. Fill the bottom of a large glass container with a layer of coarse sand or gravel. Combine one part fine sand with two parts potting soil and spread this over the top of the first layer.

    b. Sprinkle lightly with water.

    c. Place several varieties of cactus into the terrarium (it might be a good idea to wear gloves). Most nurseries carry cacti, or they can be ordered through the mail from selected seed companies and mail order nursery houses.

    d. When planting the cacti, be sure that the roots are covered completely by the sandy mixture.

    e. You and your students may decide to place several desert animals, such as lizards or horned toads in the terrarium. Be sure the animals have a sufficient quantity of food and water available.

    f. The desert terrarium can be left in the sun and does not need a glass cover. It should, however, be lightly sprinkled with water about once a week.

2. Students may enjoy creating their own "Desert Dictionary." Invite them to form small groups, with each group responsible for gathering words and definitions for several letters of the alphabet. For example:

    A—Atacama Desert
        Australian Thorny Devil
        Ananuca Lily
    B—Beetles
        Blue Gilia
    C—Camel
        California Poppy
    D—Desertification
    E—Endangered environment
    F—Frilled Lizard
        Fennec Fox

    Students may wish to contribute their class dictionary to the school library.

3. Invite students to write to one or more of the following national parks and request information about the flora and fauna that inhabit those special regions. When the brochures, flyers, leaflets, and other descriptive information items arrive, invite students to assemble them into an attractive display in the classroom or a school display case.

    Death Valley National Park
        P.O. Box 579
        Death Valley, CA 92328

    Joshua Tree National Park
        74485 National Park Dr.
        Twentynine Palms, CA 92277

Great Basin National Park
Baker, NV 89311

Big Bend National Park
Big Bend, TX 79834

4. Students may wish to visit a local gardening center or nursery. Invite them to purchase a small cactus plant (these are typically very inexpensive). Have them carefully observe their respective cacti: What shape is it? Does the shape change as it grows? What do the needles look like? Students may wish to observe cactus features with a magnifying lens and record their observations in a "Desert Journal."

WETLANDS

    Wetlands are magnificent and diverse environments. They are home to an astonishing variety of plant and animal life, some of it found nowhere else on the planet. Scientists have estimated that more than 5,000 different kinds of plants and trees can be found in wetlands and that nearly one-third of all the animal species in the world inhabit wetlands areas.

Wetlands are defined as a mingling of water and land. The water may be standing (as in a pond or marsh) or it may be slowly moving (as in the Everglades). The water may be only a few inches deep or up to several feet in depth. Most of the wetlands in the United States are located in the Southeast, the Gulf Coast, the Northeastern coastal states, and certain areas in the upper Midwest. It is estimated that there are currently 95 million acres of wetlands in this country.

Literature Resources

Asch, Frank. *Sawgrass Poems*. San Diego, CA: Harcourt Brace, 1996.

Cone, Molly. *Squishy, Misty, Damp and Muddy: The In-Between World of Wetlands*. San Francisco: Sierra Club Books for Children, 1996.

Hickman, Pamela. *Wetlands*. Toronto: Kids Can Press, 1993.

Hirschi, Ron. *Where Are My Swans, Whooping Cranes, and Singing Loons?* New York: Bantam Books, 1992.

Liptak, Karen. *Saving Our Wetlands and Their Wildlife*. New York: Watts, 1991.

Silver, Donald. *One Small Square: Pond*. New York: W. H. Freeman, 1994.

Staub, Frank. *America's Wetlands*. Minneapolis, MN: Carolrhoda, 1995.

1. Students can learn a lot about the growth and development of frogs when they raise a group of tadpoles in the classroom. Depending on the species, they will be able to observe the changes a tadpole undergoes (metamorphosis) over a period of several weeks.

Materials:

frog's eggs (Students can visit a pond in the spring and look for clumps of jelly-covered eggs. Help them to scoop up 1 to 2 dozen eggs; put the eggs in a large plastic sandwich bag along with some pond water.)

long-handled net (available at any pet store)

large glass jar (an oversized mayonnaise jar works well)

magnifying lens

pond plants

Directions:

a. Take students to a pond to obtain frog eggs, pond water, and pond plants.

b. Upon returning to the classroom, have them fill the clean jar about three-fourths full of pond water.

c. Put the eggs in the jar and place the jar in a location away from direct sunlight (the jar should be kept at room temperature).

d. Using the hand lens, invite students to observe the eggs twice a day for a week. Encourage them to record what the eggs look like and how they are developing. They may use a journal or an inexpensive scrapbook.

e. The eggs will hatch in about a week. When an egg hatches, place a pond plant into the water (the tadpoles attach themselves to the leaves of the plant).

f. Students will be able to keep the tadpoles (and watch their development) for several weeks.

If students are not able to obtain frog eggs in your local area, you can order the Grow A Frog kit (Catalog No. 54-110-0296) from Delta Education, P.O. Box 3000, Nashua, NH 03061-3000 (1-800-282-9560). At this writing the kit costs about $15.00 and includes a frog house, food, instructions, and a coupon for tadpoles.

2. Provide students with a set of index cards. On each card, the name of a wetlands plant or animal is recorded, as in the following sample list:

    algae
    mosquito
    fish larva
    insects
    leopard frog
    osprey
    bacteria
    nutrients

The cards represent the line of succession in a food chain (from algae to nutrients). Provide opportunities for students to arrange the cards in a line indicating each organism and the other organisms that are dependent on it for their survival (students may wish to attach lengths of yarn to the card to denote the relationships). Later, invite students to add more cards to the deck and create additional relationships in the food chain or food web. Additional library resources may be necessary.

3. The following experiment will help students learn about various forms of pollution and its effects on an environment such as a wetlands ecosystem. This activity requires adult supervision and guidance.

    Provide students with four empty and clean baby food jars. Label the jars "A," "B," "C," and "D." Prepare each jar as follows. Fill each jar halfway with aged tap water (regular tap water that has been left to stand in an open container for 72 hours). Put a $\frac{1}{2}''$ layer of pond soil into each jar, add one teaspoon of plant fertilizer, then fill each jar the rest of the way with pond water and algae. Allow the jars to sit in a sunny location or on a window sill for two weeks.

    Next, work with students to treat each separate jar as follows:

    Jar "A":   Add 2 tablespoons of liquid detergent.
    Jar "B":   Add enough used motor oil to cover the surface.
    Jar "C":   Add $\frac{1}{2}$ cup of vinegar.
    Jar "D":   Do not add anything.
    Allow the jars to sit for four more weeks.

    Students will notice that the addition of the motor oil, vinegar, and detergent prevents the healthy growth of organisms that took place during the first two weeks of the activity. In fact, those jars now show little or no growth taking place, whereas the organisms in jar "D" continue to grow. Detergent, motor oil, and vinegar are pollutants that prevent wetlands organisms from obtaining the nutrients they need to continue growing.

- The detergent illustrates what happens when large quantities of soap are released into a wetlands area.

- The motor oil demonstrates what happens to organisms after an oil spill.

- The vinegar shows what can happen to organisms when high levels of acids are added to a wetlands area.

PHYSICAL SCIENCE

Thematic Units

SIMPLE MACHINES

GENERALIZATIONS/PRINCIPLES:

1. There are six basic simple machines.

2. Simple machines are the foundation upon which more complex machines are built.

3. Many technological advancements were inspired by nature.

4. Technology is always changing, always evolving.

CONCEPTS:

cause and effect

change

interaction

MATERIALS:

Primary Literature Selections

Gates, Phil. *Nature Got There First: Inventions Inspired by Nature*. New York: Kingfisher, 1995.

Lampton, Christopher. *Bathtubs, Slides, Roller Coasters: Simple Machines That Are Really Inclined Planes*. Brookfield, CT: Millbrook Press, 1991.

Lampton, Christopher. *Marbles, Roller Skates, Doorknobs: Simple Machines That Are Really Wheels*. Brookfield, CT: Millbrook Press, 1991.

Parker, Steve. *53½ Things That Changed the World and Some That Didn't*. Brookfield, CT: Millbrook Press, 1995.

Secondary Literature Selections

Barton, Byron. *Machines at Work*. New York: Crowell, 1987.
> A wonderful introduction to the various types of machines used in and around a construction site.

Bender, Lionel. *Invention*. New York: Knopf, 1991.
> This book deals with inventions: what they do, how they work, and who invented them. The inventions range in origin from early Egyptian to present day.

Laithwaite, Eric. *Force: The Power Behind Movement*. New York: Watts, 1986.
> An interesting and enlightening look into principles of gravity, inertia, and friction. Also covered are simple machines and the various forces that help us survive.

Lampton, Christopher. *Seesaws, Nutcrackers, and Brooms: Simple Machines That Are Really Levers*. Brookfield, CT: Millbrook Press, 1991.
> Levers are all around us—crowbars, wheelbarrows, and shovels. This book describes the many ways levers are used in everyday life.

Macauley, David. *The Way Things Work*. Boston: Houghton Mifflin, 1988.
> A unique and insightful inspection of the way everyday objects work. Scientific principles are highlighted and discussed in language youngsters can understand.

Parker, Steve. *Everyday Things and How They Work*. New York: Random House, 1991.
> This book is a wonderful resource and reference guide for any youngster seeking to discover how common items work and operate.

Taylor, Barbara. *Machines and Movement*. New York: Warwick Press, 1990.
> This book is a compendium of lots of well-illustrated experiments and projects for creating simple devices based on simple machines.

Weiss, Harvey. *Machines and How They Work*. New York: Crowell, 1983.
> This book describes how the six simple machines are used in everyday life. Readers are provided with instructions for creating their own simple machines.

Zubrowski, Bernie. *Raceways: Having Fun with Balls and Tracks*. New York: Morrow, 1985.
> No youngster will want to pass up this book. The author demonstrates how homemade raceways illustrate the principles of velocity and acceleration.

Zubrowski, Bernie. *Wheels at Work: Building and Experimenting with Models of Machines.* New York: Morrow, 1986.

This book is a marvelous addition to youngsters' study of machines and their construction. Provides many opportunities for readers to create their own machines.

INITIATING ACTIVITY:

Create a duplicable chart similar to the one in figure 7.1. Provide students (individually or in small groups) with copies of the chart and invite them to keep track throughout the unit on the various types and examples of simple machines they locate in their homes, neighborhood, community, on vacation, or at school (a few examples have been provided). You may wish to challenge students to locate at least ten examples for each of the six categories. Another option would be to organize a scavenger hunt, during which students search out examples of simple machines in and around the school within a designated time period (30 minutes, for example). Be sure to plan time at the end of the unit so that students can review their respective lists and share thoughts and ideas about the value and utility of simple machines in everyday life.

SIMPLE MACHINE	EXAMPLES
Lever	shovel
Pulley	clothesline
Wheel & Axle	doorknob
Inclined Plane	stairs
Wedge	knife
Screw	drill

Fig. 7.1. Simple machines tracking chart.

GENERAL ACTIVITIES:

1. Provide students with definitions and examples of what simple machines are and what they do. The following definitions can be written on a large chart and posted in the classroom:

   a. Lever—A lever is used to lift, move, or press different objects. It is a bar that pivots on a fixed point called a *fulcrum.*

   b. Pulley—A pulley is a wheel with a rope or line moving around it. It is used to raise objects.

   c. Wheel and Axle—This simple machine is a combination of two wheels, a large one connected to a small one. The small one is really the axle. It is used to move objects or increase power.

   d. Inclined Plane—This simple machine is a slanting surface or ramp that enables something to move from one level to another.

   e. Wedge—A wedge is two inclined planes placed back to back. It is used to spread an object apart or to raise an object.

     f.   Screw—A screw is basically an inclined plane that is wrapped around a post. It is used to fasten objects together or to increase power.

2.   Ask students to make up six file folders for permanent display on a bulletin board or in a file box. Label each of the folders with the name of a simple machine. Invite students to collect photographs and illustrations of examples of simple machines from several old magazines (or keep an eye out for current magazines and newspapers), each example can be filed in one of the folders. Provide regular opportunities for students to discuss their collections and offer reasons for assigning selected photos to a particular folder.

3.   Have students create individual charts similar to the one used in the Initiating Activity for this unit. Invite them to take a field trip through their homes and identify the simple machines in use in each room. Which room has the most simple machines in use—kitchen, living room, bedroom, etc.? Which room has the least number of simple machines?

4.   Make a technology time line. Provide students with a long sheet of newsprint taped to one wall of the classroom. Encourage them to record the dates of major technological advances (and provide accompanying illustrations), particularly those involving the development of machines that incorporate one or more simple machines in their design. Invite students to consult the references in this unit as well as any books in the school or public library. Following are a few examples to get them started:

     Discovery of the wheel—3,500 B.C.

     Sails and sailboats—5,000 B.C.–3,200 B.C.

     Sundial—500 B.C.

     Mechanical clock—A.D. 725

     Horse-based vehicles—A.D. 800–900

     Printing press—1454

     Spinning wheel—1530

     Steam engine—1700s

     Cotton gin—1793

     Bicycle—1816

     Internal combustion engine—1880

5.   Invite a carpenter to visit the classroom and bring several of his or her tools to share. Ask this individual to describe how certain types of work are made easier through the use of selected tools. Students should be encouraged to prepare a list of potential questions (concerning simple machines) prior to the visit.

PRIMARY LITERATURE SELECTIONS:

Title: Nature Got There First:
Inventions Inspired by Nature

Author: Phil Gates

Bibliographic Information: New York: Kingfisher, 1995

Summary: A magnificent book that should be in the library of every school and every classroom. This book is a wondrous look at simple, everyday inventions and objects, each of which was inspired by an action, event, or feature found in the natural world. For example: tropical trees inspired cathedral structure, armadillos inspired armored cars, rattlesnakes inspired burglar alarms, and dolphins inspired sonar. This is a must-have book for any science program.

1. Invite students (in pairs or small groups) to select one of the "natural" inventions mentioned in the book. Ask each group to prepare an advertising campaign for that device. What features should be emphasized? What are the benefits to human beings? What inventions might result from a study of that device? The advertising campaign can be in the form of a written ad or a video production.

2. Gliders were invented as a result of humans' observations of birds. Invite students to create their own homemade gliders with the following activity: Cut two 2"-wide strips (lengthwise) from an index card. Form each of the two strips into loops (one loop should be considerably smaller than the other). Secure each loop with a paper clip. Slip the paper clip fastened to one loop over the end of a drinking straw. Slip the other loop in the same way over the other end of the straw. (See fig. 7.1.) Using the small loop as the front of the glider, each student can throw their invention in the air and watch it glide (this may take a little practice to perfect). If appropriate, you may wish to explain Bernoulli's Principle (why objects such as birds, airplanes, and gliders tend to stay aloft) to students.

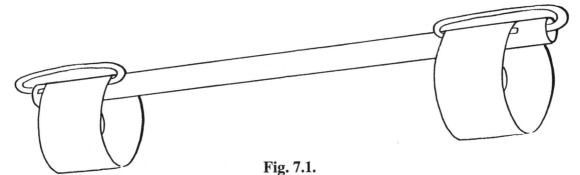

Fig. 7.1.

3. Helicopters were invented after humans watched certain types of seeds whirl through the air. Students may wish to create their own miniature helicopters with the following activity: Cut a ½" x 5" strip from an index card. Fold the strip (lengthwise) into three equal sections. Position the flaps so that the strip looks like an "S." Fasten a paper clip directly in the middle of the middle section. (See fig. 7.2.) Slip the paper clip into one

end of a drinking straw. Holding the straw upright (the paper "S" will be on top) between your hands, twirl it back and forth and then release it quickly. It will twirl upward toward the ceiling in a fashion similar to that of a helicopter.

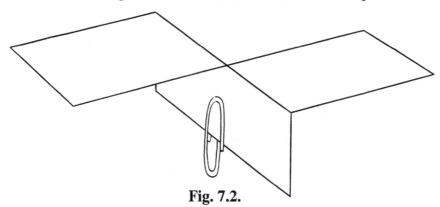

Fig. 7.2.

4. After reading the book, invite students to make a list of ten inventions discussed in the book. Encourage students to describe how people might be able to live or survive if those inventions had not been inspired by nature or had not been invented at all.

5. Invite each individual to select one natural device and write a technical description of that object for someone who has never seen it before. Encourage students to describe what their object looks like, how it functions, its specifications, and its operation. Students may wish to assemble a technical manual for a rattlesnake rattle, cactus needles, a squid, or a beaver's teeth, for example. Invite them to discuss any difficulties they have in describing a natural item in comparison to a mechanical invention.

Title: Bathtubs, Slides, Roller Coasters: Simple Machines That Are Really Inclined Planes

Author: Christopher Lampton

Bibliographic Information: Brookfield, CT: Millbrook Press, 1991

Summary: Inclined planes are all around us, from the stairs we climb in our houses to the roller coasters we ride at amusement parks. This book introduces readers to the wide variety of inclined planes that dominate our everyday lives. A real eye-opening book.

1. Build an inclined plane in your classroom. Lean one end of a board on a stack of books while the other end rests on the floor. Then invite one or more students to lift a heavy object (a box with some bricks in it, for example). Invite them to discuss the difficulties they have with this assignment. Then place that heavy object at the bottom of the inclined plane and invite students to push it up the ramp. Afterwards, encourage them to discuss how much easier it was to push the item up the ramp than to lift it straight up.

2. Invite students to create an advertisement for a set of stairs. Encourage them to look at sample magazine advertisements and create an original that emphasizes all the benefits of owning a set of stairs. How will those stairs make life easier? How will those stairs increase the productivity or comfort of the owner? How will those stairs pay for themselves in work or time saved? Have students arrange their advertisements in an attractive bulletin board display.

3. If possible, arrange for students to visit a construction site. Encourage them to list all the various ways that inclined planes are used in and around the construction site. How are the inclined planes making the work easier for the construction workers? What would they be unable to do if they did not have a simple machine such as an inclined plane?

4. Invite students to prepare a Venn diagram that lists the uses of inclined planes 100 years ago versus the uses of inclined planes today. What are the similarities? What are the differences? Encourage students to discuss how inclined planes have made certain jobs and work projects easier.

Title: Marbles, Roller Skates, Doorknobs: Simple Machines That Are Really Wheels

Author: Christopher Lampton

Bibliographic Information: Brookfield, CT: Millbrook Press, 1991

Summary: From the cars we drive, the can openers we use, and the toys we play with, wheels (and axles) are a normal and natural part of our everyday lives. This wonderful book alerts young readers to the array of inventions and devices that employ the wheel and axle and how these inventions have made our lives easier and more productive.

1. Invite each student to maintain a personal diary of all the different types of wheels and axles that he or she uses in the course of one day. Examples may range from getting to school on a school bus to the pencil sharpener in the classroom to the roller blades used on the driveway. Encourage students to speculate how their lives might be different (on a daily basis) if they did not have, or couldn't use, those wheels and axles.

2. Ask students to research the various uses of wheels from a historical perspective. What were some early uses of wheels by prehistoric peoples? How might early explorers have used wheels? How did wheels figure into certain wars or other significant historical events? Encourage students to share their findings with the class.

3. Challenge students to create a "Rolling Alphabet" book. Encourage students to think of at least one item or invention that uses one or more wheels for each letter of the alphabet. For example: A = Airplane; B = Bicycle; C = Can opener; etc.

4. Wheels come in all shapes and sizes. Invite students (individually or in small groups) to create a classroom "Wheel Museum." Students may wish to bring in objects or

items from home, search through garage or yard sales, or borrow selected items from their friends for possible inclusion in the museum. Encourage students to decide how the items will be grouped, for example, (a) from a historical perspective, (b) based on size, or (c) efficiency.

Title: 53½ Things That Changed the World and Some That Didn't

Author: Steve Parker

Bibliographic Information: Brookfield, CT: Millbrook Press, 1995

Summary: From common inventions such as the toilet, the clock, the screw, and the telephone to less familiar inventions such as the blast furnace, the combine harvester, and the atomic bomb, this book provides readers with some incredible insights into the devices that have made our lives easier. Each invention is described in colorful detail, with the emphasis on history, how the device works, and its effects on modern life.

1. Provide youngsters with a simple, everyday object and ask them to create 10 new uses for it. For example, a wire coat hanger can become a giant safety pin, a back scratcher, a bath towel holder, a giant cookie cutter, a very large toothpick, a baton, a plant hanger, a free-form sculpture, a wand, or a paper picker-upper.

2. Invite students to select one of the inventions detailed in the book and prepare a brief oral report on the significance of the item to or the effects that item has had on society. For example, how has the telephone changed the way people communicate with each other? How has it made our lives easier? In what ways has it allowed us to do things we previously were unable to do?

3. Invite students to select any five of the inventions mentioned in the book and explain how they would be able to live or survive today if that invention had not been created many years ago. For example, how would their lives be different if the plow had never been invented? If nobody had ever designed the screw, how would our lives today be changed? Youngsters may wish to present an oral report or a brief one-page description of their ideas.

4. Youngsters may wish to create their own car with the following activity:

Push one end of a rubber band through the hole in a spool of thread (this can be accomplished by pushing it through the hole using a large paper clip that has been straightened out). When one end of the rubber band pokes out of the other end of the spool, slip it onto a medium-sized paper clip. Tape this clip to the far end of the spool.

Slip the rubber band at the near end of the spool through a jumbo paper clip. Turn this clip with your finger to wind it. Be careful that the rubber band doesn't bunch up inside the spool. (See fig. 7.3.)

After the rubber band is twisted into the hole, keep winding for about 15 to 25 additional turns. Place the car on a table top or other flat surface and release it. It will dash across the surface. (A rubber band wrapped around the middle of the spool will provide more traction for the car.)

After students have created and practiced with this basic car, invite them to make design changes that will make the car go faster, in a straighter line, or more smoothly. What items can they add to the car that will improve its performance? How is their invention similar to any of the inventions mentioned in the book? What are some of the practical uses of their invention? Can their invention be used as part of a larger invention? If so, what would that invention be?

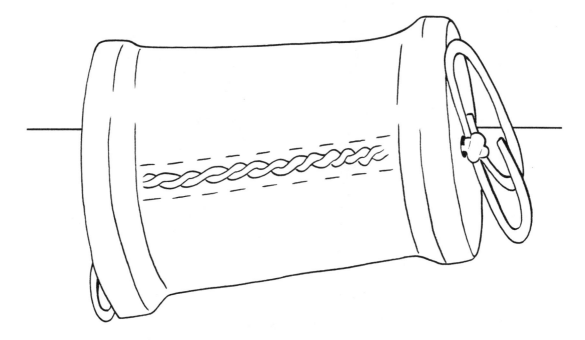

Fig. 7.3.

CULMINATION:

Using information collected during the Initiating Activity, as well as data learned during the various activities throughout this unit, invite students to prepare a production (video, slide-tape program, or informational brochure, for example) on "The Uses of Simple Machines in Our Everyday Lives." Students may wish to share this final project with another class or donate it to the school library. Encourage them to emphasize how our lives have been made easier through the use of these simple machines and the numerous complex machines that employ a combination of simple machines.

Mini-Units

INVENTIONS AND INVENTORS

People have been inventing things for thousands of years. Many of those inventions have been both useful and helpful creations (lightbulbs, zippers, telephones); others have been questionable at best (brain scanners, electric toilet seats). However, the creative process is continually alive through the inventions of people, both famous and infamous. Students, too, will enjoy creating their own inventions as well as studying the inventive process.

Literature Resources

Ardley, Neil. *How Things Work*. New York: Wanderer Books, 1984.

Berder, Lionel. *Eyewitness Books—Invention*. New York: Knopf, 1991.

Caney, Steven. *The Invention Book*. New York: Workman, 1985.

Giblin, James. *From Hand to Mouth: How We Invented Knives, Forks, Spoons, and Chopsticks and the Table Manners to Go with Them.* New York: Crowell, 1987.

Macauley, David. *The Way Things Work.* Boston: Houghton Mifflin, 1988.

Wulffson, Donald. *The Invention of Ordinary Things.* New York: Lothrop, Lee & Shepard, 1981.

1. Set up a table with: roll of tape, lightbulb, pencil, tennis ball, comb, small radio, roll of film, batteries, etc. (10 to 12 items). Ask students:

   a. Why is this collection here? What do all these objects have in common?

   b. What are some things that are not inventions?

   c. Who can be an inventor?

   d. Why do people invent?

   Invite students to speculate on the different types of inventions that could be created using just the materials on the table. What inventions could be created with these materials in combination with other materials?

2. Encourage students to keep a diary of everything they do in the morning, making notes on what they use (for example, light switch, etc.). Then invite them to write a diary as if they lived 100 years ago. A good resource for this activity is *The Last Hundred Years: Household Technology* by Daniel Cohen (New York: M. Evans, 1982). Encourage students to compare and contrast their reports.

3. If possible, arrange a trip to the music room to investigate the inventions. Invite the music teacher to give a brief history of a few selected instruments.

4. Challenge students to send messages to each other using nonconventional materials (such as sticks scratching mud, etc.). Next, divide the students into two groups and set up a relay race. One group can use a rubber stamp (for example) to print a message, while another group writes the same message by hand. Invite students to observe the difference in time and accuracy that was magnified by the invention of movable type and the printing press.

5. Invite students to research simple inventions, such as the wheel, a gear, a pulley, and how they work. A good resource is *EUREKA! An Illustrated History of Inventions from the Wheel to the Computer* by Edward DeBono (New York: Holt, Rinehart & Winston, 1974).

6. Provide small groups of students with one or more simple objects and invite them to create several new uses for it. For example, a coat hanger can become a giant safety pin, a back scratcher, a bath towel holder, a giant cookie cutter, etc.

7. Invite students to choose an invention and write a critical report on its use and the effect it has had on our society.

LIGHT AND COLOR

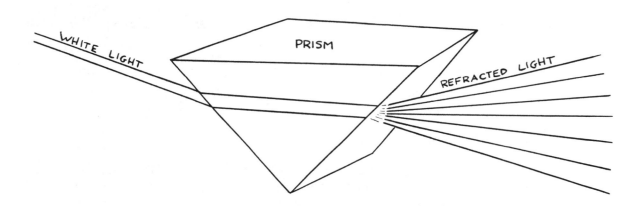

By definition, light is a visible form of energy. White light, the most common form of light, is actually a combination of all the colors of the rainbow (red, orange, yellow, green, blue, indigo, and violet). Both white light and the colors of light in it are referred to as the *visible spectrum*.

People see colors because of what happens when light hits different objects and because white light is made of all the colors. Objects absorb, or take in, some of the light that hits them. Objects also reflect, or bounce back, some light. An opaque object (one through which light cannot pass) reflects whatever light it does not absorb. The color of the object is actually the color of the light it reflects. For example, a green shirt absorbs all the colors of the spectrum except green; green is the color it reflects, and hence it is the color we see.

Literature Resources

Branley, Franklyn. *Color: From Rainbows to Lasers.* New York: Crowell, 1978.

Darling, David. *Making Light Work: The Science of Optics.* New York: Dillon Press, 1991.

Jennings, Terry. *Light and Dark.* New York: Gloucester Press, 1991.

Laurence, Clifford. *The Laser Book.* New York: Prentice-Hall, 1986.

Taylor, Barbara. *Color and Light.* New York: Watts, 1990.

1. Visit a local toy store or hobby store and obtain a glass prism. Let students use the prism to create rainbows throughout the classroom. By holding the prism in a beam of white light the colors of the rainbow are separated and can be shown on a piece of paper or on a nearby wall. (You can also obtain a very inexpensive prism [Catalog No. 57-160-4679] from Delta Education, P.O. Box M, Nashua, NH 03061 [1-800-258-1302]).

2. Invite students to make a chart with the words "TRANSPARENT," "TRANSLUCENT," and "OPAQUE" listed across the top (transparent objects are those in which light passes through readily—glass, clear plastic; translucent objects are those in which some light passes through, but you cannot see clearly—waxed paper, shower doors; opaque objects permit no light to pass through—wood, steel). Encourage each student to take a field trip through his or her home and make a list of objects that could be placed in each of those categories. Which category has the fewest number of items? Which has the most?

3. Mirrors have smooth, shiny surfaces that form good images (light is reflected off a mirror at the same angle or direction at which it hit the surface). Discuss with students the various ways in which mirrors are used in everyday life. How many different ways do we use mirrors (bathrooms, cars, dentist, cameras, etc.) in our lives? Challenge students to develop a list of as many different uses for mirrors as possible. What are the benefits of this accurate reflection of light?

4. Pour some whole milk into a saucer. Around the perimeter of the milk, quickly add two drops of each of the following four food colors: red, green, blue, and yellow. Swiftly place one or two drops of liquid detergent into the middle of the milk. Invite students to observe what happens. The colors will start swirling around until they eventually form a grayish mixture. This occurs because the fat molecules in the whole milk hold the water droplets (in the food color). When the detergent is added, it begins to break apart those fat molecules. As the fat molecules separate from each other they also "pull" the water molecules away from one another. As the water molecules separate, they swirl and mix in the milk.

WORK AND ENERGY

In scientific terms, *work* is done only when a force (a push or a pull) makes something move. When we rake leaves, work is done. When we climb a mountain, work is done. However, if we push against a solid brick wall, no work is done, because nothing moves. *Energy* is defined as the ability to do work. Humans get their energy from the food they eat, cars get their energy from gasoline, a hair dryer gets its energy from electricity. We often speak of two types of energy: *kinetic energy*, which is the energy of motion (a ball moving through the air); and *potential energy*, which is stored energy (a rubber ball that is squeezed has potential energy that is released when it rebounds). All objects can have both potential and kinetic energy.

Literature Resources

Ardley, Neil. *The Science Book of Energy*. San Diego, CA: Harcourt Brace, 1992.

Ardley, Neil. *The Science Book of Motion*. San Diego, CA: Harcourt Brace, 1992.

Bailey, Donna. *What Can We Do About Conserving Energy?* New York: Watts, 1992.

Challoner, Jack. *Energy*. New York: Dorling Kindersley, 1993.

Gardner, Robert. *Energy Projects for Young Scientists*. New York: Watts, 1987.

Gutnik, Martin. *The Energy Question: Thinking About Tomorrow*. Hillside, NJ: Enslow, 1993.

Taylor, Barbara. *Energy and Power*. New York: Watts, 1990.

Zubrowski, Bernard. *Messing Around with Water Pumps and Siphons*. Boston: Little, 1981.

Zubrowski, Bernard. *Raceways: Having Fun with Balls and Tracks*. New York: Morrow, 1985.

1. Obtain several different objects of different weights (a book, a small brick, a cooking utensil—each should be between one and three pounds in weight). Tie a string around each object and fasten a rubber band to the object. Invite selected students each to lift one object by the rubber band. When the band is stretched to its fullest, measure its length with a ruler. Use the same (or an identical rubber band) for each of the other objects (measuring the length of each when a different object is lifted). Help students conclude that the longer the rubber band becomes, the greater the amount of energy needed to lift an object. Explain that heavier objects, therefore, require more energy to lift them.

2. Students can demonstrate friction by rubbing their hands together rapidly. The heat that results occurs because of the friction between the two hands. Have students move pairs of other objects together, such as a wood block moved across a brick several times, a coffee cup rubbed across a carpet, or a shoe rubbed across concrete. Invite students to touch one of the two objects and note the amount of heat generated. That heat is the result of friction between the objects.

3. Challenge students to make a list of examples of when energy is used but work is not done. For example, pushing against the side of the house, trying to open a jar lid without success. Talk with students about some of the different kinds of work that are done around the house each day by family members. Ask students to determine if the amount of work done is equal to the amount of energy used (most often, there will usually be more energy used than work accomplished).

4. Neil Ardley (see Literature Resource listing) has written a number of excellent books on work and energy. Invite students to select one or more of those books from the school or public library and create one or more of the machines and/or mechanical devices in Ardley's books. Provide opportunities for students to note the efficiency of their respective machines and the relationship (or ratio) between energy (produced) and work (accomplished).

MAGNETS AND MAGNETISM

A magnet is defined as anything that pulls iron-bearing material to it. Magnetism is the force around a magnet. Basically, magnets are of two types, natural and artificial. Natural magnets, or lodestones, are a type of iron ore known as magnetite. They occur in nature and have north and south poles, as do the magnets we use in our homes and schools. Artificial magnets are usually made of steel or alnico (an alloy of aluminum, nickel, copper, and cobalt). These types of magnets are commonly in the shape of a bar or horseshoe. Most of the magnets we use on our refrigerator doors and in our toys are alnico magnets.

Literature Resources

Adler, David. *Amazing Magnets*. Mahwah, NJ: Troll, 1983.

Challand, Helen. *Experiments with Magnets*. Chicago: Childrens Press, 1986.

Jennings, Terry. *Magnets*. New York: Gloucester Press, 1990.

Kent, Amanda. *Physics*. New York: EDC, 1984.

Taylor, Barbara. *Electricity and Magnets*. New York: Watts, 1990.

Whyman, Kathryn. *Electricity and Magnetism*. New York: Gloucester Press, 1985.

1. Obtain a sheet of thin cardboard and some iron filings (available at toy, hobby, or hardware stores). Draw a simple outline of a person's face on the cardboard (head, eyes, nose, mouth, ears). Place four water glasses on a table and place the cardboard so the corners rest on the edges of the glasses. Sprinkle some iron filings in the middle of the illustration. Provide students with a strong bar magnet (available at most larger toy stores) and invite them to move it underneath the cardboard so that the iron filings can be moved around the face. Encourage students to put a beard, mustache, eyebrows, and other "hair" on various locations on the face.

2. Students may wish to create their own magnetic compass. Rub a bar magnet lengthwise on a sewing needle (in one direction only). Carefully stick the needle partway through the top of a small piece of sponge (about one inch square). Mix a few drops of liquid detergent into a small bowl of water. Place the sponge and needle assembly in the bowl, on edge. The needle should be parallel to the water, but not touching it. The sponge and needle should float in the center of the bowl. (See fig. 7.4.) If they don't, add one or more drops of detergent until they do. After the needle stops moving, it is pointing to the earth's magnetic north pole.

3. If possible, visit a yard or garage sale and obtain one or two small motors. Invite students to disassemble the motors and locate the magnets inside each. Explain to students that most motors use similar magnets in the generation of electricity.

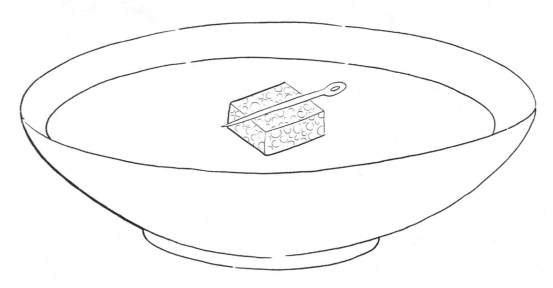

Fig. 7.4.

SPACE SCIENCE

Thematic Units

SPACE EXPLORATION

GENERALIZATIONS/PRINCIPLES:

1. The solar system consists of nine (known) planets and one sun.

2. The universe consists of several different types of celestial bodies.

3. Humans explore space in a variety of ways.

4. We are constantly learning more and more about the universe in which we live.

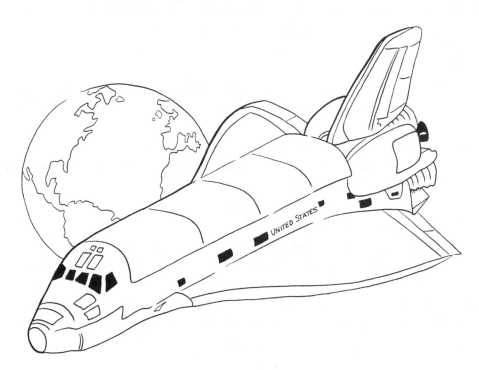

185

CONCEPTS:

cause and effect

patterns and motions

movement

MATERIALS:

Primary Literature Selections

Beasant, Pam. *1000 Facts About Space*. New York: Kingfisher, 1992.

Cole, Joanna. *The Magic School Bus Lost in the Solar System*. New York: Scholastic, 1990.

Ride, Sally, with Susan Okie. *To Space and Back*. New York: Lothrop, Lee, & Shepard, 1986.

Simon, Seymour. *Our Solar System*. New York: Morrow Junior Books, 1992.

Secondary Literature Selections

Barrett, Norman S. *The Picture World of Rockets and Satellites*. New York: Watts, 1990.
    Lots of great photographs highlight this colorful introduction to rockets and satellites.

Barrett, Norman S. *The Picture World of Space Shuttles*. New York: Watts, 1990.
    The amazing space shuttle and its history are profiled in this colorful and engaging book.

Barrett, Norman S. *The Picture World of Space Voyages*. New York: Watts, 1990.
    This book is a terrific introduction to the U.S. space program and what has been discovered as a result of space voyages.

Barton, Byron. *I Want to Be an Astronaut*. New York: HarperCollins, 1989.
    A very brief introduction to the life of an astronaut. A good first book.

Berliner, Don. *Living in Space*. Minneapolis, MN: Lerner, 1993.
    How do astronauts go to the bathroom, brush their teeth, or live with others in close quarters? This book explains all.

Fraser, Mary Ann. *One Giant Leap*. New York: Holt, 1993.
    The voyage and landing of the Apollo 11 moon mission are told through wonderful illustrations and engaging text.

Gallant, Roy. *The Macmillan Book of Astronomy*. New York: Macmillan, 1986.
    A complete guide to all the planets, stars, asteroids, comets, and meteors of our solar system, filled with many photographs and illustrations.

Gibbons, Gail. *Planets*. New York: Holiday House, 1993.
    A brief but thorough introduction to the planets, particularly suited to young readers.

Gustafson, John. *Planets, Moons and Meteors*. New York: Messner, 1992.
    A wonderfully detailed text filled with photographs and engaging activities highlights this valuable resource.

Vogt, Gregory. *Apollo and the Moon Landing*. Brookfield, CT: Millbrook Press, 1991.
    Manned explorations to the surface of the moon are detailed in an easy-to-read text.

Vogt, Gregory. *Space Stations*. New York: Watts, 1990.
    From their earliest beginnings to futuristic designs, space stations are detailed in this delightful book.

Wood, Tim. *Out in Space*. New York: Aladdin Books, 1990.
    A good introduction to the solar system; the reader takes an imaginary trip through space.

INITIATING ACTIVITY:

Involve students in a Solar System Scavenger Hunt. Create index cards, each of which includes an intriguing fact about each planet or the sun without identifying the heavenly body (see the following samples). There should be enough index cards so that each student gets one, and there should be an equal number of cards for each planet and the sun. Provide students with sufficient opportunities to consult books listed throughout this unit, as well as any in the classroom or school library, to identify which body is being described. Based upon the heavenly body described on his or her index card, each student should then get into the appropriate planet/sun group and share the information on the index card. Here are some facts you may wish to include on the cards:

The Sun

    1.3 million times the size of the Earth.
    Uses 4,000,000 tons of hydrogen every second.
    Temperature is as high as 27,000,000°F.
    The inner atmosphere is the chromosphere, the outer atmosphere is the corona.

Mercury

    One day on this planet is almost as long as a year.
    Almost airless planet.
    At night the temperature falls to -300°F.
    Covered with craters from meteoroid collisions.

Venus

    Called the Evening Star or Morning Star.
    Rotates from east to west.
    Sometimes called Earth's sister planet.
    The hottest planet of the solar system.

Mars

    Named for the Roman god of war.
    Doesn't have canals, as once believed.
    May have had elementary forms of life.
    Soil contains iron oxide.

Jupiter

    Has giant windstorm called the Great Red Spot.
    Four of its moons are big enough to be seen from Earth through binoculars.
    One of its moons has exploding volcanoes.
    Has sixteen moons.

Saturn

Its rings are made of thousands of smaller rings within rings.
Has the most moons of any planet.
One of its moons is the only moon in the solar system to have an atmosphere.
Takes 30 years to orbit the sun.

Uranus

The planet is lying on its side in space.
Right now the south pole is in the midst of 42 years of constant sunlight.
Discovered by William Herschel in 1781.
Shines with a greenish-blue color.

Neptune

Has the strongest winds ever measured on a planet.
Its moon is colder than any known object in the solar system.
Is the planet furthest from the sun until 1999.
Was discovered because of its gravitational pull on Uranus.

Pluto

Has an odd, tilted orbit.
Smallest, coldest planet in the solar system.
Takes 247.7 years to revolve around the sun.
Was discovered in 1930.

GENERAL ACTIVITIES:

1. Through this experiment, students will learn how a rocket works. Thread one end of a 20-foot-long string through a straw. Fasten that end low on a table leg. Fasten the other end high on a wall. Label the area high on the wall the space station. Blow up a balloon and fold over the open end and fasten it with a paper clip. Fasten the balloon to the straw with tape. (See fig. 8.1.) Hold the balloon near the floor end of the string, quickly remove the paper clip, and let go.

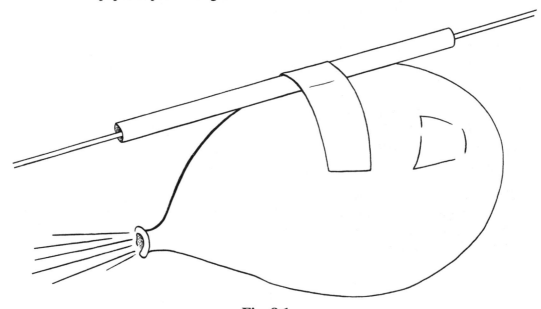

Fig. 8.1.

2. To demonstrate the orbits of satellites, cut a garbage bag so that a single thickness can be stretched over the top of a round garbage can. Tie a string around the can, to hold the bag in place. Put a baseball in the middle to represent a planet. Using a marble as a satellite, launch the marble into orbit from a cardboard tube. The marble will roll around the outside edges of the plastic (and eventually toward the baseball [planet]). (See fig. 8.2.) *Note:* You may have to practice several times to achieve the desired effect.

3. Invite each student to make a travel brochure about a planet, moon, or star to interest people in visiting that celestial body. Youngsters may wish to use reference books in the library or the ones referred to throughout this unit to compile their information.

4. Depending where you are located, invite a college professor specializing in space exploration to visit the class. Encourage students to brainstorm some questions they would like to ask.

5. Invite each students to select and research one of the world's space pioneers, to learn about his or her background, contributions, successes, failures, motivations, and any other relevant and pertinent data. Following the research, invite students to take on the role of their selected pioneer and share his or her views on the importance of the space program and its future. Some space pioneers include (but are not limited to) the following:

Fig. 8.2.

Edward (Buzz) Aldrin, Jr.

William A. Anders

Neil Armstrong

Guton S. Bluford, Jr.

Frank Borman

Scott M. Carpenter

Michael Collins

Gordon Cooper

Robert L. Crippen

Yuri Gagarin

John H. Glenn, Jr.

Robert H. Goddard

Virgil Grissom

Johannes Kepler

James A. Lovell, Jr.

Sharon (Christa) MacAuliffe

Sir Isaac Newton

Sally K. Ride

Alan B. Shepard

Wally Schirra

Valentina Tereshkova

Edward J. White

Wernher von Braun

James W. Young

6. Ask students to create a space time line. As students read about the advances in space exploration, invite them to add selected events (e.g., manned space missions, unmanned space exploration missions, space shuttles, etc.) to the time line. For each event, encourage students to include the name of the mission, the dates, the astronauts/cosmonauts (if appropriate), the main purpose(s) of the mission, and its most significant contributions. Invite students to illustrate each of the events they highlight.

7. Involve students in experiments that will help them better understand the solar system and space travel. Here are three excellent books to get you started:

Gustafson, John. *Planets, Moons and Meteors*. New York: Messner, 1992.

Schatz, Don. *The Astronomy Activity Book*. New York: Simon & Schuster, 1991.

VanCleave, Janice. *Astronomy for Every Kid*. New York: Wiley, 1991.

8. Play music or songs that deal with the theme of space. These may include "Aquarius" from the play *Hair*, or the themes from *Star Trek*, *Star Wars*, or *2001, A Space Odyssey*. Take time to discuss with students how the music captures the mood of space. Invite students to create their own modern dance, interpretive rendition, or artistic endeavor related to the music.

PRIMARY LITERATURE SELECTIONS:

Title: Our Solar System

Author: Seymour Simon

Bibliographic Information: New York: Morrow Junior Books, 1992

Summary: A wonderful book containing up-to-date information about the sun and the planets, moons, asteroids, meteoroids, and comets that travel around our sun. The compelling text is complemented by vivid and detailed photographs from both manned and unmanned space missions.

1. Invite students to identify each of the heavenly bodies on the cover of the book. In groups, encourage them to select one object and create a small replica of it (from papier mâché). Involve the entire class in a brainstorming session to discover what they know about each planet and the sun. Attach a list of responses to the appropriate replica.

2. Tie a bagel to a piece of string about 10 feet long. Slide the other end of the string through a spool of thread. (See fig. 8.3.) The bagel represents a planet and the spool represents the sun. Invite a student to hold the spool with one hand and the end of the string with the other hand. Ask the student to twirl the bagel in a circular motion around his or her head (this is an outdoor activity). Invite the student to notice the "gravitational pull" of the bagel (planet) as it "orbits" the spool (sun). The students will be able to feel that pull on the string. Also, planets that are close to the sun (pull the bagel closer to the spool as it is spinning) have greater gravitational pull than planets that are further from the sun (allow the bagel to spin further away from the spool).

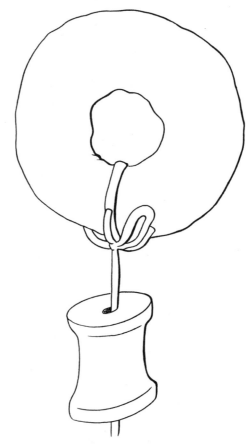

Fig. 8.3.

3.   The front of the book contains a chart with all types of information regarding the planets and the sun. Duplicate the chart and invite each student to create five questions that involve a comparison of the planets/sun.

4.   Invite students to create statistical puzzles regarding the planets and the sun. For example: "The sun is _____ times bigger than all the planets put together." (Answer: 600 times). The chart in the book will assist students in creating and solving the puzzles.

5.   Invite small groups of students to create an advertising campaign for each of the nine planets. For example: What type of information should be shared with the public? Should real estate be offered on a selected planet? How would environmental concerns be advertised? What are the most significant features of each planet that should be promoted to the general public? Can a planet be advertised as a travel destination?

6.   Based on the photographs of the planets, involve students in selecting one of the planets/sun and creating a map of its surface. Encourage students to label unique features on the planet.

Title: To Space and Back

Author: Sally Ride with Susan Okie

Bibliographic Information: New York: Lothrop, Lee & Shepard, 1986

Summary: This book, directed to a young audience, answers many questions space enthusiasts may ask. The author, Sally Ride, describes her own personal adventures in space. Also described is the life of an astronaut, and mention is made of the remarkable men and women who have chosen to explore space.

1.   Invite student pairs to construct a telephone with two styrofoam cups and thin string. Punch a small hole in the bottom of each cup and put the string through the hole of each cup tying a large knot. Encourage students to take turns talking into the cups. Invite students to discuss how the sound travels along the line and compare it to an astronaut's headset. *Note:* The string must be taut.

2.   Bring a few sleeping bags, belts, earmuffs, and pairs of sunglasses to class. Divide these items among students working in small groups. Invite students (one at a time) in each group to zip themselves inside the sleeping bag with their arms outside. Another student within the group can make notes of the experimenter's feelings and comments. Next, the students in the sleeping bags can put on the earmuffs and sunglasses. Finally, a member of each group can strap the belt around the sleeping bag with the experimenter's arms inside. Discuss as a class the reasons why astronauts sleep this way in space. You may want to review the concept of gravity, too.

3.   Encourage students to draw pictures of themselves as space shuttle crew members. Invite them each to write a letter to his or her family back on Earth. They may wish to tell the family what it feels like on the shuttle as well as what they do.

4.   Invite students to create their own space shuttles. Split open large plastic jugs so that one side is still attached. Cut cardboard semicircles and glue them inside to make decks. Cut holes for hatches and make toothpick ladders to go through the hatches. Label the decks "flight deck," "living deck," and "storage deck."

5.   Encourage students to practice exercises that are like astronauts running a treadmill. Invite students to place their hands on a wall and push while they run in place. Encourage students to design and create a series of exercises for astronauts in space. What considerations need to be kept in mind (e.g., space limitations, zero gravity, etc.)?

6.   To show students what dried food is like and the difference in weight, do an experiment with two apples. Take one apple and put it in a cool place. Peel the other and cut it into six round slices. Push a threaded needle through each apple slice and hang the slices to dry. Encourage students to make predictions of what will happen to the apples. Check the apples daily. When the apples are dried, compare their combined weight with that of a whole fresh apple.

Title: The Magic School Bus Lost in the Solar System

Author: Joanna Cole

Bibliographic Information: New York: Scholastic, 1990

Summary: A fantasy adventure in which Miss Frizzle and her class take a wild and crazy ride through the solar system in their magical bus. Lots of facts, terrific illustrations, and a delightful text make this book an essential reference tool for any solar system explorations.

1.   After reading this book, invite students to compile a *Book of Facts About the Solar System*. Encourage students to illustrate their pages and bind them together in book form. As an alternative, students may elect to create an *ABC* book based on the solar system.

2.   Throughout the book, the students on the bus write short papers describing some aspect of space. Invite each student to select one of the papers and elaborate on it by researching the subject more fully. They may wish to use references from this unit or those in the school or classroom library.

3.   Encourage students to create a travel brochure and map of the solar system to assist those who are visiting—or lost!

4.   Invite students to compare the relative sizes of the earth and the sun. This can be done by getting a very long piece of string. Form the string into a circle (on the playground or field) that is 27 feet in diameter. This circle represents the sun. Take a regular bagel and place it on the ground next to the circle. A normal bagel is approximately 3 inches in diameter. The bagel represents the planet Earth. Because the sun is 108 times larger than the planet Earth, this circle/bagel model is an accurate representation of these two celestial bodies and their relative sizes.

5.   Encourage students to keep a pictorial diary of the phases of the moon. Every three or four days, for a month, invite selected students to take pictures of the moon and keep track of the date and time the picture(s) was taken. Encourage students to create a booklet on the moon and accompany each photo with a descriptive simile or metaphor (for example: the full moon lights up the sky like a giant firefly).

Title: 1000 Facts About Space

Author: Pam Beasant

Bibliographic Information: New York: Kingfisher, 1992

Summary: Fun and informative, this book is crammed with facts and exciting data about the stars, landing on the moon, the history of astronomy, comets and meteorites, and the future of space discovery. Page after page of colorful illustrations make this an ideal book for browsing again and again.

1.   After students have had an opportunity to read this book, invite selected groups to compile a list of the "Top Ten" space facts. They can base their selection of facts on those that are (a) most interesting, (b) most unusual, (c) most amazing, (d) most incredible, or other criteria as they may decide. These lists may be organized into a larger book to be donated to the school library.

2.   An excellent magazine of outer space and astronomy for elementary students is *Odyssey* (AstroMedia Corporation, 625 E. St. Paul Ave., P.O. Box 92788, Milwaukee, WI 53202). For older students and adults just beginning to explore the heavens, there's *Astronomy* (AstroMedia Corporation, 625 E. St. Paul Ave., P.O. Box 92788, Milwaukee, WI 53202). The premier magazine for amateur astronomers is *Sky & Telescope* (Sky Publishing Corp., 49 Bay State Road, Cambridge, MA 02238). If possible, obtain some back issues of one or more of these magazines and share them with your students.

3.   A most interesting sky map known as the Sky Challenger can be obtained from Discovery Center (Lawrence Hall of Science, University of California, Berkeley, CA 94720 [write for a catalog]). This instrument, with several interchangeable wheels, provides many different views of the night sky. After students have had an opportunity

to use this instrument, a similar one, or a star map, they may want to create their own star maps. This can be done by cutting away the end of a shoe box. Provide students with black construction paper and ask each one to copy the location of a cluster of stars or constellation onto the paper (locations can be marked with white chalk). Prick the paper at each spot with a needle (enough to let light through). Cover the end of the shoe box with the construction paper (each piece can be temporarily held on with masking tape) and ask each student to stand in front of a light source and look through a small hole cut in the opposite end of the shoe box. Each of the constellations can then be placed at the end of the box for student viewing. Have students compare what they see in their star box with the actual constellations in the night sky.

4. Students may enjoy creating some sun pictures. Invite each student to design an illustration or cut letters from a piece of paper. Place one or more small pieces of tape on the back of each picture or letter and affix them to individual sheets of construction paper (large 12″ x 18″ sheets are recommended). Place each sheet outside or in a sunny window. Invite students to note the amount of fading that occurs over a period of several days. After one or two weeks, invite students to remove the illustrations or letters from the construction paper and notice the contrast between the faded portion of the paper and the portion that was covered. The resultant sun pictures can be displayed in the classroom.

5. Perhaps the best and most informative set of children's books on the planets have been written by Seymour Simon. Books such as *Mars*, *Jupiter*, *Saturn*, *Uranus*, and *Neptune* are not only accurate and up-to-date, but are also filled with mind-boggling photographs and illustrations that will stimulate any reader's curiosity. All of the books are published by William Morrow and Co. (105 Madison Ave., New York, NY 10016) and should be available in any public school or community library. Plan to get some and share them with your students.

6   You may wish to obtain some astronomical posters and charts on the solar system and other celestial objects for your classroom. Most are inexpensive and provide wonderful views of various parts of the universe. The following companies offer posters. Write to them and request their catalogs: Celestial Arts (231 Adrian Rd., Millbrae, CA 94030); Nature Company (P.O. Box 7137, Berkeley, CA 94707); Sky Publishing Company (49 Bay State Rd., Cambridge, MA 02238); Edmund Scientific (101 East Gloucester Pike, Barrington, NJ 08007); and Astronomical Society of the Pacific (1290 24th Ave., San Francisco, CA 94122).

7. You can help students understand some of the comparative distances between the planets with the following activity. Take the students to the high school football field. Invite one student (the "sun") to stand on the end zone line at one end of the field. Ask each of nine other students to take on the role of one of the nine planets and to place themselves at the following distances away from the "sun":

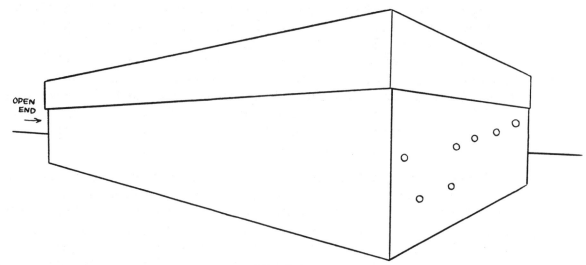

Fig. 8.4.

Planet	Distance from "Sun"
Mercury	2½ ft.
Venus	4½ ft.
Earth	6½ ft.
Mars	10 ft.
Jupiter	11⅓ yds.
Saturn	20½ yds.
Uranus	41½ yds.
Neptune	65 yds.
Pluto	86 yds.

Emphasize to students that the sun is the center of our solar system. Therefore, the planets are not strung out in a straight line as in this re-creation. In fact, if the school is near a very large, open field, you can set up this demonstration with the "planets" arranged in many different directions.

CULMINATION:

Students can be invited to select one or more of the following activities and projects:

1. Invite students to hold a mini-debate in which they discuss the following issue: Should funding for space exploration and colonization be continued when money is so badly needed to solve social problems such as hunger, crime, and diseases on Earth?

2. Invite students to collect different stories, fables, and legends about the solar system or universe that have originated from different cultures and societies. A terrific resource is *Tales of the Shimmering Sky* by Susan Milord (Charlotte, VT: Williamson, 1996). This particular book has 10 global folktales and legends about the sun, the moon, and the stars, along with a variety of hands-on learning activities. Students may wish to assemble their collection into a class book for donation to the school library.

3. Invite students to work in small groups to create a scrapbook of articles and clippings about space exploration. These articles can be obtained from the local newspaper, news magazines, or science periodicals (e.g., *Discover* magazine). Invite students to discuss how the scrapbook could become an important feature of their space exploration studies.

4. Invite students to discuss which of the planets would be most interesting to explore. Which planet would be least interesting to explore? Encourage students to provide reasons and rationale for their opinions.

5. If possible, invite students from a local college or university to share their knowledge about space exploration with your class. Students taking an astronomy or space science course may wish to share thoughts and information with your students. Encourage your students to prepare a list of possible questions prior to the arrival of the guest speakers.

Mini-Units

EARTH, SUN, AND MOON

The three celestial bodies with which students are most familiar are a planet, a star, and a satellite. Typically, youngsters' first explorations into space include a study and examination of these three objects. It is not surprising, either, that much of what scientists know about our solar system is based on data gathered from the sun, moon, and our own earth.

Literature Resources

Asimov, Isaac. *How Did We Find Out About the Solar System?* New York: Walker, 1983.

Asimov, Isaac. *Why Does the Moon Change Shape?* Milwaukee, WI: Gareth Stevens, 1991.

Bendick, Jeanne. *The Sun, Our Very Own Star.* Brookfield, CT: Millbrook Press, 1991.

Branley, Franklyn. *The Sun, Our Nearest Star*. New York: Crowell, 1988.

Branley, Franklyn. *What the Moon Is Like*. New York: Crowell, 1986.

George, Michael. *The Sun*. Mankato, MN: Creative Education, 1991.

Lauber, Patricia. *How We Learned the Earth Is Round*. New York: HarperCollins, 1990.

Simon, Seymour. *The Moon*. New York: Four Winds, 1984.

Simon, Seymour. *The Sun*. New York: Morrow, 1986.

Stacy, Tom. *Sun, Stars and Planets*. New York: Random House, 1990.

1. Divide students into three small groups. Provide each group with a raisin, an orange, and a beach ball. Invite each group to designate the order of these three items so that they represent the relative sizes of the earth, sun, and moon. Invite groups to share their deliberations with the class.

2. It takes approximately eight minutes for sunlight to reach the earth. Challenge students to sit quietly for eight minutes with their eyes closed, pretending that they are rays of sunlight traveling to earth. After the eight minutes are up, invite the whole class to generate a list of things they saw on their journey.

3. Invite each student to select a letter of the alphabet. Encourage students to work together, brainstorming and/or researching lists of earth, sun, or moon terms that begin with the selected letters. Compiled lists can be combined into a class dictionary.

4. Because there is no atmosphere on the moon, sound cannot travel. Invite students to think of 10 different ways they could communicate with others (fellow astronauts, for example) without the use of sound (e.g., hand signals, flags, etc.). Invite students to demonstrate their ideas to each other.

5. Choose one student each day to find out the moon's temperature for that day. This can be done by using the American Express Travel Service phone number: 1-900-WEATHER; a touch-tone phone is necessary. After dialing, press the letters MOO: this is the access code for the moon. The caller will receive a temperature reading for the moon. *Note*: There is a per-minute charge for this call.

6. In one corner of the classroom, set up a reading corner containing a variety of earth, sun, and moon books (see the Literature Resources section of this mini-unit). If possible, invite selected parents to record the books on cassette tape and create an ongoing library of recorded books. More titles can be added throughout the year.

7. Students may wish to create their own sundials. Provide each child with a sheet of paper and a sharpened pencil. The students can place the sheets of paper on the ground and push the pencils straight through the paper into the ground. At the top of each hour, invite students to mark on the papers where the pencil's shadow falls. Students may wish to check their sundials over the course of several days.

STARS AND CONSTELLATIONS

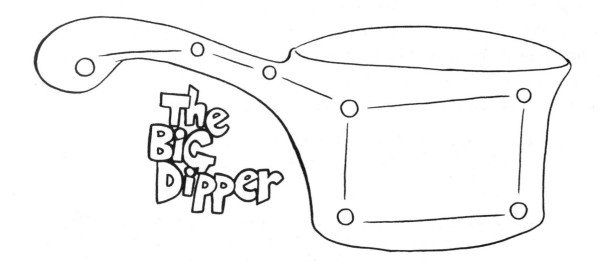

From the beginning of time, humans have studied the night sky. To early watchers of the sky, the stars held a magical fascination and the patterns they formed were a constant and awe-inspiring sight. Even today, with our technological advances in astronomy, we are still amazed at the wonder and beauty of the night sky. Youngsters, too, find the study of stars and constellations to be a delightful part of their scientific investigations.

Literature Resources

Branley, Franklyn. *Star Guide*. New York: Crowell, 1987.

Branley, Franklyn. *Superstar*. New York: HarperCollins, 1990.

Gallant, Roy. *The Private Lives of the Stars*. New York: Macmillan, 1986.

Gibbons, Gail. *Stargazers*. New York: Holiday House, 1992.

Gustafson, John. *Stars, Clusters, and Galaxies*. New York: Messner, 1992.

Hort, Lenny. *How Many Stars in the Sky?* New York: Tambourine, 1991.

Lampton, Christopher. *Stars and Planets*. New York: Doubleday, 1988.

Reigot, Betty. *A Book About Planets and Stars*. New York: Scholastic, 1988.

Rosen, Sidney. *How Far Is a Star?* Minneapolis, MN: Carolrhoda, 1992.

Simon, Seymour. *Stars*. New York: Morrow, 1986.

1. There are several legends and folktales about the stars. Invite students to read one or more of the following: *A Song of Stars* by Tom Birdseye (New York: Holiday House, 1990); *The Star Maiden: An Ojibway Tale* by Barbara Esbensen (Boston: Little, Brown, 1988); *The Lost Children* by Paul Goble (New York: Bradbury, 1993); or *Legend of the Milky Way* by Jeanne Lee (New York: Holt, 1982). Invite students to discuss any similarities between these legends, how they may have started, and why they may be important to selected cultures or groups of people.

2. After reading a book about constellations, invite each student to make a journal entry about the evolution and life history of a selected constellation. They may pick whichever constellation they wish to be.

3. Invite students to make a bulletin board of constellations. Arrange the stars to form a constellation shape and glue or pin strands of yarn between the stars to help accentuate the shapes.

4. Encourage students to write and illustrate a story about their lives as stars. They may wish to include what they may see happening on Earth or around them in the sky.

5. Invite each student to tape a piece of acetate to a window in his or her home. On one selected night, encourage each student to stand approximately three feet behind the sheet of acetate and locate several different stars (they may wish to identify that exact position by placing a piece of masking tape on the floor). Ask each student to mark the location of those stars on the acetate using a permanent marker. Invite students, on a once-a-week basis, to stand at that same location and, with a different color marker, mark the location of each of the same stars on the acetate. After several weeks, invite students to bring in their acetate sheets and discuss them in class. Students may note that the stars seem to have moved (their marked positions on the acetate sheets will be different from week to week). Actually, the stars haven't moved—the earth has!

6. Invite students to create a book of "Star Facts" in which they include interesting facts about the stars and constellations (for example, "What is the brightest star in our universe?" "What is the nearest star?" "How are stars created?" " What is a star composed of?"). Students may wish to illustrate each fact included.

PLANET EARTH

Four and a half billion. It's a number almost too large to comprehend. Yet that's how many years the earth has been in existence. During that time it has undergone some remarkable changes. Rocks have formed, primeval seas have ebbed and flowed across vast continents, and dramatic weather conditions have contributed to the geography and structure of our planet. Still, it's amazing to realize that this planet is but one particle in a universe of stars, satellites, and other celestial bodies. The beauty of our world and its place in the universe are areas ripe for exploration.

Literature Resources

Brown, Julie. *Exploring the World.* Milwaukee, WI: Gareth Stevens, 1990.

Brown, Robert. *The Changing Face of Earth.* Milwaukee, WI: Gareth Stevens, 1990.

Ford, Adam. *Spaceship Earth.* New York: Lothrop, 1981.

Gallant, Roy. *Our Restless Earth.* New York: Watts, 1986.

Goodman, Billy. *Natural Wonders and Disasters.* Boston: Little, Brown, 1991.

Hirst, Robin, and Sally Hirst. *My Place in Space.* New York: Watts, 1990.

Stacy, Tom. *Earth, Sea and Sky.* New York: Random House, 1990.

1. Students may enjoy receiving some aerial photographs of the planet Earth taken from satellites, space shuttles, and other space craft. Invite them to write to the Earth Resources Observation Systems Data Center (U.S. Geological Survey, Sioux Falls, SD 57198) and request information on the availability of specific photos.

2. If students are interested in maps and mapping, write to the American Association for the Advancement of Science (1776 Massachusetts Ave., NW, Washington, DC 20036) and encourage them to ask for the "Maps and Mapping" pamphlet, which is part of the Association's Opportunities in Space series.

3. Obtain a medium-size styrofoam ball from a local hobby or art store. Poke a pencil through the ball. Have a selected student trace a large circle on paper with the pencil. Explain to him or her that the ball is moving like the earth revolving around the sun. Then have the student spin the ball on the pencil. This represents the earth rotating. Invite the student to retrace the original circle while spinning the ball. This demonstrates the revolution (the earth spinning around on its axis once every 24 hours) and rotation (the earth moving around the sun once every year) of the earth.

4. Invite students to assemble a collection of "Amazing Facts About the Earth." This book can be made part of the classroom library or donated to the school library. Here are a few facts to get students started:

    • The average orbital speed of the earth around the sun is 66,641 mph.

    • The earth receives only one-half of one-billionth of the sun's radiant energy.

    • Because of the rotational velocity of the earth, a person standing on the equator is moving at a speed of 1040 mph.

THE SOLAR SYSTEM

Students enjoy learning about the solar system—the planets and their moons, the sun, and the other bodies that move around in space. The solar system includes our sun, the nine planets (Mercury, Venus, Earth, Mars, Jupiter, Saturn, Uranus, Neptune, and Pluto) and their moons, comets (large chunks of ice and dust that orbit the sun), asteroids (rocks that orbit the sun), meteors (small pieces of rocks that enter the earth's atmosphere), and meteorites (any part of a meteor that reaches the surface of the earth). Obviously, there are many objects in our solar system and many objects still waiting to be discovered.

Literature Resources

Asimov, Isaac. *How Did We Find Out About Neptune?* New York: Walker, 1990.

Beasant, Pam. *1000 Facts About Space*. New York: Kingfisher, 1992.

Harris, Alan, and Paul Weissman. *The Great Voyager Adventure: A Guided Tour Through the Solar System*. New York: Messner, 1990.

Lampton, Christopher. *Stars and Planets*. New York: Doubleday, 1988.

Landau, Elaine. *Mars*. New York: Watts, 1991.

Levy, David, consulting ed. *Stars and Planets*. New York: Time-Life Books, 1996.

Simon, Seymour. *Mars*. New York: Morrow, 1987.

Simon, Seymour. *Uranus*. New York: Morrow, 1987.

Stott, Carole. *Space*. New York: Watts, 1995.

Wood, Tim. *Out in Space*. New York: Aladdin Books, 1990.

1. Invite youngsters to assemble a "Book of Facts" about the solar system, based on information obtained from their readings. Students may decide to organize the book by assigning one planet or celestial body to each chapter. Here are some possible facts for inclusion in the book:

   • The surface temperature on Mercury can reach 425°C.

   • There are two other planets besides Saturn that have rings.

   • The original name for the planet Uranus was "Herschel."

   • Thousands of meteorites bombard Earth every year.

   • It takes Pluto nearly 250 earth years to orbit the sun.

   • The tail of a comet can extend for about 90 million miles (the distance between the sun and Earth).

2. Students may enjoy conducting some library research to determine the origin of the names of the planets. For whom were the planets named? Who is responsible for naming the planets? Are there any similarities in the names of the planets? If a new planet were to be discovered, how would it be named?

3. Students may be interested in obtaining some information or printed materials on the travels and discoveries of spacecraft, such as the Voyager and Viking spacecraft. Invite students to write to the NASA Jet Propulsion Laboratory (California Institute of Technology, Pasadena, CA, 91109). Provide opportunities for students to discuss the materials with the entire class.

4. The first trip from the earth to the moon took approximately four days. Invite students to calculate the time it would take for a rocket ship to travel from the earth to each of the nine planets. Use an average rocket speed of 40,000 miles per hour for the calculations. After students have computed the approximate times, encourage them to discuss some of the preparations and provisions that would have to be considered before some of the longer manned voyages. What difficulties might be encountered?

WOMEN IN SPACE

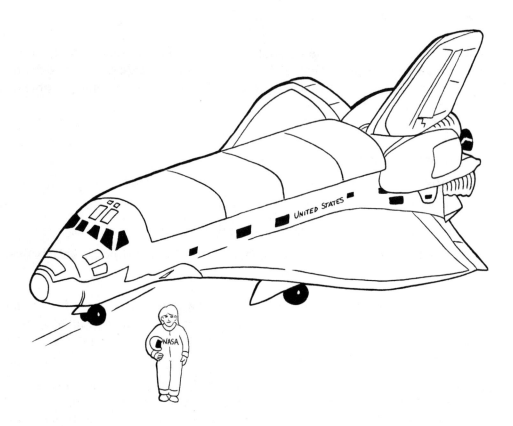

Space travel has come a long way from the crude-looking spherical object large enough to hold only one human passenger to today's space shuttles that carry entire teams of astronauts into space for weeks at a time. Our thinking about the qualifications of astronauts has also changed; no longer are men the only passengers on space missions! Women have assumed a greater role in the space program, providing girls with positive role models and a wealth of opportunities to reach for the stars as they set their occupational goals.

Literature Resources

Armbruster, Ann, and Elizabeth Taylor. *Astronaut Training*. New York: Watts, 1990.

Baird, Anne. *Space Camp: The Great Adventure of NASA Hopefuls*. New York: Morrow, 1992.

Billings, Charlene. *Christa McAuliffe*. Hillside, NJ: Enslow, 1986.

Bobdar, Barbara. *On the Shuttle: Eight Days in Space*. Buffalo, NY: Firefly Books, 1993.

Ride, Sally, with Susan Okie. *To Space and Back*. New York: Lothrop, Lee & Shepard, 1986.

1. Students will note that there are not a lot of books written about women astronauts. Invite students to discuss reasons for this. Is it because there haven't been a lot of women in space (compared with men)? Is it because young readers are not interested in the subject? Is it because girls are not particularly interested in reading about space travel? After students have reached some conclusions, they may wish to draft a letter to one or more publishers to express their feelings.

2. As a follow-up to activity #1, invite students to write to one or more of the authors of the books listed in this mini-unit (letters can be sent in care of each author's publisher). Encourage students to inquire about the research that was necessary for the authors to prepare their respective manuscripts and whether any follow-up books on women astronauts are planned for the future.

3. Invite students to create a special SPACE AGE award for the woman astronaut they feel made the greatest contribution to the space program. Who would they choose? What qualifications did this individual have that made her stand out from the others? Were her qualifications comparable to, or different from, the qualifications of her male counterparts? *Note:* This activity will surely generate some healthy classroom discussions.

4. After students have read some of the books listed in this mini-unit, invite them to select one woman astronaut and write a newspaper article as though they were this person, to reflect her feelings about exploring space, concerns, highlights, frustrations, etc. Encourage students to assemble several articles into a classroom newspaper.

APPENDIX

Resources for Thematic Instruction

 Top Ten Teacher Resources

The following books provide a wonderful collection of experiments, children's literature, discoveries, and explorations into all dimensions of the elementary science curriculum. Available in most libraries, bookstores, curriculum centers, and teacher supply stores, they offer a host of exciting ways to energize your science program and make it dynamic. All of these books are recent publications and represent the best teacher resource materials in elementary science instruction.

1. *Integrating Science and Language Arts: A Sourcebook for K-6 Teachers* by Donna Shaw and Claudia Dybdahl. (Boston: Allyn & Bacon, 1996) [ISBN: 0-205-16072-7].

   In response to teachers' needs for ideas on how to integrate the subject areas of science and language arts, the authors of this sourcebook provide motivating ideas for units that merge the disciplines of science and language. In this hands-on, activity-based book, the authors give you ideas and a framework for units that you can select and modify to fit your individual classroom.

2. *The Complete Guide to Thematic Units: Creating the Integrated Curriculum* by Anita Meinbach, Liz Rothlein, and Anthony D. Fredericks. (Norwood, MA: Christopher-Gordon Publishers, 1995) [ISBN: 0-926842-42-0].

   This book is a practical guide to developing thematic units that challenge students and promote an integration of the entire elementary curriculum. Eight ready-to-use thematic units in science, social studies, math, and language arts are included, along with practical charts, graphs, and other aids for teacher-created units.

3. *Resources for Teaching Elementary School Science* by National Academy of Sciences/ Smithsonian Institution. (Washington, DC: National Academy Press, 1996) [ISBN: 0-309-05293-9].

   This book is an annotated guide to hands-on, inquiry-centered curriculum materials and sources of help for teaching science from kindergarten through sixth grade. The guide annotates about 350 curriculum packages, describing the activities involved and what students learn.

4. *More Thematic Units for Creating the Integrated Curriculum* by Liz Rothlein, Anthony D. Fredericks, and Anita Meinbach. (Norwood, MA: Christopher-Gordon Publishers, 1996) [ISBN: 0-926842-53-6].

   A companion volume to *The Complete Guide to Thematic Units: Creating the Integrated Curriculum*, this book offers eight new thematic units in science, social studies, math, and language arts. Units include "Dinosaurs," "Multicultural Understanding," "Special Children," "Counting and Computation," and "Saving Our Environment," among others.

5. *Science Through Children's Literature: An Integrated Approach* by Carol M. Butzow and John Butzow. (Englewood, CO: Teacher Ideas Press, 1989) [ISBN: 0-87287-667-5].

   An exciting and valuable resource for the teacher seeking to integrate more children's literature (principally fiction) into the science program. A detailed look at a whole language approach to science education. This book should be on every teacher's desk.

6. *From Butterflies to Thunderbolts: Discovering Science with Books Kids Love* by Anthony D. Fredericks. (Golden, CO: Fulcrum Publishing, 1997) [ISBN: 1-55591-946-4].

   This book will be a perfect companion for every elementary teacher seeking innovative, creative, and dynamic ways to integrate science and language arts. A wonderful potpourri of engaging activities and projects highlight this resource, which focuses on the best fiction and nonfiction literature for children. A "must-have" book!

7. *Intermediate Science Through Children's Literature: Over Land and Sea* by Carol M. Butzow and John Butzow. (Englewood, CO: Teacher Ideas Press, 1994) [ISBN: 0-87287-946-1].

   A companion book to the best-selling *Science Through Children's Literature*, this volume provides a wealth of interactive projects for students in grades 4 through 7. Focusing on land and ocean studies, this resource is an invaluable guide for any teacher looking for fresh ideas and engaging activities.

8. *Every Teacher's Science Booklist: An Annotated Bibliography of Science Literature for Children* edited by Bernice Richter and Pam Nelson. (New York: Scholastic, 1994) [ISBN: 0-590-49381-7].

   An annotated bibliography of hundreds of science trade books (each one rated) constitutes the bulk of this outstanding resource. This is a reference you'll turn to again and again. Don't pass this one by—it's well worth the money.

9. *IDEAAAS Sourcebook for Science, Mathematics and Technology Education* edited by Barbara Walthall. (Washington, DC: American Association for the Advancement of Science, 1995) [ISBN: 0-87168-545-0].

   This is an incredible resource! Packed with information from cover to cover, this is an ideal guide to materials, supplies, agencies, producers, and professional societies—anything and everything related to science and science education. A magnificent guide to places and people.

10. *Eyeopeners II: Children's Books to Answer Children's Questions About the World Around Them* by Beverly Kobrin. (New York: Scholastic, 1995) [ISBN: 0-590-48402-8].

    More than 800 children's books are profiled in the pages of this delightful and much-needed resource. These books represent the best of the best, and the text includes full annotations and proven strategies for using these books in the classroom. This guide will be a staple of your professional library.

Science Periodicals for Students

Following are the names and addresses of some of the best science magazines for children. These periodicals are excellent resources for student projects and activities within and throughout any thematic unit or mini-unit. Make sure your school library subscribes to several of these and be sure to recommend them to parents as gifts for holidays and birthdays.

Audubon Adventure
National Audubon Society
613 Riverville Rd.
Greenwich, CT 06830
(6 issues per year)

Chickadee
Young Naturalist Foundation
255 Great Arrow Ave.
Buffalo, NY 14207-3082
(10 issues per year)

Dolphin Log
Cousteau Society
8440 Santa Monica Blvd.
Los Angeles, CA 90069
(6 issues per year)

Kids Discover
Box 54206
Boulder, CO 80312-4206
(monthly)

Kind News
The Humane Society of the United States
67 Salem Rd.
East Haddam, CT 06423-0362
(9 issues per year)

National Geographic World
National Geographic Society
17th and M St., NW
Washington, DC 20036
(monthly)

Naturescope
National Wildlife Federation
1912 16th St., NW
Washington, DC 20036
(monthly)

Odyssey
Kalmbach Publishing Co.
Box 1612
Waukesha, WI 53187
(monthly)

Otterwise
Box 1374
Portland, ME 04104-1374
(quarterly)

Owl
Young Naturalist Foundation
255 Great Arrow Ave.
Buffalo, NY 14207-3082
(10 issues per year)

Planet Three
Foundation, Inc.
Box 52
Montgomery, VT 05470
(10 issues per year)

Ranger Rick
National Wildlife Federation
1400 16th St., NW
Washington, DC 20036-2266
(monthly)

Science Weekly
2141 Industrial Parkway No. 202
Silver Spring, MD 20904
(weekly during school year)

Scienceland
Scienceland, Inc.
501 Fifth Ave., Suite 2108
New York, NY 10017-6102
(8 issues per year)

3-2-1 Contact
Children's Television Workshop
One Lincoln Plaza
New York, NY 10023
(10 issues per year)

Wonderscience
American Chemical Society
1155 16th St., NW
Washington, DC 20036-4800
(monthly)

Your Big Backyard
National Wildlife Federation
1400 16th St., NW
Washington, DC 20036
(monthly)

Zoobooks
Wildlife Education, Ltd.
930 West Washington St.
San Diego, CA 92103
(10 issues per year)

 **Web Sites**

The following World Wide Web sites can provide you with valuable background information, a wealth of science resources, scores of up-to-date lesson plans, and numerous tools for expanding any area of science education. They can become important adjuncts to any literature-based science curriculum and can be used by teachers and students alike. Use them to keep your thematic units and mini-units fresh and up-to-date.

Note: These Web sites were current and accurate as of the writing of this book. Please be aware that some may change, others may be eliminated, and new ones will be added to the various search engines that you use at home or at school.

General

http://www.afredericks.com

This Web site is designed to provide busy classroom teachers with the latest information, the newest activities, the best resources, and the most creative projects in elementary science. It's updated frequently with hundreds of exciting ideas.

http://www.nsta.org

This is the Web site for the National Science Teachers Association, the professional organization for all teachers of science.

http://www.askanexpert.com/askanexpert

This site allows you and your students to pose questions to specific scientists, including astronomers, biologists, geologists, meteorologists, volcanologists, and zoologists, to name a few.

http://www.enc.org

This is the Eisenhower National Clearinghouse for Math and Science Education. It includes detailed descriptions of curriculum materials and links to other education sites on the Internet.

http://www.learner.org

A wonderful and all-inclusive resource for teachers of science, with one of the most extensive and versatile search engines found on the Web. This Web site was established to help schools and communities improve math and science education. Click on to SAMI and discover a searchable database with easy access to curriculum resources, lesson plans and projects, and more.

http://server2.greatlakes.k12.mi.us

An incredible collection of teacher resources available for downloading. Included are lesson plans, computer software, Hyper-Card files, news resources, thematic units, guest speakers, field trips, and student-created material resources.

http://www.teachers.net/lessons

> Take a lesson, leave a lesson at the Teachers Net Lesson Exchange. The lessons cover all subjects and grade levels; the site includes links to the teachers who posted the lessons.

http://www.pacificnet.net/~mandel

> A wonderful place to share ideas, concerns, and questions with educators from around the world. The material is updated weekly and you'll be able to obtain lesson plans in every curricular area. Also included are teaching tips for both new and experienced teachers.

Animals

http://www.Seaworld.com

> This is an animal information database maintained by Sea World/Busch Gardens. Scores of animals are listed, along with biological classification and scientific facts about each one.

http://netvet.wustl.edu/e-zoo.htm

> The Electronic Zoo contains hundreds and hundreds of resources, research links, publications, organizations, mailing lists, newsgroups, and search engines on animals. Complete and thorough.

Dinosaurs

http://www.hi.is/~hbh/

> The Educational Dinosaur Guide offers dozens of links to educational resources on the Net for both teachers and students. A "blue ribbon" winner—perfect for any classroom.

http://www.dinosociety.org

> WOW—it's all here! You can tap into the vast resources of the Dinosaur Society to create some incredible lessons and wonderful explorations for any group of students.

Rainforests

http://www.ran.org/ran/kids_action/index.html

> Developed by the Rainforest Action Network, this site offers an excellent overview of rainforest life, ideas on how kids can become involved in preservation efforts, and a question-and-answer section.

http://kids.osd.wednet.edu/Marshall/rainforest_home_page.html

> A magnificent Web site developed by students in Olympia, Washington. Here you and your students will discover tons of information along with lesson plans and resource materials. A super site!

Human Body

http://www.innerbody.com/indexbody.html

> This site offers scores of interactive and educational views of the human body. Included are more than 100 illustrations (with animations) and thousands of descriptive links.

http://www.nlm.nih.gov/research/visible/visible_human.html

> The Visible Human Project offers complete, anatomically detailed, three-dimensional representations of the male and female human body. Dozens of links and scores of additional information is provided on this all-inclusive site.

Four Seasons

http://www.princeton.edu/Webweather/ww.html

> On this Web site students can discover the current as well as future weather patterns for specific areas (cities or states) of the United States. Included are Weather Service satellite maps.

http://www.4seasons.org.uk/mainmenu.htm

This Web site has three school-based projects on the four seasons along with a range of environmental education resources for schools. These projects are all related to weather in England and would make interesting compare/contrast activities with U.S. seasonal patterns.

Weather

http://athena.wednet.edu/curric/weather

Lots and lots of instructional materials, links, resources, lesson plans, multimedia programs, and education programs on every aspect of the weather can be found on this site. A magnificent research tool.

http://www.weatheronline.com

An incredible Web site that has just about every type of resource and information that you need for weather studies. Scores of links and tons of data highlight this powerful site.

Changing Earth

http://volcano.und.nodak.edu

This Web site offers students opportunities to e-mail volcanologists, keep up to date on the latest volcanic eruptions, and discover how volcanoes work. Teachers can get complete lesson plans on volcanoes.

http://quake.wr.usgs.gov

This site has up-to-the-minute information on earthquakes around the world. Included are maps, earthquake preparedness information, earthquake facts, and loads of data from the United States Geological Survey.

Oceans

http://inspire.ospi.wednet.edu:8001/curric/oceans

The site offers instruction units and projects on a variety of topics—tracking drifter buoys, investigating ocean currents, ocean color, and plant life in the ocean.

http://seawifs.gsfc.nasa.gov/ocean_planet.html

The Web site is a listing of oceanography-related resources that can be found on the Internet. Exploration of these resources will turn up a surprising variety of information.

Simple Machines

http://seamonkey.ed.asu.edu/~hixson/index/machines.html

A great resource with lots of student links to other sites including demonstrations, graphics, examples, resources, explanations, activity pages, and experiments with simple machines.

http://viking.stark.k12.oh.us/~greentown/simpmach.htm

This site provides several links to other sites on simple machines. It includes lesson plans, activities, teacher resources, and lots of practical information.

Space Exploration

http://seds.lpl.arizona.edu/nineplanets/nineplanets/nineplanets.html

This Web site is loaded with an incredible array of space science information, including overviews of all the planets, sound files and video links, and loads of pictures and facts.

http://www2.ari.net/home/odenwald/cafe.html

The Astronomy Cafe bills itself as "the Web site for the astronomically disadvantaged." You'll bill it as outstanding. It's chock full of resources, links, questions and answers, books, essays, information, and much more on practically every aspect of space science.

SUBJECT INDEX

ABOUT THE AUTHOR

Tony is a nationally recognized science educator well known for his energetic, fast-paced, and highly practical presentations for strengthening science instruction. His dynamic and stimulating seminars have captivated thousands of teachers from coast to coast and border to border. His background includes extensive experience as a classroom teacher, curriculum coordinator, staff developer, author, professional storyteller, and university specialist in children's literature, language arts, and science education.

Tony has written more than 30 teacher resource books in a variety of areas, including the hilarious *Tadpole Tales and Other Totally Terrific Treats for Readers Theatre* (Teacher Ideas Press, 1997), the highly acclaimed *From Butterflies to Thunderbolts: Discovering Science with Books Kids Love* (Fulcrum, 1997), and the best-selling *The Complete Science Fair Handbook* (Addison-Wesley, 1990), which he coauthored with Isaac Asimov.

Not only is Tony an advocate for the integration of children's literature throughout the elementary science curriculum, he is also the author of such award-winning children's books as *Weird Walkers* (NorthWord, 1996), *Exploring the Oceans* (Fulcrum, 1998), and *Clever Camouflagers* (NorthWord, 1997). He is currently a professor of education at York College in York, Pennsylvania, where he teaches methods courses in science and language arts. Additionally, he maintains a Web site (www.afredericks.com) with hundreds of exciting resources, dynamic activities, and creative projects for elementary science instruction.